T0272456

WAFFEN-SS DIVISIONS

TANKS, SELF-PROPELLED GUNS, ARMOURED CARS

IDENTIFICATION GUIDE

WAFFEN-SS DIVISIONS

TANKS, SELF-PROPELLED GUNS, ARMOURED CARS

CHRIS BISHOP

amber
BOOKS

This edition published in 2024

First published in 2007 as *The Essential Vehicle Identification Guide: Waffen-SS Divisions 1939–45*

Published by
Amber Books Ltd
United House
London N7 9DP
United Kingdom
www.amberbooks.co.uk
Facebook: amberbooks
YouTube: amberbooksltd
Instagram: amberbooksltd
X(Twitter): @amberbooks

ISBN: 978-1-83886-351-7

Printed in China

PICTURE CREDITS:

All artworks and photographs courtesy Amber Books Ltd, except the following:

AirSeaLandPhotos: 6, 8, 9, 13(t), 28, 37(t), 39(b), 44(t), 56(t), 59(t), 70, 77(t), 83, 92(t),
99(t), 105(t), 106(b), 117(t), 120(t), 124, 134, 138, 143(t), 161(t), 162, 170, 176(t)

Contents

Introduction

The history of the SS (*Schutzstaffel*) falls into distinct phases. Formed as a security force to keep order at party meetings, then developing into the *Führer's* bodyguard, the SS was not a large organization in the 1920s. By the time Hitler came to power, however, it had grown to around 25,000 men, a tiny number compared to the millions of SA (*Sturmabteilung*) members.

AFTER 1933, THE SS GREW RAPIDLY, in the process splitting into three main groups. The *Allgemeine-SS*, or 'General' SS, initially took control of the police and security forces. It was also responsible for administering the rapidly growing SS economic empire, and took a leading role in investigating and promoting Himmler's racial theories. The *Allgemeine-SS* retained the characteristic black unifom long after other SS branches had switched to grey.

Separate from the *Allgemeine-SS*, the *Totenkopf-verbände* were the camp guards and have been most responsible for the horrible reputation the SS has kept since the end of the war. These brutal units were created after the SS won a turf fight with the SA for control of the concentration camps. The first camps were being built almost as soon as the Nazis came to power, and at Dachau the *Totenkopf* guards evolved many of the systems and techniques by which the SS terrorized Europe.

Armed SS

The Armed SS was established after Hitler came to power in 1933. Neither Hitler nor Himmler trusted the German generals, and they saw the SS as a military force personally loyal to the *Führer*, which he could use as a counterweight to the Army. Composed of well-trained troops of unquestioned loyalty to the party and the *Führer*, the Armed SS initially comprised the members of Hitler's bodyguard and the *Leibstandarte*, together with a number of *Politischen Bereitschaften*, or Political Emergency Squads, whose primary function had been to use

◀ **Ardennes offensive**
A PzKpfw V 'Panther' Ausf E from the II SS Panzer Corps advances down a snow-covered Belgian road as part of the attempt to push the Allies back to the English Channel, December 1944.

▲ **Cherkassy encirclement**

Men from the 5th SS Division *Wiking* man a PzKpfw IV amidst the fighting in the Cherkassy pocket, January 1944. More than 75,000 German troops were trapped in the encirclement, with some 35,000 – including troops from the *Wiking* Division – managing to break out in February.

violent measures against party opponents. These became the *SS-Verfügungstruppe*, or SS-VT.

By the time of the *Anschluss* with Austria in March 1938, the Armed SS had grown dramatically. In addition to the 2600 men of the *Leibstandarte*, there were three SS-VT *Standarten*, or regiments, derived from the *Politischen Bereitschaften*. The three regiments were given the names *Deutschland*, *Germania* and *Der Führer*, and were trained and equipped as motorized infantry.

Becoming known as the *Waffen-SS* in 1940, the Armed SS would be by far the largest branch of Himmler's personal empire, eventually numbering 38 divisions. Through its ranks passed nearly one million men of 15 nationalities. The premier formation of the *Waffen-SS*, the *Leibstandarte Adolf Hitler*, provided guards of honour for visiting VIPs before the war, but they were more than parade-ground warriors. The *Waffen-SS* took part in

12 major campaigns and were noted for their tough fighting qualities and aggressive leadership.

Chain of command

Assigned to Army control in combat, the SS had an entirely separate chain of command away from the battlefield. Answering to the *Reichsführer-SS* Heinrich Himmler, and through him to the *Führer*, the Armed SS was controlled by the *SS-Führungshauptamt* (FHA), the SS Operations Department. This was one of a dozen or so Main Offices via which the SS spread its tentacles throughout German society.

Headed by *SS-Obergruppenführer und General der Waffen-SS* Hans Jüttner, the FHA was split into four main groups. *Amtsgruppe* A was responsible for organization, personnel and supply. *Amtsgruppe* B was responsible for training. *Amtsgruppe* C controlled the inspectorates for various branches of the service, including infantry and mountain troops, cavalry, artillery, combat engineers, armoured troops, signals troops and various support and training services. *Amtsgruppe* D controlled SS medical services.

Surprisingly, the *Waffen-SS* had great difficulty in acquiring adequate equipment, at least in the early years of the war. Although classed as motorized formations, large parts of the SS went into battle on foot, with horsedrawn supplies – although in this they were hardly any different from the bulk of the German Army.

SS equipment was procured through the Army, and since the Army saw the SS as a potential rival, it was reluctant to supply the latest weapons. Some SS units used commandeered Czech weapons, and as the war progressed they also made extensive use of captured equipment. It was not until the last years of the conflict that the *Waffen-SS* received any preferential treatment, and by then they were hardly a separate organization.

Combat role

Originally looked on with distrust by the Army, the SS became more and more a part of the *Wehrmacht*. Armed SS units had always been under Army control on the battlefield; now, *Waffen-SS* equipment and organization were the same as those of the Army. SS units were interchangeable with Army units, and senior SS officers adopted Army ranks.

By the end of the war, first-line SS Panzer and Panzergrenadier divisions were among the largest and most powerful in the German armed forces. SS cavalry and mountain divisions had been formed, and hundreds of thousands of foreign volunteers found a home in the SS, until parts of it were more like a German 'Foreign Legion' than the elite of the German race.

The *Waffen-SS* had moved a long way in 20 years. Hitler's personal thugs became the parade soldiers of the 1930s, who in turn evolved into the well-equipped, million-strong army of 1944.

In the early days at least, Armed SS members retained the fanaticism that had been bred into them, which they translated into fighting spirit. They were regarded as an elite, only the best physical specimens being allowed to join. They were tough, and they were dedicated, influencing the course of World War II out of all proportion to their numbers.

They were also fanatical and ruthless. Being fanatics, they were responsible for many atrocities.

▶ **SS Panzer commander**

SS-Gruppenführer Paul Hausser (centre, inside turret), shown here inspecting a PzKpfw III from the *Das Reich* Division, led that division from its formation until October 1941, when he became commander of the I SS Panzer Corps.

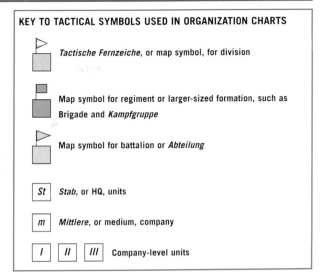

KEY TO TACTICAL SYMBOLS USED IN ORGANIZATION CHARTS

Tactische Fernzeiche, or map symbol, for division

Map symbol for regiment or larger-sized formation, such as Brigade and *Kampfgruppe*

Map symbol for battalion or *Abteilung*

St   *Stab*, or HQ, units

m   *Mittlere*, or medium, company

I *II* *III*   Company-level units

But as the war went on, it became harder to distinguish the SS from the soldiers alongside whom they served. By 1945, the survivors were a close-knit, battle-wise force with a full range of modern weapons, including tanks and artillery.

Chapter 1

The First SS Divisions

Hitler's bodyguard, the *Leibstandarte,* was the first unit of what would eventually become the Armed, or *Waffen*-, SS. Hitler and Himmler did not trust the German Army, and saw the SS as a military force personally loyal to the *Führer,* which he could use as a counterweight to the Army. The Armed SS was the largest branch of the organization. It would eventually number some 39 divisions, and one million men of 15 nationalities passed through its ranks. Taking the name *Waffen-SS* in the spring of 1940, it took part in 12 major campaigns and was noted for its tough fighting qualities and aggressive leadership.

◀ **Kharkov defence**

Panzergrenadiers from the *Das Reich* Division climb on board a StuG assault gun amidst the protracted fighting around Kharkov in March 1943. The II SS *Panzerkorps*, which included divisions *Das Reich*, *Leibstandarte* and *Totenkopf*, was used to stem the Soviet advance following the retreat from the Volga and Caucasus after the defeat at Stalingrad.

1st SS Panzer Division LSSAH

Between March 1933 and May 1945, the *Leibstandarte SS Adolf Hitler* grew from a bodyguard of 120 men protecting the *Führer* to the 1st SS Panzer Division, an outsized and immensely powerful armoured formation more than 20,000 strong.

EQUIPPED WITH THE most modern weapons that German industry could produce, it was led by some of the toughest and most controversial figures in German military history – men like *SS-Oberführer* Kurt 'Panzer' Meyer, *SS-Obersturmbannführer* Joachim 'Jochen' Peiper and *SS-Obersturmbannführer* Max Wunsche. But the man who did most to shape the character of *Leibstandarte* was its first commanding officer, Josef 'Sepp' Dietrich. Dietrich, one of the earliest members of the SS, had been Hitler's driver and bodyguard, and was to rise to become an Army commander.

The *Leibstandarte* initially wore the black uniform of the *Allgemeine-SS* with the *Totenkopf* cap badge. The first armed SS guard unit was the *SS-Stabswache Berlin*, later renamed the *Wachtbataillon Berlin*. This became the *Leibstandarte SS Adolf Hitler* (SS Bodyguard Regiment Adolf Hitler) in

ORGANIZATION

Inf.Rgt LSSAH — St

I. — St — I II III
II. — St — I II III
III. — St — I II III
IV. — St — I II III

IG.Kp — St — I II III
Pzjr.Kp — St — I II III
Krd.Kp — St — I II III

HQ ORGANIZATION

Inf.Rgt LSSAH — HQ

Auf | Pnr | Krd | Nch | Mu | le.I

Commanders

Obergruppenführer Josef 'Sepp' Dietrich
1933 – July 1943

Brigadeführer Theodor Wisch
July 1943 – August 1944

Brigadeführer Wilhelm Mohnke
August 1944 – February 1945

Brigadeführer Otto Kumm
February 1945 – May 1945

INSIGNIA

In German, 'dietrich' is slang for a skeleton key, so to honour their commander the division adopted a shield with a key as its insignia.

Waffen-SS Divisional insignia were usually enclosed within a standard shield although this was not always applied on vehicles.

Because insignia were often painted on to vehicles in the field, they occasionally varied from the standard, sometimes being modified to fit a specific space.

When Dietrich was awarded the Oakleaves to the Knight's Cross in 1941, the division honoured their commander by adding oakleaves to its insignia.

As a security measure in the build up to Kursk, units involved in the operation used special formation markings to replace their standard insignia.

Divisional History	Formed
SA Stabswache	1923
SA Stosstrupp Adolf Hitler	1923
Stabswache	1925
Schutzstaffel	1925
SS-Stabswache Berlin	1933
SS-Sonderkommando Berlin	1933
Adolf Hitler-Standarte	1933
Leibstandarte Adolf Hitler	1933
Leibstandarte-SS Adolf Hitler	1934
Infanterie-Regiment Leibstandarte SS Adolf Hitler (mot)	1938
SS-Division Leibstandarte-SS Adolf Hitler	1941
SS-Panzergrenadier-Division Leibstandarte-SS Adolf Hitler	1942
1.SS-Panzer-Division Leibstandarte-SS Adolf Hitler	1944

▶ **Motorcycle reconnaissance company**

Although *Leibstandarte* was originally a ceremonial unit, from 1936 it was equipped as a motorised infantry formation as its combat role developed.

September 1933. Two months later, on the tenth anniversary of the Munich Putsch, its members took an oath of personal allegiance to Adolf Hitler.

In the early days, the purpose of the *Leibstandarte* was ceremonial – standing like black statues outside the main buildings in Berlin or executing crisp drill movements as honour guards for visiting VIPs. But its capacity for violent action was never far from the surface. In June 1934, Dietrich and his men – using weapons and transport supplied by the Army – were used by the Nazi party in the 'Night of the Long Knives', the bloody purge that eliminated senior *Sturmabteilung* leaders and other political enemies.

Armed SS

When it was decided to set up a private Nazi army, the *Leibstandarte* provided the core of the new 'Armed SS'. In December 1934, it was expanded to regimental size and began to move away from its political bodyguard function to a more conventional military role. It participated in the bloodless occupation of the Rhineland in March 1936, and a motorized battalion under Sepp Dietrich took part in the invasion of Austria in March 1938.

▶ **Leichte Lkw 1t Opel Blitz 2.0-12**

Leibstandarte SS Adolf Hitler / I.Bataillon

In 1934, the LSSAH had to borrow trucks from the Army to take part in the 'Night of the Long Knives'. By 1938, it was a fully motorized formation, though many of its vehicles were commercial models like the Opel Blitz introduced in that year.

Specifications

Crew: 1	Engine: Opel 1920cc 6-cylinder petrol
Weight: 3.29 tonnes (3 tons)	(36hp)
Length: 6.02m (19ft 9in)	Speed: 80km/h (50mph)
Width: 2.27m (7ft 5in)	Range: 410km (255 miles)
Height: 2.18m (7ft 2in)	Radio: None

▶ **Schwerer Panzerspähwagen 6-Rad (SdKfz 231)**

Spähpanzerwagen-Zug LSSAH

Although nominally an infantry regiment, the LSSAH was in effect a motorized division in miniature, with artillery, reconnaissance, pioneers and support units. In addition to a motorcycle company, LSSAH had its own armoured car platoon.

Specifications

Crew: 4	Magirus petrol (60-80hp)
Weight: 5.9 tonnes (5.35 tons)	Speed: 70km/h (43mph)
Length: 5.57m (18 ft 7in)	Range: 300km (186 miles)
Width: 1.82m (5ft 11.5in)	Radio: FuG Spr Ger 'a'
Height: 2.25m (7ft 4.5in)	Armament: 1 x 20mm (0.7in) cannon;
Engine: Daimler-Benz, Büssing-NAG or	1 x 7.62mm (0.3in) MG (coaxial)

Poland and France
1939–1940

As a regimental formation, *Leibstandarte* was the first *Waffen-SS* unit to see combat action in World War II – first in Poland in September 1939, then in Holland and France in May 1940.

WHEN WAR BROKE OUT in September 1939, the *Leibstandarte* was organized as a motorized infantry regiment. By this time, the Armed, or *Waffen-*, SS was wearing field grey uniform like the Army. Unlike Army units, however, its soldiers were also equipped with a range of well-designed camouflaged smocks and helmet covers – which were later to become complete camouflage uniforms.

The *Leibstandarte* was distinguished from other *Waffen-SS* formations by cuff titles worn on the left sleeve of uniform jackets. The *Leibstandarte* cuff title consisted of a strip of black ribbon with a woven silver border and facsimile of the signature 'Adolf Hitler'. In day-to-day usage, the full title *Leibstandarte SS Adolf Hitler* was usually contracted to 'LSSAH' or 'LAH'.

On 1 September 1939, Hitler unleashed his forces against Poland, with the Armed SS operating under Army control. The *Leibstandarte* in particular, now expanded to regimental size, fought hard, serving as a motorized regiment attached to von Rundstedt's Army Group South. *Leibstandarte* was part of the Tenth Army, under the command of fanatical Nazi General von Reichenau.

Casualties were high, however, as the attacking philosophy instilled into the SS by Felix Steiner meant that commanders often threw caution to the wind in order to achieve their aims. Army

commanders were particularly critical of the leadership capabilities of junior SS officers.

War in the West

When the war moved west, the bulk of the Armed SS was deployed. *Leibstandarte* was attached to the right flank of the 227th Infantry Division with von Bock's forces, which also controlled the SS-VT Division.

The *Leibstandarte* was the first SS unit into action, crossing the Dutch border just after dawn on 9 May. LAH linked up with German paratroopers in the Dutch city of Rotterdam.

After Holland, it was deployed to France. The SS had no part to play in the opening stages of the drive

▶ **Gepanzerter Selbstfahrlafette für Sturmgeschütz 7.5-cm Ausf B (SdKfz 142)**

Panzersturmbatterie LSSAH

At the end of April 1940, a battery of six 7.5cm (3in) assault guns was assigned to the LSSAH's 5th Battalion, though it was not formally incorporated into the unit until July, after France had been defeated.

Specifications

Crew: 4	Engine: Maybach HL120TR
Weight: 21.6 tonnes (21.1 tons)	Speed: 40km/h (25mph)
Length: 5.38m (17.7ft)	Range: 160km (99.4 miles)
Width: 2.92m (9.6ft)	Radio: FuG15 or FuG16
Height: 1.95m (6.4ft)	

through the Ardennes. However, the *Leibstandarte* was one of the regiments attached to the 1st Panzer Division, which drove across northern France to the sea at Boulogne.

After Dunkirk, the three SS units were withdrawn for a couple of days of rest, before being moved yet again to take part in the Battle of France. *Leibstandarte* and the two SS divisions were attached to *Panzergruppe Kleist*, which was planning its advance towards the Marne. On 8 June, the *Leibstandarte* drove through Soissons towards the

Aisne. The *Leibstandarte* continued the chase through central France, taking Clermont-Ferrand on 20 June. They overran the large French airbase near the city, capturing hundreds of *Armée de l'Air* aircraft as well as a number of Polish Air Force machines that had fled westwards the year before. LSSAH ended the campaign at St Etienne on 24 June.

LAH was expanded to brigade strength in August 1940, and at this time its members were told by their *Führer*, 'It will be an honour for you, who bear my name, to lead every German attack.'

▼ LSSAH Artillery Regiment

By May 1940, the *Leibstandarte* had grown to the size of a brigade, and had been redesignated as the Reinforced LSSAH. The unit's artillery assets originally came from the 4th Battalion, SS Artillery Regiment, but by August of 1940 this had grown to the size of a regiment itself, with two battalions of light and heavy field howitzers and an anti-aircraft, or Flak, battery attached to the 2nd Battalion.

I.*Bataillon*

II.*Bataillon*

▶ **Panzerspähwagen (Fu) 8-Rad (SdKfz 232)**

Aufklärungs-Abteilung LSSAH

The SdKfz 232 was the radio version of the heavy SdKfz 231 eight-wheeled armoured car introduced in the late 1930s. It usually operated in support of the lighter and more numerous four-wheeled reconnaissance vehicles.

Specifications	
Crew: 4	Speed: 85km/h (52.8mph)
Weight: 9.1 tonnes (8.3 tons)	Range: 300km (186 miles)
Length: 4.67m (15ft 4in)	Radio: FuG12 plus FuG Spr Ger 'a'
Width: 2.2m (7ft 2in)	Armament: 1 x 20mm (0.7in) KwK
Height: 2.35m (7ft 8in)	30/38 L/55 cannon; 1 x 7.92mm
Engine: Büssing-NAG L8V	(0.3in) MG (coaxial)

Balkans and Greece
APRIL–MAY 1941

The *Wehrmacht's* plans to invade the USSR were interrupted by the Balkans campaign, in which German troops were called upon to come to the aid of Mussolini's Italian forces.

IN FEBRUARY 1941, THE *LEIBSTANDARTE*, which by now had grown from an outsized regiment into a mechanized brigade, was moved from its winter quarters at Metz. It travelled by rail to Sofia in Bulgaria, where it would join Field Marshal Wilhelm List's Twelfth Army. On 6 April 1941, it crossed the border as one of the lead elements in the invasion of southern Yugoslavia.

Most of the Twelfth Army would attack southwards out of southern Bulgaria into Greece, while the rest of the army, led by the *Leibstandarte*, drove westwards into Kosovo and Macedonia.

Along with the 9th Panzer Division, the LSSAH formed General Stumme's XL Panzer Corps. The *Leibstandarte* and the Panzers headed westwards, driving through Macedonia towards Skopje. This force overran southern Yugoslavia to reach the Greek frontier at Monastir on 10 April. Their aim was to put a barrier in the way of any Greek armies coming to help the Yugoslavs.

South into Greece

Only one corps of List's Twelfth Army had entered Yugoslavia: the other two corps would attack though Macedonia, piercing or bypassing the Greek defences. The XXX and XLVIII Corps drove directly to the Aegean, punching clean through the Greek defences. A British armoured brigade deployed in the north was ordered to fall back along the eastern coast.

Meanwhile, *Leibstandarte* and the 9th Panzer Division were ordered south along the Albanian border. A smaller German force presented a further threat to the Greek defenders, making a series of landings on the Greek islands along the Turkish coast.

REGIMENTAL ORGANIZATION, EARLY 1941

Inf.Rgt LSSAH
St | Mu

I.
St
I | II | III

II.
St
I | II | III

III.
St
I | II | III

IV.
St
I | II | III

Auf.Abt
St
I | II | III

Art.Rgt
St
I | II | III

Pnr.Btl
St
I | II | III

Nach.Abt
St
I | II | III

Nsch.Die

SUPPORT ORGANIZATION

Nsch-Dienste

St

Wrk | Bet | 1 | 2 | 3

The Italian Army undertook a new offensive that was timed to coincide with the *Führer's* intervention. The Greek 'Army of Epirus', outgunned, started to give way.

The *Leibstandarte* performed outstandingly well. On 11 April, it had forced its way through the Monastir gap after a close-quarter, hand-to-hand battle with the small force of Australian and New Zealand troops who had been rushed north. By the 14th, the brigade was engaging the Greek 21st Division defending the Klissura Pass. The Greek resistance was extremely tough, and it was not until a young *Sturmbannführer* named Kurt Meyer infiltrated the LSSAH reconnaissance company along goat tracks over the mountains that the tide turned.

Victory

The Greek Government accepted defeat on 19 April, and the British announced their withdrawal from the mainland, although Crete would continue to be held. An orderly evacuation was imperilled on 26 April by a daring *coup de main*. German paratroops attacked the bridge over the Corinth Canal.

By this time, the *Leibstandarte* had reached the Gulf of Corinth, where Kurt Meyer commandeered two caiques (Greek fishing boats) and organized a ferry across the gulf. Swinging eastwards, the SS troops cleared the southern edge of the gulf before linking up with the paratroopers of the 2nd Fallschirmjäger Regiment.

However, the bridge was blown up and the British retreat continued into the Peloponnese, where a last stand at Kalamata ended with 7000 British and Commonwealth troops laying down their arms after exhausting their ammunition.

During the Greek campaign, the *Leibstandarte* won a reputation for being hard but fair – a reputation that was to change dramatically on the Eastern Front. Following a victory parade in Athens, the unit returned to barracks in Czechoslovakia.

▼ Panzerjäger I
V.Bataillon LSSAH / Panzerjäger-Kompanie (Sf)
The Czech 47mm (1.8in) anti-tank gun was fitted to the chassis of the tiny Panzer I to create one of the first self-propelled tank-hunters. From May 1940 until at least the end of 1941 or early 1942, the 5th Battalion of the *Leibstandarte* had nine of these vehicles in its *Panzerjäger* company.

Specifications

Crew: 3	Engine: Maybach HL62TR
Weight: 8.9 tonnes (8.1 tons)	Speed: 40km/h (25mph)
Length: 4.8m (15ft 8in)	Range: 200km (124 miles)
Width: 2.22m (7ft 4in)	Radio: FuG5
Height: 1.99m (6ft 6in)	Arament: 1 x 47mm (1.8in) gun

▶ Panzerkampfwagen I Ausf B (SdKfz 101)
Panzerjäger-Abteilung LSSAH / 1.Kompanie / Stab
By the time the LSSAH was authorized to raise a three-company Panzer troop in February 1942, the Panzer I was long out of frontline service. However, it was issued to the commanders of *Panzerjäger* companies and battalions.

Specifications

Crew: 3	Engine: Maybach HL62TR
Weight: 8.9 tonnes (8.1 tons)	Speed: 40km/h (25mph)
Length: 4.8m (15ft 8in)	Range: 200km (124 miles)
Width: 2.22m (7ft 4in)	Radio: FuG5
Height: 1.99m (6ft 6in)	

On the Eastern Front
1941–1942

Thanks to its involvement in the Balkans, *Leibstandarte* was still refitting when the invasion of the Soviet Union was launched in June 1941. However, it was quickly sent to the front.

BY THE OPENING OF Operation *Barbarossa* in June 1941, LAH was a division in strength, but not in name (although by September 1941 it was unofficially being referred to as the *SS-Division LSSAH*, and by the end of the year it had in fact been redesignated).

Waffen-SS units were deployed among the various Army commands. Field Marshal Gerd von Rundstedt, commanding Army Group South, was allocated the *Leibstandarte SS Adolf Hitler* and the *Wiking* Division, which were with General Ewald von Kleist's 1st Panzer Group.

Between July and November 1941, *Leibstandarte* fought non-stop from the Polish border to Kherson near the Black Sea and then along the Sea of Azov to Rostov on the Don.

In mid-November, when the majority of III Panzer Corps had caught up with the spearhead units, the assault on Rostov began. The capture of this essential communications link by the *Leibstandarte* Division was assured when it took a vital bridge over the River Don. Soviet engineers had mined the rail bridge with demolition charges, but it was still intact. Its imminent destruction was, apparently, being

▶ **PzKpfw II für 7.62-cm Pak36(r) (SdKfz 139)**
Panzerjäger-Abteilung LSSAH / 1.Kompanie
Known as the Marder III, the combination of a captured Soviet gun mounted on a modified Czech tank chassis saw service on the Eastern Front from April 1942 until phased out in the summer of 1944.

Specifications	
Crew: 4	Engine: Praga EPA or EPA/2
Weight: 11.76 tonnes (10.67 tons)	Speed: 42km/h (26mph)
Length: 5.85m (19ft 2in)	Range: 185km (115 miles)
Width: 2.16m (7ft 0in)	Radio: FuG Spr 'd'
Height: 2.50m (8ft 2in)	Armament: 1 x 76.2mm (3in) FK296

considered by Soviet engineers. Seeing a locomotive standing by the bridge with a full head of steam, *SS-Hauptsturmführer* Springer, commanding the 3rd Company, SS-Panzergrenadier Regiment of the *Leibstandarte* Division, ordered his men to open fire with every weapon available, peppering the engine and releasing high-pressure steam from countless holes. The ensuing confusion provided the cover required to storm the bridge. Springer and his men went on to remove the demolition charges, ensuring the bridge's safety.

Pushed back for the first time

However, the Soviet winter counteroffensive pushed LAH out of the city and back over the River Mius, all but destroying the division in the process. Its performance in the fierce fighting on the Eastern

ORGANIZATION

National markings were enlarged on captured tanks to reduce the risk of 'friendly fire' incidents, though not always successfully since troops often fired at the shapes of tanks long before seeing any markings.

Front won the *Leibstandarte* considerable respect from the Army for its combat ability, but the hardness of its men was also reflected in the increasing number of atrocities they committed.

Vengeance was a major motive for slaughter: over three days in April 1942, the *Leibstandarte* murdered 4000 Soviet POWs in retaliation for the killing of six of their own.

▶ **Panzerkampfwagen T-34 747(r)**

Panzer-Regiment LSSAH / I.Bataillon

Captured Soviet T-34s were pressed into service by most German formations. When the LSSAH 1st Panzer Battalion was transferred west to be reorganized in April 1943, it took six damaged Panzers and two T-34s.

Specifications

Crew: 4	Engine: V-2-34
Weight: 24 tons (23.6 tonnes)	Speed: 40km/h (25mph)
Length: 6.58m (21ft 6in)	Range: 430km (267 miles)
Width: 2.98m (9ft 8in)	Radio: 10R
Height: 2.57m (8ft 4in)	

▶ **Mittlere Schützenpanzerwagen (SdKfz 251/1)**

2.Panzergrenadier-Regiment LSSAH / III.Bataillon

The three *Schützen* companies and the heavy company of the 3rd Battalion of the 2nd Regiment were issued with half-tracks when the division was upgraded to Panzergrenadier status in November 1942.

Specifications

Crew: 2 plus 12 troops	Engine: Maybach HL42TUKRM
Weight: 9.9 tonnes (9 tons)	Speed: 53km/h (33mph)
Length: 5.98m (19ft 7in)	Range: 300km (186 miles)
Width: 2.1m (6ft 11in)	Radio: FuG Spr Ger 1
Height: 1.75m (5ft 8in) or 2.16m	Armament: 1/2 x 7.62mm
(7ft) including MG shield	(0.3in) MG

Kharkov and Kursk
1943

The mauled LAH was withdrawn to France in June 1942. There it was partly re-equipped with armour and designated a *Panzergrenadier,* or armoured infantry, division.

IN THIS NEW ROLE, IT RETURNED to Russia in January 1943 as part of the XXXVIII Panzer Corps under Field Marshal von Manstein. In February 1943, after the fall of Stalingrad, the LAH played a critical part in the battle for Kharkov. Following the battle – Germany's last major victory on the Eastern Front – Josef Goebbels recorded in his diary that Hitler 'was exceptionally happy about the way the *Leibstandarte* was led by Sepp Dietrich. This man has personally performed real feats of heroism.'

Leibstandarte was part of the southern pincer attempting to pinch off the Kursk salient in July 1943. It bypassed Belgorod and reached Teterevino

before being forced to withdraw. In the intense fighting, the division knocked out about 500 Soviet tanks. The Soviet forces moved from the defensive at Kursk to a huge rolling summer and winter offensive.

2nd SS Panzer Regiment, July 1943	Strength
PzKpfw II	4
PzKpfw III (short barrel)	3
PzKpfw III (long barrel)	10
PzKpfw IV (long barrel)	67
PzKpfw VI Tiger	13

▶ **Panzerkampfwagen III Ausf M (SdKfz 141/1)**

Panzer-Regiment LSSAH / II.Bataillon / Battalion Adjutant

There were more than 400 long-barrelled Panzer IIIs serving in German frontline units at the start of the Kursk offensive in July 1943.

Specifications	
Crew: 4	Engine: Maybach HL120TRM petrol
Weight: 25.4 tonnes (23 tons)	(300hp)
Length: 6.41m (21ft)	Speed: 40km/h (25mph)
Width: 2.95m (9ft 7in)	Range: 155km (96 miles)
Height: 2.44m (8ft)	Radio: FuG5

▶ **Panzerkampfwagen IV Ausf H (SdKfz 161/2)**

Panzer-Regiment LSSAH / II.Bataillon / 1.Kompanie

At the beginning of the Kursk action, the *Leibstandarte*'s 2nd Panzer Battalion had three medium Panzer companies with a total of 10 Panzer IIIs and 52 Panzer IVs, and a heavy company with nine Panzer VI Tigers.

Specifications	
Crew: 5	Speed: 38km/h (23.6mph)
Weight: 27.6 tonnes (25 tons)	Range: 210km (130.5 miles)
Length: 7.02m (23ft 0in)	Radio: FuG5
Width: 2.88m (9ft 5in)	Armament: 1 x 75mm (3in) KwK
Height: 2.68m (8ft 10in)	40/43; 2 x 7.92mm (0.3in) MG
Engine: Maybach HL120TRM	(one hull-mounted, one coaxial)

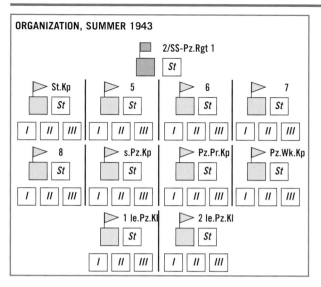

ORGANIZATION, SUMMER 1943

2/SS-Pz.Rgt 1

St.Kp | 5 | 6 | 7

8 | s.Pz.Kp | Pz.Pr.Kp | Pz.Wk.Kp

1 le.Pz.Kl | 2 le.Pz.Kl

To Italy

After being stopped by fierce Soviet resistance at Kursk, *Leibstandarte* was sent to Italy. Re-equipped and redesignated as a full Panzer division, the LAH was again sent to rescue the crumbling situation on the Eastern Front.

The LAH played a significant part in the relief of the Cherkassy pocket, where 50,000 Germans, including men of the *Waffen-SS* Division *Das Reich*, had been trapped by the Soviet advance. About 35,000 survivors were able to break out and link up with advanced guards of the *Leibstandarte*.

▼ Medium Panzer Company

At the time of the Battle of Kursk, the 1st Battalion of *Leibstandarte's* Panzer regiment had been returned to the West to re-equip with new Panzer V Panthers. The unit had transferred all of its tanks to the 2nd Battalion, which had four medium Panzer companies plus a company of Tigers. Most of the Panzer strength was provided by long-barrel Panzer IVs with a small number of Panzer IIs and IIIs serving in staff companies and platoons.

Stab

1.*Zug*   2.*Zug*   3.*Zug*   4.*Zug*

▶ **Panzerkampfwagen V Ausf A (SdKfz 171)**

1.SS-Panzer-Regiment / I.Panzer-Abteilung

The LSSAH sent the men of its 1st Panzer Battalion back to Germany, where they were to re-equip with the new PzKpfw V Panther tank.

Specifications

Crew: 5	Speed: 46km/h (28.6mph)
Weight: 50.2 tonnes (49.5 tons)	Range: 200km (124.3 miles)
Length: 8.86m (29ft 0in)	Radio: FuG5
Width: 3.4m (11ft 2in)	Armament: 1 x 75mm (3in) KwK42
Height: 2.98m (9ft 10in)	L/70; 2 x 7.92mm (0.3in) MG (one
Engine: Maybach HL230P30	hull-mounted, one coaxial)

▶ **Panzerkampfwagen VI Ausf E (SdKfz 181)**

1.SS-Panzer-Regiment / II.Panzer Abteilung / 13.schwere Kompanie / Stab

The 13th (Heavy) Tank Company of the LSSAH's Panzer regiment at Kursk was equipped with Tiger I heavy tanks.

Specifications

Crew: 4	(300hp)
Weight: 25.6 tonnes (25 tons)	Speed: 40km/h (25mph)
Length: 6.77m (22ft 2in)	Range: 210km (130 miles)
Width: 2.92m (9ft 7in)	Radio: FuG15 or FuG16
Height: 2.15m (7ft)	Armament: 1 x 75mm (3in) StuK 40
Engine: Maybach HL120TRM petrol	L/48 gun

Normandy
JUNE 1944

By the beginning of 1944, the *Leibstandarte* Division was a shadow of the well-armed, nearly full-strength force that had spearheaded Operation *Citadel* at Kursk in 1943.

IT WAS WITHDRAWN to western Europe to rest and refit, becoming a fully fledged Panzer division in the process. In the summer of 1944, the 1st SS Panzer Division *Leibstandarte* was based near Bruges in Belgium. Following the D-Day landings in Normandy, it was ordered to northwest France to form part of the I SS Panzer Corps.

By 17 June, the *Leibstandarte* had arrived from Bruges to join the battle for Caen. It suffered badly at the hands of Allied aircraft, as well as from naval gunfire and continuous action against overwhelming British, Canadian and US forces.

On 6 July, one month after the Allied landings, the LSSAH was fully committed to the campaign. Over the next three days, it would repulse a British assault, and when the 12th SS Division was pulled out of the line for a rest, the *Leibstandarte* took over the defence of the Caen sector. Between 18 and 21 July, the 1st SS Panzer Division met the major Allied offensive known as Operation *Goodwood*, driving back the British 7th and 11th Armoured Divisions and inflicting heavy casualties in the process.

The constant battering against the German right flank had been costly to the Anglo-Canadian forces, and seemed to have made little progress. The *Leibstandarte* men were still holding their positions on the Caen-Falaise highway, standing firm against repeated attacks from Montgomery's 21st Army Group. By this time, the formation's Panzer strength had fallen to 33 Panthers, 30 Mark IV Panzers and 22 *Sturmgeschütz* assault guns. Around 1500 men had been killed, wounded, captured or were missing.

The relative weakness of the German units in the western sector of the front was fairly obvious to the Americans, who were far from being the amateur incompetents imagined by Rommel. And General Omar N. Bradley was certainly not going to pass up this opportunity.

At the end of July, in spite of bad weather, Bradley readied the US First Army to punch through the German lines west of St Lô. Known as Operation *Cobra,* the breakout began on 24 July 1944.

Mortain counterattack

Obergruppenführer Paul Hausser's Seventh Army was ordered to counterattack. On 4 August, they struck westwards. The attack was reinforced on 6 August by the 1st SS Panzer Division. *Leibstandarte* had been relieved on the Caen sector and had marched across the battlefield to continue the thrust. Bradley, now promoted to command the 7th Army Group, sensed the danger and threw in two corps from the US First Army. There was bitter fighting at Mortain, but Avranches was not reached by the Germans.

The attacks were finally stopped by artillery fire and by a devastating series of attacks by Allied fighter bombers. On 7 August, the LSSAH attack was shattered by Hawker Typhoons of the RAF's 245th Squadron. By the 10th, the *Leibstandarte* was on the defensive at St Barthelemy, and Sepp Dietrich was

asking the *Führer* for permission to pull back. Permission was refused.

Waffen-SS losses had been appalling. Divisions that had entered the fray with hundreds of tanks and thousands of men were reduced to little more than battalion strength: the *Leibstandarte* lost all its tanks and artillery. The Battle of Normandy finally ended on 21 August, with surviving German divisional units pulling back to the Seine.

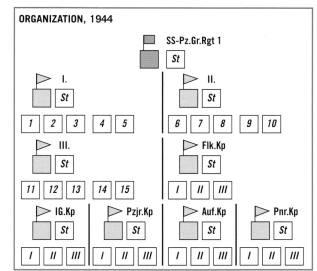

▶ **7.5cm Sturmkanone 40 Ausf F/8 (SdKfz 142/1)**

SS Sturmgeschütz Abteilung 1 / I. Kompanie

The *Leibstandarte* had been operating assault guns in small numbers since 1940. These had been organized into a *Sturmgeschütz-Abteilung* in 1942, and in 1943 it was designated as the 1st SS StuG Battalion.

Specifications

Crew: 4	Engine: Maybach HL120TRM petrol (300hp)
Weight: 25.6 tonnes (23.3 tons)	Speed: 40km/h (25mph)
Length: 6.77m (22ft 2in)	Range: 210km (130 miles)
Width: 2.92m (9ft 7in)	Radio: FuG15 or FuG16
Height: 2.15m (7ft)	Armament: 1 x 75mm (3in) StuK 40 L/48 gun

▶ **15cm sIG33 (Sf) auf PzKpfw I Ausf B (SdKfz 101)**

1.SS-Panzergrenadier-Regiment / 17.sIG-Kompanie

Late in 1943, LSSAH's Panzergrenadier regiments had a heavy infantry gun company, but by the summer of 1944 these had been transferred into the regiments' heavy infantry companies.

Specifications

Crew: 4	Engine: Maybach NL38TR
Weight: 9.4 tonnes (8.5 tons)	Speed: 40km/h (25mph)
Length: 4.67m (15.3ft)	Range: 140km (87 miles)
Width: 2.06m (6.8ft)	Armament: 1 x 150mm (5.9in) sIG33 L/11
Height: 2.8m (9.2ft)	

◀ **Leichte Schützenpanzerwagen (SdKfz 250/9)**

SS-Panzer-Aufklärungs-Abteilung LSSAH / 2.Kompanie (Skw)

Late in 1944, the reconnaissance battalion had three half-track companies.

Specifications

Crew: 3	Speed: 60km/h (37mph)
Weight: 6.9 tonnes (6.3 tons)	Range: 320km (199 miles)
Length: 4.56m (14ft 11.5in)	Radio: FuG Spr Ger 'f'
Width: 1.95m (6ft 5in)	Armament: 1 x 20mm (0.7in) KwK 30/38 L/55
Height: 2.16m (7ft 1in)	cannon; 1 x 7.92mm (0.3in) MG (coaxial)
Engine: Maybach HL42TRKM 6-cylinder (100hp)	

 # The Ardennes

DECEMBER 1944

The defeat in Normandy did not mean that the fighting days of the LAH were over. From 16 December 1944 to 1 January 1945 it played a key part in the Ardennes against the US Army.

B Y THE CLOSE OF THE Battle of Normandy, it had been reduced to less than 30 serviceable armoured vehicles. Among the casualties was the seriously wounded Teddy Wisch. From August 1944 to February 1945, command of LAH passed to *SS-Oberführer* Wilhelm Mohnke.

By now, the *Waffen-SS* had grown to nearly a million men, enough to provide an entire armoured

▶ **Mittlere Schützenpanzerwagen (SdKfz 251/9)**

1.SS-Panzergrendier-Regiment LSSAH / I.Battalion / 1.Kompanie

In December 1944, one battalion in each of the *Leibstandarte*'s 1st and 2nd SS Panzergrenadier Regiments were mounted on half-tracks. The three Panzergrenadier companies in each battalion had two SdKfz 251/9s in their heavy platoons.

Specifications

Crew: 3	Engine: Maybach HL42TUKRM
Weight: 9.4 tonnes (8.53 tons)	Speed: 53km/h (33mph)
Length: 5.98m (19ft 7in)	Range: 300km (186 miles)
Width: 2.83m (9ft 4in)	Radio: FuG Spr Ger 'f'
Height: 2.07m (6ft 10in)	Armament: 1 x 75mm (3in) KwK L/24 gun

ORGANIZATION
▷ SS-Pzjr.Abt 1
☐ St
1 | 2 | Pzjr | Ns

army for the campaign, the Sixth Panzer Army. However, the SS and the *Leibstandarte* were no longer the elite formation of the early 1940s. Conscription had been brought in, and the division included among its reluctant recruits men from factories, the *Kriegsmarine* and the *Luftwaffe*.

SS Panzer Army

Leibstandarte was the most powerful unit in the Sixth SS Panzer Army. It had just re-equipped with massive King Tiger tanks serving alongside Panthers and long-barrel Panzer IVs. Spearheading the attack in the Ardennes was an LAH *Kampfgruppe,* or battle

group, under the command of *SS-Obersturmbannführer* Jochen Peiper. The 5000 men of *Kampfgruppe Peiper* pushed forward nearly 60km (37 miles), but their attack was eventually blunted. It was during this thrust that the *Leibstandarte* was held responsible for the murder of 71 American prisoners of war at the Malmedy crossroads.

Steady Allied pressure and air power freed by clearing weather halted and finally broke the German attack. The remnants of the *Leibstandarte* were withdrawn to Bonn to refit. The Ardennes offensive had cost the Germans nearly 100,000 dead and the Americans 76,000.

ORGANIZATION
▷ s.SS-Pz.Ab 101
☐ St
1 | 2 | 3

▶ **Medium Panzer Company**

In 1944, the nominal strength of a Panther company was 21 or 22 tanks as seen here. However, by February 1945 the four companies of the *Leibstandarte's* 1st Battalion had only 34 Panthers, an average of only eight or so tanks per company.

Stab

1.*Zug*   2.*Zug*   3.*Zug*   4.*Zug*

▶ **10.5cm leFH 18/2 auf PzKpfw II (Sf) Wespe (SdKfz 124)**

1.SS-Panzer-Artillerie-Regiment LSSAH / I.Bataillon / 3.Batterie

Even for such a favoured formation as the *Leibstandarte,* there were not enough resources to equip more than one out of the LSSAH's four artillery battalions with self-propelled artillery pieces.

Specifications

Crew: 5	Speed: 40km/h (25mph)
Weight: 12.1 tonnes (11 tons)	Range: 220km (136.7 miles)
Length: 4.81m (15ft 10in)	Radio: FuG Spr 1
Width: 2.28m (7ft 6in)	Armament: 1 x 105mm (4.1in) LeFH 18M
Height: 2.25m (7ft 4.5in)	L/28 howitzer
Engine: Maybach HL62TR	

▶ **15cm schw. Panzerhaubitze auf Geschützwagen III/IV Hummel (SdKfz 165)**

1.SS-Panzer-Artillerie-Regiment LSSAH / I.Bataillon / 1.Batterie

At the end of 1944, the LSSAH artillery regiment's 1st Battalion had one battery of 15cm (5.9in) Hummel howitzers and two batteries of 10.5cm (4.1in) Wespe light field howitzers.

Specifications

Crew: 6	Speed: 42km/h (26mph)
Weight: 26.5 tonnes (24 tons)	Range: 215km (133.6 miles)
Length: 7.17m (23ft 6in)	Radio: FuG Spr 1
Width: 2.97m (9ft 8in)	Armament: 1 x 150mm (5.9in)
Height: 2.81m (9ft 2in)	sFH 18/1 L/30;
Engine: Maybach HL120TRM (265hp)	1 x 7.92mm (0.3in) MG

 # The end in Hungary

FEBRUARY–MAY 1945

The final battle for the *Leibstandarte* came in January 1945, when the Russian winter offensive pushed into Hungary and the Sixth SS Panzer Army was deployed to retake the Balaton oilfields.

▶ **3.7cm Flak auf Pz IV (Sf) Möbelwagen (SdKfz 161/3)**

1.SS-Panzer-Regiment LSSAH / Stab-Kompanie / Flak-Zug

At the beginning of February 1945, the *Leibstandarte* had eight 3.7cm (1.5in) Flak Panzers in its Panzer regiment's HQ company.

Specifications

Crew: 6	Engine: Maybach HL120TRM
Weight: 26.5 tonnes (24 tons)	Speed: 38km/h (23.6mph)
Length: 5.92m (19.4ft)	Range: 200km (124 miles)
Width: 2.95m (9.7ft)	Radio: FuG5 and FuG2
Height: 2.73m (9ft)	

AFTER A FRUITLESS ATTEMPT to recapture the oilfields and to relieve the besieged Hungarian capital of Budapest, the Germans withdrew into Austria but were ordered to hold Vienna. When Hitler heard of the withdrawals, he flew into a rage. He ordered that the men of SS divisions should remove their cuff titles and that all promotions and decorations were to be cancelled.

Sepp Dietrich's reaction was typical and robust. When the commander of the Sixth SS Panzer Army received the signal, he considered putting all the honours into a chamber pot and sending them to Hitler, but then he simply ignored the order.

Following the news of Hitler's death, Dietrich ensured that most of the *Waffen-SS* divisions in the East were able to break contact with the advancing Russians and surrender to the Americans at Steyr in upper Austria. But the war was not over for the men of the *Leibstandarte*. They might have considered themselves the elite of the German armed forces, but to the Allies, they were all members of the SS. They faced years of captivity in POW cages after the International Military Tribunal at Nuremberg determined that the SS was an illegal organization. Many of its leading lights were tried and sentenced as war criminals, though few served their full terms.

▲ Panzerkampfwagen VI Ausf E (SdKfz 181)
501.schwere Panzer-Abteilung

In November 1944, the 101st Corps' heavy tank battalion was attached to LAH as the 501st Heavy Tank Battalion.

Specifications

Crew: 5	Speed: 46km/h (28.6mph)
Weight: 47.4 tonnes (43 tons)	Range: 200km (124 miles)
Length: 8.86m (29ft 0in)	Radio: FuG5
Width: 3.4m (11ft 2in)	Armament: 1 x 75mm (3in) KwK 42 L/70;
Height: 2.95m (9ft 8in)	2 x 7.92mm (0.3in) MG (one hull-mounted,
Engine: Maybach HL230P30	one coaxial)

Specifications

Crew: 5	Speed: 38km/h (23.6mph)
Weight: 62.8 tonnes (61 tons)	Range: 140km (87 miles)
Length: 8.45m (27ft 8in)	Radio: FuG5
Width: 3.7m (12ft 1in)	Armament: 1 x 88mm (3.5in) KwK 36 L/56;
Height: 2.93m (9ft 7in)	2 x 7.92mm (0.3in) MG (one hull-mounted,
Engine: Maybach HL210P45 (700hp)	one coaxial)

▼ Panzerkampfwagen V Ausf D (SdKfz 171)
1.SS-Panzer-Regiment LSSAH / I.Abteilung / 1.Kompanie / Stab

Although early Panther D models had largely been replaced by 1944, some survived into 1945.

2nd SS Panzer Division *Das Reich*

The *Schutzstaffel*, or SS, split into three main branches after the Nazis came to power: the *Allgemeine-*, or General SS, the *Totenkopf* concentration camp guards and the Armed SS.

THE ARMED SS WAS the largest branch of the organization. It would eventually number some 39 divisions, and one million men of 15 nationalities passed through its ranks.

Taking the name *Waffen-SS* in the spring of 1940, it took part in 12 major campaigns and was noted for its tough fighting qualities and aggressive leadership.

The premier formation of the *Waffen-SS*, the *Leibstandarte Adolf Hitler*, provided guards of honour for visiting VIPs before the war.

Initially the Armed SS was made up from Hitler's bodyguard, the *Leibstandarte*, together with a number of *Politsiche Bereitschaften*, or political emergency squads. These had been established in the 1930s as strong-arm units designed to use violent measures against political opponents.

INSIGNIA

The *Wolfsengel* or Wolf's Hook is a germanic symbol dating back to the Middle Ages, thought in folklore to represent a kind of iron trap used to catch wolves.

The horizontal version of the symbol as used by *Das Reich* was known as 'the werewolf'. It was often painted onto vehicles without a surrounding shield.

As the second SS Division, at Kursk *Das Reich* was given a symbol with two vertical uprights compared to the single upright of *Leibstandarte*.

Commanders

Gruppenführer Paul Hausser *October 1939 – October 1941*	Obersturmbannführer Christian Tychsen *July 1944*
Brigadeführer Wilhelm Bittrich *October 1941 – December 1941*	Oberführer Otto Baum *July 1944 – October 1944*
Brigadeführer Matthias Kleinheisterkamp *December 1941 – April 1942*	Brigadeführer Heinz Lammerding *October 1944 – January 1945*
Gruppenführer Georg Keppler *April 1942 – February 1943*	Standartenführer Karl Kreutz *January 1945 – February 1945*
Oberführer Hebert-Ernst Vahl *February 1943 – March 1943*	Gruppenführer Werner Ostendorff *February 1945 – March 1945*
Standartenführer Kurt Brasack *March 1943 – April 1943*	Standartenführer Rudolf Lehmann *March 1945 – April 1945*
Gruppenführer Walter Krüger *April 1943 – October 1943*	Standartenführer Karl Kreutz *April 1945 – May 1945*
Brigadeführer Heinz Lammerding *November 1943 – July 1944*	

▼ **Armoured column**

A mixture of armoured fighting vehicles from the *Das Reich* Division, including a Panzer IV (right) and a Tiger I (left), prepare to move, southern Russia, late 1943.

Members of the Armed SS were originally designated as *SS-Verfügungstruppe,* or special duty troops. The name was usually shortened to SS-VT.

By the time of the *Anschluss,* the Armed SS had grown dramatically. In addition to the 2600 men of the *Leibstandarte,* there were three SS-VT *Standarten,* or regiments, derived from the *Politische Bereitschaften.* The three regiments were given the names *Deutschland, Germania,* and *Der Führer,* and were trained and equipped as motorized infantry.

Divisional History	Formed
Die SS-Verfügungstruppe	1934
SS-Division Verfügungstruppe	1940
SS-Division Deutschland	1940
SS-Division (mot) Reich	1940
SS-Division (mot) Das Reich	1942
SS-Panzergrenadier-Division Das Reich	1942
2.SS-Panzer-Division Das Reich	1943

▶ Schwere Panzerspähwagen (SdKfz 231)

SS-Verfügungstruppe / SS-Standarte Germania / Spähpanzerwagen-Zug

The SdKfz 231 was the standard pre-war heavy armoured car that was used by motorized reconnaissance troops in Austria, Czechoslovakia, Poland and France.

Specifications

Crew: 2

Weight: 2.45 tonnes (2.23 tons)

Length: 5.10m (16ft 8in)

Width: 1.93m (6ft 4in)

Height: 1.96m (6ft 5in)

Engine: Krupp 3.3L 4-cylinder (60hp)

Speed: 70km/h (43mph)

Range: 450km (280 miles)

Radio: None

▶ Mittlere Lkw Henschel 33 3t

SS-Verfügungstruppe / SS-Standarte Der Führer

The *Der Führer* Regiment, of the SS-VT was originally raised in Vienna in 1938 after the German *Anschluss.* From the start, the *Standarte* was motorized, its troops being lorry-borne.

Specifications

Crew: 1

Weight: 6.1 tonnes (6 tons)

Length: 7.4m (24ft)

Width: 2.25m (7ft 4in)

Height: 3.2m (10ft 6in)

Engine: 10.7 L (650ci),

    6-cylinder petrol (100hp)

Speed: 60km/h (37mph)

Payload: 3 tonnes (2.95 tons)

    or 18 troops

▶ Leichte Lkw Krupp L2H143 (Kfz 69)

SS-Verfügungstruppe / SS-Standarte Deutschland

The light artillery tractor variant of the Krupp L2H43 and L2H143 was used by the Panzerjäger and infantry gun companies of the *SS-VT* regiments to tow 3.7cm (1.5in) Pak 36 anti-tank guns and 7.5cm (3in) light infantry guns.

Specifications

Crew: 2

Weight: 2.45 tonnes (2.23 tons)

Length: 5.10m (16ft 8in)

Width: 1.93m (6ft 4in)

Height: 1.96m (6ft 5in)

Engine: Krupp 3.3L 4-cylinder (60hp)

Speed: 70km/h (43mph)

Range: 450km (280 miles)

Radio: None

Poland and France
1939–1940

The motorized *Der Führer*, *Deutschland* and *Germania* Regiments of the Armed SS were attached to and under the command of German Army units in the invasion of Poland in September 1939.

BEFORE THE WAR, the SS was an exclusively volunteer force, and its physical entry standards were high. Training was along Army lines; aggression was highly prized, and exercises emphasized speed and ferocity of attack.

The three SS-VT *Standarten* displayed all of that aggression when they fought in Poland, as individual regiments attached to Army formations. *Reichsführer-SS* Himmler was unhappy about this, and won a concession from the Army that SS units would serve in SS formations, though remaining under *Wehrmacht* control when in combat.

SS-VT Division in France

After the campaign in Poland, the SS-VT units were withdrawn to East Prussia, where they were to be merged into a new division. Although the *Leibstandarte* remained separate, the three other *Standarten* would become the nucleus of the SS-VT Division, which saw action in Poland and France.

In the early stages of the campaign in the West, the SS-VT Division had been split. *Der Führer* fought alongside the *Leibstandarte* as the German X Corps

pushed through the Grebbe defensive lines en route to Amsterdam.

The other two regiments, *Deutschland* and *Germania,* were attached to the 9th Panzer Division. Operating further south, the units were tasked with pushing through heavily mined polders on the approach to Rotterdam. First combat came against Dutch units reinforced by French troops that had driven through Belgium, and the *Deutschland* Regiment performed very well in heavy fighting around the port of Flushing.

All three regiments suffered heavy casualties in unsuccessfully trying to prevent the British retreat into Dunkirk. After Dunkirk, the three SS units were withdrawn for a couple of days of rest, before being moved yet again to take part in the Battle of France. *Leibstandarte* and the SS-VT Division were attached to *Panzergruppe Kleist.*

The SS-VT Division reached the Aire River on 7 June, where it encountered some of the fiercest French resistance of the campaign. The badly mauled SS-VT retired over the Somme, before returning to prevent a breakout of French forces in Alsace.

COMBAT UNIT ORGANIZATION, 1939

STANDARTE (REGIMENTAL) ORGANIZATION, 1939

▶ Panzerkampfwagen II Ausf C (SdKfz 121)

SS-Panzertruppe Reich

The *Reich* Division was given its own Panzer troop in May 1941, soon after the division was withdrawn from the Balkans.

Specifications

Crew: 3	Engine: Maybach HL62TR
Weight: 9.8 tonnes (8.9 tons)	Speed: 40km/h (25mph)
Length: 4.81m (15.8ft)	Range: 200km (124.3 miles)
Width: 2.22m (7.3ft)	Radio: FuG5
Height: 1.99m (6.5ft)	

▶ 15cm sIG33 auf PzKpfw I Ausf B

SS-Division VT / SS-Standarte Germania / Infanteriegeschütz-Kompanie

Mounting light howitzers onto tracked chassis gave German infantry units a considerable amount of dedicated firepower, which meant that they did not have to wait for regimental or divisional assets to be assigned for their use.

Specifications

Crew: 4	Engine: Maybach NL38TR
Weight: 9.4 tonnes (8.5 tons)	Speed: 40km/h (25mph)
Length: 4.67m (15.3ft)	Range: 140km (87 miles)
Width: 2.06m (6.8ft)	Armament: 1 x 150mm (5.9in) sIG33 L/11
Height: 2.8m (9.2ft)	

▶ Leichte Panzerspähwagen MG (SdKfz 221)

SS-Aufklärungs-Abteilung

Manufactured from 1935 to 1940, the lightweight SdKfz 221 was issued to light, Panzer and motorized divisions in the early years of the war.

Specifications

Crew: 2	Engine: Horch 3.5 L petrol (75hp)
Weight: 4 tonnes (3.61 tons)	Speed: 90km/h (56mph)
Length: 4.80m (15ft 8in)	Range: 320km (199 miles)
Width: 1.95m (6ft 5in)	Radio: None
Height: 1.70m (5ft 7in)	Armament: 1 x 7.92mm (0.3in) MG

▶ Personenkraftwagen VW (Kfz 1)

SS-Division Reich

The mass-produced Volkswagen Model 82 fitted with standard military bodywork became one of the most used light vehicles in the whole *Wehrmacht*.

Specifications

Crew: 1	Engine: Volkswagen 998cc petrol (24hp). Later
Weight: 0.64 tonnes (0.58 tons)	Volkswagen 1131cc petrol (25hp)
Length: 3.73m (12 ft 3in)	Speed: 100km/h (62mph)
Width: 1.60m (5ft 3in)	Range: 600km (375 miles)
Height: 1.35m (4ft 5in)	Radio: None

Invasion of the Balkans

APRIL 1941

After a period on occupation duties, training for an invasion of Britain which never came, the SS-VT Division lost some of its units to form a new SS division, later known as *Wiking*.

FOR A SHORT TIME, the SS-VT Division was given the new title *SS-Division Deutschland,* but this was too close to the name of the Army's showpiece *Grossdeutschland* Regiment, so in January 1941 it was again renamed, becoming the *SS-Division Reich.*

The German campaign against the Balkans in 1941 would involve both *Leibstandarte* and the *Reich* Division. General Ewald von Kleist's 1st Panzer Group, an armoured army in all but name, would attack westwards from southern Romania and northern Bulgaria, directed towards Belgrade. The *SS-Division Reich* would be one of his spearhead formations.

Panzers drove westwards, the *SS-Division Reich* racing the Army's elite *Grossdeutschland* Regiment for their objectives. The SS men reached the town of Alibunar first, but heavy rains, marshy terrain and muddy roads slowed progress. On 12 April, the Germans reached the Tamis River where it joined the Danube (known as the Dunay in Yugoslavia). The delays in reaching their objectives meant that *Reich* and *Grossdeutschland* were halted on the banks of the Danube while new plans were being made.

SS-Hauptsturmführer Fritz Klingenberg, the commander of *Reich*'s motorcycle reconnaissance company, had other ideas, however. Using rubber boats to cross the Danube on 14 May, Klingenberg took 10 men into Belgrade, quickly realizing that the city was very lightly defended. The inventive SS officer claimed to be the forerunner of a powerful assault. He threatened the city's mayor with further massive aerial bombardments unless the city surrendered – neglecting to point out that his radios were not working and that his 10 men were all the assault force that there was.

The 11th Panzer Division arrived in the city a few hours later. Much to their chagrin, the Army troops found Belgrade already in the possession of one SS officer and 10 of his men.

SS arrogance

Relations between the *Reich* Division and their fellows were not good, however. All would admit that the SS men fought with vigour and great dash, but their arrogance rubbed most of the *Wehrmacht* up the wrong way. Relations were not helped by friction in the field: in one incident, a fast-moving Army convoy was about to overtake a column of SS vehicles. Wanting a clear road ahead, and not wanting to eat the Army's dust, the SS

▶ **Panzerkampfwagen III Ausf F (SdKfz 141)**

SS-Panzergrenadier-Division Das Reich / Panzer-Abteilung / Stab

The *Reich* Division acquired a Panzer troop after the Balkans campaign. By 1942, this had grown to battalion size, and in November 1942 it became a two-battalion regiment in the Panzergrenadier Division *Das Reich*.

Specifications

Crew: 5	Engine: Maybach HL120TRM
Weight: 21.8 tonnes (19.8 tons)	Speed: 40km/h (25mph)
Length: 5.38m (17.7ft)	Range: 165km (102.5 miles)
Width: 2.91m (9.5ft)	Radio: FuG5
Height: 2.44m (8ft)	

commander threatened to open fire if the Army vehicles did try to pass.

After a war that had lasted only 12 days, Yugoslavia ceased to exist as a nation. Italy and Germany annexed parts of Slovenia, while Hungary received territory northwest of Belgrade. To the east, Bulgaria acquired a large piece of land that included parts of Macedonia and northeastern Greece. Italy also received a section of the Dalmatian coast and the Bay of Kotor.

The units involved in the campaign, including the *Reich* Division, were quickly pulled out for refitting. A much larger campaign, against the Soviet Union, was about to get under way.

▼ Aufklärungs-Abteilung SS-Division Reich, Spähpanzerwagen-Kompanie

The purpose of a reconnaissance company was to discover information about the enemy, and to get that information back to higher command levels. As a result, armoured car platoons always featured vehicles with long-range radios, operating together with gun-armed vehicles which served as protection.

Schwere Zug

1.leichte Zug

2.leichte Zug

3.leichte Zug

▶ **Panzerkampfwagen IV Ausf H (SdKfz 161/2)**

2.SS-Pz.Rgt Das Reich / II.Abteilung / 6.Kompanie

Production of the Ausf H variant of the
Panzer IV began early in 1943, and the 2nd
SS Panzer Regiment had started replacing Panzer IIIs with the type
by the summer.

Specifications

Crew: 5	Engine: Maybach HL120TRM
Weight: 27.6 tonnes (25 tons)	Speed: 38km/h (23.6mph)
Length: 7.02m (23ft 0in)	Range: 210km (130.5 miles)
Width: 2.88m (9ft 5in)	Radio: FuG5
Height: 2.68m (8ft 10in)	

▶ **Schwere Spähpanzerwagen 8-Rad (SdKfz 231)**

SS-Aufklärungs-Regiment Langemark / Spähpanzerwagen-Kompanie

With a maximum speed of 85km/h (52.8mph), the SdKfz 231 had duplicate driving
controls at the rear of the vehicle. With six reverse gears matching its six forward
gears, it was just as fast going backwards as it was in advancing.

Specifications

Crew: 4	Engine: Büssing-NAG 8-cylinder petrol
Weight: 9.1 tonnes (8.3 tons)	Speed: 85km/h (52.8mph)
Length: 5.85m (19ft 2in)	Range: 300km (186 miles)
Width: 2.20m (7ft 2.5in)	Radio: FuG Ger 'a'
Height: 2.35m (7ft 8in)	Armament: 1 x 20mm (0.7in) cannon

 # With Army Group Centre
1941–1942

***SS-Division Reich* was one of the *Wehrmacht's* spearhead formations in the invasion of the
Soviet Union. It would take its final and most famous name of *Das Reich* early in 1942.**

THE *REICH* DIVISION was allotted to General Heinz
Guderian's 2nd Panzer Group and formed part of
Army Group Centre, which comprised nine Panzer
divisions, five motorized and 31–35 infantry
divisions, as well as two to three security divisions,
a cavalry division and the *Grossdeutschland* Regiment,
all under Field Marshal Fedor von Bock.

The *Reich* Division experienced considerable
difficulty in its advance. Because Army Group Centre
had not allocated it any space on the road leading to
the front line, most of its soldiers had to march on
foot through the countryside, although some of them
were able to hitch rides with Army convoys.

However, these unpromising
beginnings were soon forgotten
as *Reich* took part in the Battle
of Yelnya near Smolensk, and
then in the spearhead of the
drive to capture Moscow. *Reich*
came within a few kilometres of
the Soviet capital in November
1941. However, with Moscow
within sight of the division's
reconnaissance units, the
offensive ground to a halt in the
fierce Russian winter. *Reich* then

ORGANIZATION
▷ Pz.Tr Reich
St
mit | lei | lei | Pzw

ORGANIZATION
Krd.Rgt DR
St
I | II

ORGANIZATION

suffered massive losses as the Soviet counterattack pushed the Germans back from Moscow.

After a period of heavy combat and serious losses for the division, by now named *Das Reich*, it was pulled out of the fighting and sent to France to refit, where it would eventually be upgraded as a Panzergrenadier division. Some units remained in the East under the command of *Standartenführer* Werner Ostendorf as *Kampfgruppe Ostendorf.*

▶ **Panzerkampfwagen KV-1a 753(r)**

2.SS-Panzer-Regiment Das Reich

Although most captured Soviet KV-1 tanks were operated by Army divisions, formations like *Das Reich* would use any captured tanks in working order to supplement their own armour.

Specifications

Crew: 5
Weight: 46.6 tonnes (42.3 tons)
Length: 6.7m (22ft)
Width: 3.32m (10ft 11in)
Height: 2.7m (8ft 11in)
Engine: V-2K
Speed: 35km/h (22mph)
Range: 180km (112 miles)
Radio: 10R

 # Kharkov and Kursk
1943

While *Das Reich* was refitting in France over the summer of 1942, the decision was taken to upgrade it further. In November, it became the *SS-Panzergrenadier-Division Das Reich.*

IN THE SAME MONTH, as Germany occupied the Vichy-controlled zone of France, parts of the division took part in an attempt to prevent the scuttling of the French Fleet at Toulon. Early in 1943, *Das Reich* was transferred back to the Eastern Front, where it helped reclaim the crumbling central front around Kharkov.

Kharkov was the first major Soviet city to be liberated by the Red Army after Stalingrad. Two weeks later on 17 February, the Red Army was at Pavlograd, only 40km (25 miles) from the Dnieper – and quite close to Hitler, who was paying a flying visit to Zaporozhye. Field Marshal von Manstein had a clear plan for stabilizing the desperate situation in the East, and he persuaded the *Führer* to let him conduct the battle his way, instead of conducting the rigid defence that Hitler usually favoured. The result was a tactical masterstroke, which continues to be studied in military academies today.

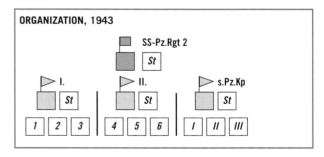

SS-Panzergrenadier-Division *Das Reich*, July 1943	Strength
PzKpfw II	1
PzKpfw III (long-barrel)	62
PzKpfw IV (long barrel)	33
PzKpfw VI Tiger	14
PzKpfw T-34(r)	25
Befehls	10

Manstein let the Soviet advance continue while he assembled a powerful striking force on its flanks, consisting of SS Panzergrenadier Divisions *Leibstandarte*, *Das Reich* and *Totenkopf* combined with five Army Panzer divisions and the *Grossdeutschland* Division. Manstein sprang his first trap on 20 February. On the day that the forward Soviet patrols reached Pavlograd, Panzers were driving up the west bank of the Donets behind them. In what he dubbed his 'backhand blow', Manstein drove east to cut off all the Soviet forces that had broken over the Donets.

▶ Panzerkampfwagen VI Ausf E (SdKfz 181)

2.SS-Panzer-Regiment Das Reich / II.Battalion / 8.Kompanie

Early in 1943, each of the *Das Reich* Panzer battalions was
assigned a heavy
company of
Tiger tanks.

Specifications

Crew: 5	Height: 2.93m (9.6ft)
Weight: 62.8 tonnes	Engine: Maybach HL210P45
(57 tons)	Speed: 38km/h (23mph)
Length: 8.45m (27.7ft)	Range: 140km (87 miles)
Width: 3.7m (12ft)	Radio: FuG5

▶ Panzerkampfwagen V Ausf A (SdKfz 171)

2.SS-Panzer-Regiment Das Reich / I.Battalion / 1.Kompanie

In May 1943, *Das Reich*'s 1st Panzer Battalion was returned to Germany to convert
to the new PzKpfw V Panther.

Specifications

Crew: 5	Speed: 46km/h (28.6mph)
Weight: 50.2 tonnes	Range: 200km (124.3 miles)
(45.5 tons)	Radio: FuG5
Length: 8.86m (29ft 0in)	Armament: 1 x 75mm (3in)
Width: 3.4m (11ft 2in)	KwK42 L/70; 2 x 7.92mm
Height: 2.98m (9ft 10in)	(0.3in) MG (one hull-
Engine: Maybach HL230P30	mounted, one coaxial)

▶ Panzerkampfwagen III Ausf M (SdKfz 141/1)

2.Pz.Rgt Das Reich / I.Bataillon / 3.Kompanie

Das Reich still had more than 60 Panzer IIIs on strength in July 1943, at the
opening of the Battle of Kursk. Most had been replaced
by Panthers by the end of the year.

Specifications

Crew: 4	Engine: Maybach HL120TRM petrol
Weight: 25.4 tonnes (23 tons)	(300hp)
Length: 6.41m (21ft)	Speed: 40km/h (25mph)
Width: 2.95m (9ft 7in)	Range: 155km (96 miles)
Height: 2.44m (8ft)	Radio: FuG5

By 3 March, the Soviets had been forced to abandon nearly 15,500 square kilometers (6000 square miles) of their recent gains. The SS Panzer Corps stormed Kharkov in mid-March, and Belgorod was retaken. By the end of the month, the four Soviet tank corps strung out between the Donets and Zaporozhye were annihilated.

Kursk

After the Third Battle of Kharkov, *Das Reich* along with other divisions was thrown into an assault into the Kursk salient, a bulge in the Soviet front line around the area of Kursk. *Das Reich* pushed 64km (40 miles) into the southern sector of the bulge, but was pulled out of the battle when the offensive was called off. *Das Reich* was again withdrawn to France, this time to refit as *SS-Panzer-Division Das Reich*.

Part of the division was left in the East as *Kampfgruppe Lammerding*. The *Kamfgruppe* was one of the units encircled by the Soviets at Cherkassy. In February 1944, the *Kampfgruppe* was transferred to France to join the rest of the division.

▲ **Kursk tank battle**

Sitting in the rear of an SdKfz 251, young Panzergrenadiers from the *Das Reich* Division prepare to engage Soviet forces at Kursk, July 1943.

▼ **Mittlere Pionierpanzerwagen Ausf D (SdKfz 251/7)**

2.SS-Panzer-Pionier-Bataillon / 1.(Skw) Kompanie

Introduced in September 1943, the Ausf D variant of the SdKfz 251 had a simplified armoured body made from fewer armoured plates, which was quicker and easier to manufacture.

Specifications

Crew: 7 or 8	Engine: Maybach HL42TUKRM
Weight: 8.9 tonnes (8.7 tons)	6-cylinder (100hp)
Length: 5.80m (19ft 0in)	Speed: 50km/h (31mph)
Width: 2.10m (6ft 11in)	Range: 300km (186 miles)
Height: 2.70m (8ft 10in)	Radio: FuG Spr Ger 1

� France
1944

The Allied landings in Normandy caught the German high command by surprise, with few of its Panzer divisions in position to attack the Allied beachhead.

QUICKLY GETTING OVER ITS surprise, OKW quickly began to move reserves to block the Allied advance. Among them were the *Waffen-SS* divisions, most with a hard core of troops seasoned in the bitter fighting on the Eastern Front.

The *Waffen-SS* Panzer divisions that took part in the Normandy battles brought with them a wealth of combat experience gained in years of vicious fighting on the Eastern Front, and many were survivors of the

greatest tank battle of all time – Kursk. One division that had further to travel than most was *Das Reich*. On 6 June, it had been on occupation duty around Cahors, near Bordeaux. By 9 June, it was on the march through the Massif Central, skirmishing with and being delayed by the Resistance all the way. On 10 June, a company of *Das Reich* men committed a massacre at Oradour-sur-Glane in reprisal for the apparent kidnapping of *Sturmbannführer* Kampfe.

2ND SS PANZER DIVISION *DAS REICH*

ORGANIZATION, 1944

Divisional strength – Normandy, May 1944	Strength
PzKpfw IV	78
PzKpfw V	79
StuG III	13
FlakPz 38	12

The SS men massacred 642 civilians, including 207 children, in one of the worst outrages to have taken place in Western Europe. Such events were far from unusual in Russia, however, and many of the *Das Reich* troopers still had an Eastern Front mindset.

Under the command of *Gruppenführer* Heinz Lammerding, *Das Reich* units began reaching the combat zone early in July, and were immediately engaged in combat with American forces at Coutances, St Lô, Percy and Mortain.

The relative weakness of the German units in the western sector of the front was obvious to the

Americans, an enemy hitherto underestimated by the Germans. General Omar N. Bradley saw a chance – and prepared to take it. At the end of July, in spite of bad weather, he readied the US First Army to punch through the German lines west of St Lô; from there, they would break out into the interior of France.

Mortain counterattack

Known as Operation *Cobra*, the breakout began on 24 July 1944 after heavy bombers of the Eighth US Air Force had carpet-bombed the German forward positions. To their amazement, given the sheer scale of the bombardment, the Americans encountered resistance – but it was only a thin grey line. By 28 July, the VII Corps under the dynamic General L. J. (Lightning Joe) Collins, together with General Troy Middleton's VIII Corps, had pushed the Germans back over 20km (12 miles).

The four Panzer divisions of Paul Hausser's Seventh Army struck westwards on 4 August, but in spite of bitter fighting the target of Avranches was not reached. The attacks were finally stopped by artillery fire and Allied fighter bombers. Most of the German armies in Normandy were now trapped in a pocket at Falaise. Many men escaped, but tens of thousands were either killed or taken prisoner. By the end of the battle, *Das Reich*'s strength had been reduced to just 450 men and 15 tanks.

▶ **Panzerkampfwagen V Ausf A (SdKfz 171)**

2.SS-Pz.Rgt / I.Abteilung / 4.Kompanie

This is the personal tank of SS-Oberscharführer Ernst Barkmann, one of the greatest tank aces of the war.

Specifications

Crew: 5	Speed: 46km/h (28.6mph)
Weight: 50.2 tonnes	Range: 200km (124.3 miles)
(45.5 tons)	Radio: FuG5
Length: 8.86m (29ft 0in)	Armament: 1 x 75mm (3in)
Width: 3.4m (11ft 2in)	KwK42 L/70; 2 x 7.92mm
Height: 2.98m (9ft 10in)	(0.3in) MG (one hull-
Engine: Maybach HL230P30	mounted, one coaxial)

▸ 10.5cm IFH 18/2 auf PzKpfw II (Sf) Wespe (SdKfz 124)

2.SS-Panzer-Artillerie-Regiment Das Reich / I.Bataillon (Sf) / 2.Batterie

The *Das Reich* Division's artillery regiment had the standard late-war table of equipment, with its 1st Battalion operating self-propelled howitzers and the 2nd, 3rd and 4th Battalions using towed guns and howitzers.

Specifications

Crew: 5	Speed: 40km/h (25mph)
Weight: 12.1 tonnes (11 tons)	Range: 220km (136.7 miles)
Length: 4.81m (15ft 10in)	Radio: FuG Spr 1
Width: 2.28m (7ft 6in)	Armament: 1 x 105mm (4.1in) LeFH
Height: 2.25m (7ft 4.5in)	18M L/28 howitzer
Engine: Maybach HL62TR	

▸ Mittlere Schützenpanzerwagen (SdKfz 251/9)

4.SS-Panzergrenadier-Regiment Der Führer / III.Bataillon / 11.Kompanie

Known unofficially as the *Stummel,* or Stump, the SdKfz 251/9 was designed to provide flexible short-range fire support for the heavy companies of Panzergrenadier battalions.

Specifications

Crew: 3	Speed: 53km/h (33mph)
Weight: 9.4 tonnes (8.53 tons)	Range: 300km (186 miles)
Length: 5.98m (19ft 7in)	Radio: FuG Spr Ger 'f'
Width: 2.83m (9ft 4in)	Armament: 1 x 75mm (3in) KwK
Height: 2.07m (6ft 10in)	L/24 gun
Engine: Maybach HL42TUKRM	

▲ King Tigers, Normandy 1944

Tiger IIs from an SS division rest between actions amidst the heavy fighting in Normandy following the Allied landings on 6 June 1944.

Battle of the Bulge
DECEMBER 1944

After being all but destroyed in Normandy, *Das Reich* was rebuilt in the Eifel region of Germany, in readiness to take part in Germany's last major offensive in the West.

PULLED BACK ACROSS THE SEINE and then into positions behind the West Wall fortifications along the German-French border, the 2nd SS Panzer Division prepared for the operation to punch through the Ardennes Forest in December 1944.

Led by *SS-Oberstgruppenführer* Josef 'Sepp' Dietrich, the newly established Sixth SS Panzer Army contained I and II SS Panzer Corps. Attached to II Corps, the *Das Reich* Division had finished crossing the Rhine by 24 November and, along with the 9th SS Panzer Division *Hohenstaufen,* took up positions south of I Corps near Losheim. I Corps consisted of the 1st and 12th SS Panzer Divisions, along with three Army formations. In addition, Dietrich commanded LXVII Corps of two more *Heer* divisions.

Problems bedevilled *Das Reich* and other divisions, even in the early stages of the offensive. Rushing into the battle zone, the SS units quickly became bogged down in traffic jams induced by petrol shortages. To reach Antwerp, the Germans needed to refuel their vehicles at least five times. However, Hitler provided his forces with enough petrol for only two refuellings. To maintain the secrecy of the operation, the *Führer* had forbidden the establishment of fuel dumps close to the front line.

On 20 December, *Obergruppenführer* Bittrich, commander of II SS Corps, directed *Das Reich* to relieve the 560th Volksgrenadier Division, which was attempting to capture the Baraque de Faiture crossroads. After accomplishing this task, the SS division was to push northwest through Manhay and establish a bridgehead across the River Ourthe at Bomal. By this time, Heinz Lammerding had resumed command of *Das Reich*. Coming within sight of the River Meuse, the division was halted, and then slowly smashed by fierce Allied counterattacks.

2.SS-Panzer-Division *Das Reich*	Strength
PzKpfw IV	28
PzKpfw V	58
StuG III/IV	28
FlakPz IV (2-cm)	4
FlakPz IV (3.7-cm)	4

REGIMENTAL ORGANIZATION, 1944

3.SS-Pz.Gren.Rgt Deutschland

St

| I | II | III | Flk | sIG | Pnr |

▶ **7.5cm Sturmgeschütz 40 Ausf G (SdKfz 142/1)**

2.SS-Panzer-Regiment Das Reich / II.Battalion / 8.Kompanie

One company of *Das Reich*'s 2nd Panzer Battalion was equipped with assault guns in May 1944; the other three companies had Panzer IVs.

Specifications

Crew: 4
Weight: 26.3 tonnes (23.9 tons)
Length: 6.77m (22ft 2in)
Width: 2.95m (9ft 8in)
Height: 2.16m (7ft 0in)
Engine: Maybach Hl120TRM

Speed: 40km/h (25mph)
Range: 155km (96.3 miles)
Radio: FuG 15 and FuG 16
Armament: 1 x 75mm (3in) StuG L/48 cannon

On 4 January, Bittrich ordered the 2nd SS Panzer Division *Das Reich* to leave the battle zone and serve as a reserve unit.

However, many of the division's regiments and battalions, which had been dispersed to other organizations at various sectors throughout the Ardennes, did not initially hear about this order and remained at the front lines. As a result, some of them suffered more losses when the Americans opened a major offensive five days later.

▶ **Mittlere Schützenpanzerwagen Ausf D (SdKfz 251/22)**

2.SS-Panzerjäger-Abteilung Das Reich / 1.Kompanie

Towards the war's end, Adolf Hitler ordered that every vehicle capable of carrying a 7.5cm (3in) Pak 40 be put into production. The SdKfz 251 was easy to modify: the entire Pak 40 (minus its wheels) was simply bolted on the half-track's loadbed.

Specifications

Crew: 4 or 5	Speed: 50km/h (31mph)
Weight: 8 tonnes (7.28 tons)	Range: 300km (186 miles)
Length: 5.98m (19ft 7in)	Radio: None
Width: 2.1m (6ft 11in)	Armament: 1 x 75mm (3in) PaK 40
Height: 2.25m (7ft 4.5in)	L/46 anti-tank gun; 1 x 7.92mm
Engine: Maybach HL42TUKRM	(0.3in) MG (rear-mounted)
6-cylinder petrol (100hp)	

▶ **Sanitätswagen Opel Blitz S (Kfz 31)**

2.SS-Krankenwagen-Kompanie

Das Reich's ambulance company had three detachments, which operated with the 1st and 2nd SS Medical Companies and the 1st SS Field Hospital.

Specifications

Crew: 1	Engine: Opel 6-cylinder petrol
Weight: 3.29 tonnes (3 tons)	(73.5hp)
Length: 6.02m (19ft 9in)	Speed: 80km/h (50mph)
Width: 2.27m (7ft 5in)	Range: 410km (255 miles)
Height: 2.18m (7ft 2in)	

 # End of the Reich

1945

Pulled out of the Ardennes, *Das Reich* was transferred into Germany to refit once again. However, in February it received orders to take part in the last German offensive of the war.

EARLY IN DECEMBER 1944, the Red Army invaded Hungary and reached a point along the River Danube 30km (18.6 miles) south of Budapest. Before the bulk of the Communist forces could cross the river, German formations arrived in time to stall the advance and establish the 'Margarethe Positions', a series of defensive lines arrayed from the Plattensee (Lake Balaton) to the Hungarian capital. In response, Stavka redirected the Soviet offensive and concentrated its forces at a bend in the Danube north of Budapest.

The Red Army took the Hungarian capital on 12 February. With this task accomplished, the Soviets were now able to commit most of their forces to an invasion of the oil-refining region of southern Hungary. If this area were to fall into Russian hands, the Third *Reich* would forfeit its only remaining source of fuel and thus be unable to continue the war. The loss of Hungary would also deprive the Germans of a vital grain-producing area.

To prevent such a catastrophe from befalling Germany, Hitler pulled his *Waffen-SS* divisions from the Western Front and dispatched them to the 'Margarethe Positions'. In fact, the Sixth SS Panzer Army had received orders to that effect even before the fall of Budapest. For the last time in the war, the *Das Reich* Division and other SS formations were to participate in a desperate counteroffensive that stood little chance of success against powerful and determined adversaries. Hitler called the attack Operation *Spring Awakening*.

Operation *Spring Awakening*

Unfortunately for the Germans, the Red Army would not be surprised by Operation *Spring Awakening*. When intelligence reports indicated the presence of

Das Reich and other SS divisions within the area, Stavka advised its field commanders to expect an attack that would be launched sometime between late February and early March.

Because of the soft terrain, the grenadiers had to attack on 6 March without aid from the divisional armoured units. Despite this, the SS battalions over-ran several lines of trenches and captured useful high ground. But as the German grenadiers pressed forward, the Red Army threw more reinforcements in their way, and the advance gradually slowed down and stalled.

Although the SS infantry units continued to press forward into the Red Army, senior officers in Army Group South eventually realized that the offensive did not stand any realistic chance of success.

On 16 March, the Soviets counterattacked with overwhelming force. It effectively brought Operation *Spring Awakening* to an inglorious end. Suddenly, the soldiers of the *Das Reich* Division found themselves fighting enemies that were attacking from three directions. After pushing back the Sixth *(Wehrmacht)*

▶ **Panzerkampfwagen IV Ausf H (SdKfz 161/2)**

2.SS-Pz.Rgt Das Reich / II.Battalion / 5.Kompanie

In December 1944, just before the beginning of the Ardennes offensive, *Das Reich* had 28 Panzer IVs in two companies of its 2nd Battalion. The other two companies had StuGs.

Specifications	
Crew: 5	Speed: 38km/h (23.6mph)
Weight: 27.6 tonnes (25 tons)	Range: 210km (130.5 miles)
Length: 7.02m (23ft 0in)	Radio: FuG5
Width: 2.88m (9ft 5in)	Armament: 1 x 75mm (3in) KwK
Height: 2.68m (8ft 10in)	40/43; 2 x 7.92mm (0.3in) MG
Engine: Maybach HL120TRM	(one hull-mounted, one coaxial)

▶ **Flakpanzer IV/2-cm Flakvierling Wirbelwind**

2.SS-Panzer-Artillerie-Regiment Das Reich / Stab / Flak-Zug

The Whirlwind was allocated to the anti-aircraft platoons attached to the staff companies of Panzer regiments and divisions. The quad 2cm (0.7in) turrets were mounted on obsolescent Panzer IV Ausf F and G chassis.

Specifications	
Crew: 5	Engine: Maybach HL120TRM
Weight: 24.3 tonnes (22 tons)	Speed: 38km/h (23.6mph)
Length: 5.9m (19ft 5in)	Range: 210km (130 miles)
Width: 2.9m (9ft 6in)	Radio: FuG2 and FuG5
Height: 2.76m (9ft)	

Army, Soviet armoured forces drove around Szekesfehervar and practically encircled the Sixth SS Panzer Army.

Das Reich spent the rest of the war fighting for survival from Dresden to Prague and on to Vienna. In the end, most of the division managed to escape to the West to surrender to the Americans. Before surrendering, elements of *Das Reich* helped large numbers of civilians in Prague escape the Red Army.

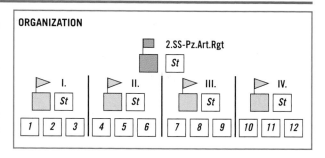

ORGANIZATION

2.SS-Pz.Art.Rgt

St

I.   St   II.   St   III.   St   IV.   St

1   2   3   4   5   6   7   8   9   10   11   12

▼ Panzer Artillery Regiment, Self-propelled Battalion

Das Reich's artillery regiment had four artillery battalions. Even at the height of the war, German production bottlenecks meant that all but the 1st Battalion were equipped with towed artillery pieces, with 10.5cm (4.1in) IFH18s in the 2nd and 3rd Battalions and 15cm (5.9in) sFH18 howitzers and 10cm (3.9in) sK18/40 long-range guns in the 4th Battalion. The 1st Battalion, however, was fully self-propelled. In May 1944, when it was at its peak strength just before the Normandy landings, the battalion had 12 Wespes in two batteries and six Hummels in a third heavy battery. The battalion's staff battery had no guns.

1. *Batterie*

2. *Batterie*

3. *Batterie*

3rd SS Panzer Division *Totenkopf*

Even before the outbreak of World War II, *Reichsführer-SS* Heinrich Himmler had been pressing to expand the Armed SS against fierce opposition from the German Army.

THE PERFORMANCE OF THE SS UNITS in Poland meant that in October 1939 Hitler gave Himmler permission to raise two new divisions. However, Army opposition remained intense, and since in law the Army had first right to conscript all German nationals, the SS struggled to find the manpower it needed. There were two sources of recruits that were under Himmler's control – the police and the concentration camp guards.

Originally classed as being part of the armed SS, Theodore Eicke's *Totenkopfverbände* had in effect become a separate organization, very different from the ferociously disciplined members of the Armed SS. Tasked with guarding and running Nazi concentration camps, the *Totenkopf* men took pride in their total lack of military virtues. The guards took their cue from their commander, Theodor Eicke.

Eicke, a psychopathic killer before being recruited by Himmler, had been a failure as a soldier and a policeman. Eicke hated professional army officers almost as much as he hated Marxists and Jews.

Death's Head Guards

In his Death's Head guards – recruited from unemployed malcontents, embittered farmhands and simple thugs – Eicke found pupils eager to learn his personal brand of brutality.

In October 1939, Eicke was ordered to raise a division from the Death's Head *Standarten,* five of which were then in existence at Dachau,

Commanders

Gruppenführer Theodor Eicke *1 November 1939 – 7 July 1941*	Gruppenführer Heinz Lammerding *27 April 1943 – 15 May 1943*
Oberführer Matthias Kleinheisterkamp *7 July 1941 – 18 July 1941*	Brigadeführer Max Simon *15 May 1943 – 22 October 1943*
Brigadeführer Georg Keppler *18 July 1941 – 19 September 1941*	Gruppenführer Herman Priess *22 October 1943 – 21 June 1944*
Obergruppenführer Theodor Eicke *19 September 1941 – 26 February 1943*	Brigadeführer Hellmuth Becker *21 June 1944 – 8 May 1945*
Brigadeführer Herman Priess *26 February 1943 – 27 April 1943*	

▲ **Pak 36 anti-tank training**

Soldiers from the *Totenkopf* division take part in an anti-tank drill in France, May 1940. *Totenkopf* troops would soon discover that this versatile weapon was ineffective against heavily-armoured British Matilda tanks near Arras.

▶ **Mittlere Lkw Opel Blitz 3000S Type S**

SS Totenkopf Infanterie Regiment 1 (mot) / II Bataillon

Built as a result of the Schell Program of 1938, examples of the Type S commercial standard 4x2 truck were constructed by Borgward, Magirus and Mercedes-Benz as well as by Opel.

Specifications

Crew: 1	Engine: Opel 6-cylinder petrol
Weight: 3.29 tonnes (3 tons)	(73.5hp)
Length: 6.02m (19ft 9in)	Speed: 80km/h (50mph)
Width: 2.27m (7ft 5in)	Range: 410km (255 miles)
Height: 2.18m (7ft 2in)	Radio: None

Mauthausen, Sachsenhausen, Buchenwald and Frankenberg.

On 1 November 1939, the *SS-Division Totenkopf* was officially raised, and began training at Dachau. A number of SS-VT troops were transferred into the division to provide a core of well-trained, combat-experienced troops. They were needed, since the new division was plagued with disciplinary problems. In December 1939, further reinforcements came from the former *Totenkopf-Standarte Götze,* which had seen combat with the *SS-Heimwehr Danzig* in the early stages of the Polish campaign.

The *Totenkopf* Division had to struggle to acquire weapons from the Army. The generals had to some extent come to accept the *Leibstandarte* and the SS-VT as real fighting men. They saw the *Totenkopf*'s former concentration camp guards as paramilitaries or police at best, and as simple thugs lacking in any military virtue at worst. It took a direct order from Hitler before the Army could be persuaded to supply the new SS unit with artillery and anti-tank guns.

Divisional History	Formed
Totenkopf-Standarten 1, 2 and 3	1937
SS-Division Totenkopf	1939
SS-Panzergrenadier-Division Totenkopf	1942
3.SS-Panzer-Division Totenkopf	1943

INSIGNIA

An ancient military symbol appropriated by the SS, the *Totenkopf* or Death's head was naturally used by the *Totenkopf* Division on its vehicles.

As the third SS division, the *Totenkopf*'s temporary divisional identification symbol used on its tanks at Kursk had three upright 'fingers'.

▶ **Leichte Panzerspähwagen 2cm (SdKfz 222)**

SS-Aufklärungs-Abteilung Totenkopf

In France in 1940, *Totenkopf* had a single light armoured car platoon, but by the time of Operation *Barbarossa* in June 1941 it had an armoured car company and by 1944 the reconnaisance battalion also had an extra armoured car platoon.

Specifications

Crew: 3

Weight: 5.3 tonnes (4.8 tons)

Length: 4.8m (15ft 8in)

Width: 1.95m (6ft 5in)

Height: 2.00m (6ft 7in)

Engine: Horch 3.5L or 3.8L petrol

Speed: 85km/h (52.8mph)

Range: 300km (186 miles)

Radio: FuG Spr Ger 'a'

Armament: 1 x 20mm (0.7in) KwK 30 L/55

cannon; 1 x 7.92mm (0.3in) MG (coaxial)

 # Battles in France

MAY 1940

In the opening stages of the campaign in the West, the *Totenkopf* Division of the SS was held back as part of von Rundstedt's reserves in Army Group A.

THE *TOTENKOPF* DIVISION had been assigned to General Max Weichs's Second Army, but the army commanders felt that a newly formed, untried division would be of little use in the campaign, and in the early phases of planning it was expected that the SS men would never play more than a reserve

role. However, when Weichs inspected the division early in April, he was pleasantly surprised. Theodor Eicke, the divisional commander, had put the *Totenkopf* through an intensive period of training in February and March. By April, he had begged, stolen and borrowed enough modern equipment to ensure

3RD SS PANZER DIVISION *TOTENKOPF*

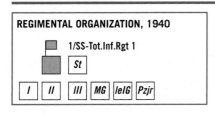

REGIMENTAL ORGANIZATION, 1940

1/SS-Tot.Inf.Rgt 1

St

| I | II | III | *MG* | *IeIG* | *Pzjr* |

that *Totenkopf* could match the best Army mechanized unit. The hard training had another effect on the thuggish former camp guards who made up much of the division: disciplinary cases, which had been running higher than in any other SS unit, were reduced considerably.

On 16 May, the *Totenkopf* Division was ordered into Belgium. As a mechanized force, it could keep up with the fast-moving Panzers, so it was sent to join General Hermann Hoth's XV Panzer Corps, consisting of the 5th and 7th Panzer Divisions.

Struggling though roads crowded with military traffic and fleeing refugees, Eicke's men made slow going. Reaching Le Cateau on the 19th, they entered combat against French tanks and Moroccan troops the next day. In a series of hard engagements, the *Totenkopf* lost 16 killed and 53 wounded. However, any respect due to the division's fighting abilities had

to be tempered by the *Totenkopf*'s attitude to the French colonial troops they faced: refusing to take 'subhuman Negroes' prisoner, they shot surrendering Moroccan soldiers out of hand.

Arras tank attack

The extended German formations were moving fast, but stretched thin, meaning that they were vulnerable to a determined Allied counterattack. On 21 May, five British brigades attacked out of Arras, the counterthrust being led by 74 Matilda infantry tanks. After a period of unbroken success, the British attack came as an unwelcome shock. Eicke ordered his artillery to engage the British over open sights, but a number of inexperienced *Totenkopf* men fled in panic. The British were eventually forced back by a combination of Ju-87 *Stuka* attacks and by Rommel's use of the powerful 8.8cm (3.5in) Flak gun in the anti-tank role, but German confidence had been severely dented, and the poor performance of some *Totenkopf* units was an embarrassment to the SS.

Over the next five days, the *Totenkopf* pressed forward towards the Lys Canal at Bethune, stubborn

▶ **Panzerkampfwagen III Ausf F (SdKfz 141)**

Panzer-Truppe Totenkopf / I.Bataillon / Stab

Totenkopf acquired an armoured troop of one medium company and two light companies when the division was reorganized in May 1941. The A12 marking indicates that this was the battalion adjutant's vehicle.

Specifications

Crew: 5	Engine: Maybach HL120TRM
Weight: 21.9 tonnes (19.8 tons)	Speed: 40km/h (25mph)
Length: 5.38m (17ft 8in)	Range: 165km (103 miles)
Width: 2.84m (9ft 4in)	Radio: FuG5
Height: 2.44m (8ft)	

▶ **Leichte Personenkraftwagen VW (Kfz 1)**

SS-Kraftrad-Regiment (VW) Totenkopf

Under the 1941 reorganization, the motorized infantry companies of the division's motorcycle regiment were re-equipped in part with Volkswagen *Kübels* in place of motorcycles with sidecars.

Specifications

Crew: 1	Engine: Volkswagen 998cc petrol (24hp). Later
Weight: 0.64 tonnes (0.58 tons)	Volkswagen 1131cc petrol (25hp)
Length: 3.73m (12ft 3in)	Speed: 100km/h (62mph)
Width: 1.60m (5ft 3in)	Range: 600km (375 miles)
Height: 1.35m (4ft 5in)	Radio: None

British opposition inflicting significant casualties in the process. On 27 May, they reached the hamlet of Le Paradis, which was being held by 100 members of the Royal Norfolk Regiment.

The British defended their positions with vigour, retreating through a farm complex to make a stand from a large cowshed. The British fought hard, and when they surrendered, the *Totenkopf* men herded their prisoners down to a field alongside another barn. Two machine guns opened up, mowing down the 100 British soldiers in cold blood.

After Dunkirk, all three SS formations were assigned to von Kleist's *Panzergruppe*. After attacking across the Aisne, the *Panzergruppe* aimed southeast towards Dijon, its purpose being to cut off any French armies in Alsace. The *Totenkopf* Division was capturing many prisoners, though colonial troops were often slaughtered out of hand. The division encountered serious resistance only once, at Tarare near Lyon, where the reconnaissance battalion fought a vicious little action with African troops before taking several thousand prisoners.

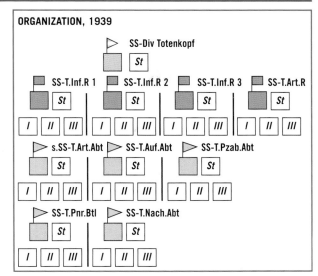

Totenkopf ended the campaign in southwest France. There they were to remain on occupation duties until being transferred east to form part of Operation *Barbarossa*.

 # Operation *Barbarossa*

JUNE–SEPTEMBER 1941

In April 1941, the *Totenkopf* Division was ordered east to join *Generalfeldmarschall* Wilhelm Ritter von Leeb's Army Group North, which was the northern wing of Operation *Barbarossa*.

EICKE USED THE YEAR between the French campaign and the Russian campaign to strengthen the firepower of his division. He converted the motorized infantry regiments into self-contained *Kampfgruppen*, or battle groups, thus giving them a greater degree of independence and flexibility. *Totenkopf*'s Flak capability was expanded and Eicke gained the long-promised allotment of enough 150mm (5.9in) heavy artillery pieces to assemble a heavy battalion in *Totenkopf*'s artillery regiment.

For the Russian campaign, the division was attached to Erich Höpner's 4th Panzer Group, the vanguard of Field Marshal Wilhelm Ritter von Leeb's Army Group North, which was tasked with advancing on Leningrad. Höpner's group, which contained XLI and LVI Panzer Corps led by Max Reinhardt and Erich von Manstein respectively,

would lead the attack through the Baltic States to Leningrad.

Russian combat

The division entered combat mopping up Soviet stragglers behind the advancing German Panzers, and was then used to plug the widening gap between Höpner's Panzers and the Sixteenth Army. *Totenkopf* smashed its way into the Stalin Line on 6 July and found the defensive network was particularly extensive in its sector. Heavy losses were sustained, but it forced its way through, establishing a bridgehead over the River Velikaya by nightfall. On 12 July, the *Totenkopf* Division moved into reserve at Porkhov. On 21 July, the advance began once again, moving through the dark forests and swamps of the region to the west of Lake Ilmen. From 8 August, the Soviets began a morale-sapping campaign, initiating night-time counterattacks. Rest in any form was all but impossible, as the *Totenkopf's* troops had to use all of their efforts during the day to force the determined defenders back.

On 22 August, the advance resumed as the *Totenkopf* Division crossed the Polist River and pushed eastwards towards the Rivers Lovat and Pola. The *Totenkopf* Division's advance continued, with its reconnaissance battalion reaching the Pola River at Vasilyevschina just as the rains commenced. Almost immediately, the division's vehicles were bogged down in the mud. The Soviets hit the *Totenkopf* Division with determined assaults, which it then spent two days desperately beating off. But the advance was being slowed all the time.

By 12 September, in the face of considerable stiffening resistance and ferocious counterattacks by the Soviet forces, the *Totenkopf* Division was once more forced onto the defensive. It became clear that *Barbarossa* would not defeat the Red Army. As the weather deteriorated, the *Waffen-SS* braced itself for its first winter in Russia.

▼ 10.5cm leichte Feldhaubitze (leFH18)

SS-Artillerie-Regiment Totenkopf / I.Bataillon / 1.Batterie

Until the division was upgraded to Panzergrenadier status at the end of 1942, its artillery regiment was exclusively equipped with towed artillery. Three battalions used leFH18s; the fourth was equipped with heavy howitzers.

Specifications

Crew: 3	Muzzle Velocity (AP): 540m/s (1770fps)
Weight: 2 tonnes (1.8 tons)	Range: HE: 12,325m (13,478 yards)
Length: 3.3m (10ft 11in)	Ammunition: Armour-piercing, high explosive
Calibre: 105mm (4.1in)	

▶ Kleine Panzerbefehlsfwagen (SdKfz 265)

Panzer-Truppe Totenkopf / Stab

Initially issued to Panzer staff units at all levels from company to brigade, the small command tank based on the Panzer I was used only at regimental and divisional level from 1941 to 1942.

Specifications

Crew: 3	Engine: Maybach NL38TR
Weight: 6.5 tonnes (6 tons)	Speed: 40km/h (25mph)
Length: 4.42m (14ft 6in)	Range: 170km (105 miles)
Width: 2.06m (6ft 8in)	Radio: FuG2 and FuG6
Height: 1.99m (6ft 6in)	

▶ 5cm Panzerabwehrkanone (Pak 38)

1.SS-Infanterie-Regiment Totenkopf / Stab-Kompanie / Panzerjäger-Zug

The Panzerjäger platoons attached to the headquarters companies of the division's two motorized infantry regiments in 1941 and 1942 each had three Pak 38s to provide last-ditch protection against enemy tanks.

Specifications

Crew: 3	Muzzle Velocity (AP): 835m/s (2900fps)
Weight: 1.2 tonnes (1.13 tons)	Range: AP: 1800m (1968 yards), HE: 2.6km
Length: 3.2m (10ft 5in)	(1.6 miles)
Calibre: 50mm (2in)	Ammunition: Armour-piercing, high explosive

Soviet Union
1941–1942

The early advances through the Baltic States soon began to slow down. By the end of 1941, a fierce series of counterattacks saw the *Totenkopf* surrounded in the Demjansk pocket.

DURING THE AUTUMN AND WINTER OF 1941, the Soviets launched a number of operations against the German lines in the northern sector of the front. During one of these operations, the division was encircled for several months near Demjansk in what would come to be known as the Demjansk pocket.

Under orders from the German Sixteenth Army, the *Totenkopf* Division was divided up and deployed at various crisis points piecemeal. With the objective of strengthening the Sixteenth Army's flanks, two infantry battalions were sent to Demjansk. The *Totenkopf* Division's infantry reconnaissance battalions were deployed at Staraya Russia, which they were ordered to hold at all costs.

Kessel battles

During these *Kessel*, or 'kettle', battles, *Totenkopf* suffered so greatly that, due to its reduced size, it was re-designated *Kampfgruppe Eicke*. The division was involved in ferocious fighting to hold the pocket. *SS-Hauptscharführer* Erwin Meierdress of the *Sturmgeschütz-Batterie Totenkopf* formed a *Kampfgruppe* of about 120 men and held the strategic town of Bjakowo despite repeated determined enemy attempts to capture the town.

During these battles, Meierdress personally destroyed several enemy tanks in his StuG III. He was

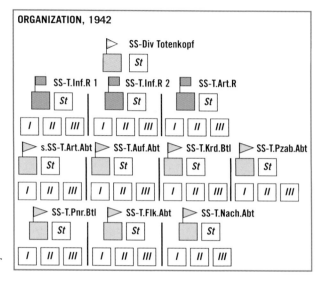

awarded the Iron Cross for his actions during this period. In April 1942, the division broke out of the pocket and managed to reach friendly lines.

Once the Soviet ring around Demjansk finally closed, General Graf von Brockdorff-Ahlefeldt took command of the troops within the pocket. The remaining *Totenkopf* Division units within the pocket were split into two battle groups, which were constructed from *Totenkopf* Division and Army

▶ **Panzerkampfwagen II Ausf C (SdKfz 121)**

3.SS-Panzer-Regiment / 2.leichte Kompanie

In June 1942, the *Totenkopf*'s Panzer troop was enlarged to become the 3rd SS Panzer Regiment *Totenkopf*. A handful of Panzer IIs served with the regimental staff and with company headquarters.

Specifications	
Crew: 3	Speed: 40km/h (25mph)
Weight: 9.8 tonnes (8.9 tons)	Range: 200km (124.3 miles)
Length: 4.81m (15ft 10in)	Radio: FuG5
Width: 2.22m (7ft 4in)	Armament: 1 x 20mm (0.7in) KwK 30 or 38
Height: 1.99m (6ft 6in)	L/55 cannon; 1 x 7.92mm (0.3in) MG (coaxial)
Engine: Maybach HL62TR (140hp)	

personnel. The troops were supplied from the air by the *Luftwaffe*, and in spite of fierce Soviet attacks, the pocket held out until relieved in April 1942.

Huge losses

At Demjansk, about 80 per cent of its soldiers were killed in action. The remnants of the division were pulled out of action in late October 1942 and sent to France to be refitted. While there, the division took part in Case *Anton*, the takeover of Vichy France in November 1942. For this operation, the division was supplied with a Panzer regiment and redesignated *3.SS-Panzergrenadier-Division Totenkopf.*

Thanks to the persuasive efforts of Himmler and *SS-Obergruppenführer* Paul Hausser, all SS Panzergrenadier divisions received a full regiment of Panzers, so were full strength Panzer divisions in all but name. The division remained in France until February 1943, when its old commander, Theodor Eicke, resumed control.

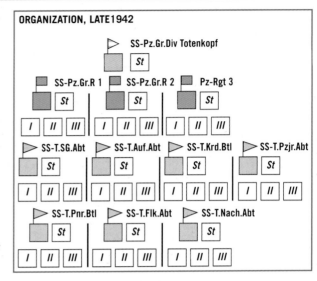

ORGANIZATION, LATE 1942

▶ **Panzerkampfwagen III Ausf H (SdKfz 141)**

3.SS-Panzer-Regiment / I.Abteilung / 2.Kompanie

The Panzer III provided the bulk of *Totenkopf's* Panzer strength in 1942 and 1943, Over 80 were in operation at the end of 1942, with 63 remaining on strength in July 1943 at the time of the Kursk offensive.

Specifications

Crew: 5	Speed: 40km/h (25mph)
Weight: 24 tonnes (21.8 tons)	Range: 165km (103 miles)
Length: 5.4m (17ft 7in)	Radio: FuG5
Width: 2.95m (9ft 7in)	Armament: 1 x 75mm (3in) KwK 37
Height: 2.44m (8ft)	L/24 gun; 2 x 7.92mm (0.3in) MG
Engine: Maybach HL120TRM	(one hull-mounted, one coaxial)

▶ **Schwere Panzerspähwagen 7.5cm (SdKfz 233)**

SS-Panzer-Aufklärungs-Abteilung Totenkopf / Stab

In September 1942, *Totenkopf* became a Panzergrenadier division. By 1944, the reconnaissance battalion's staff company was operating three close-support armoured cars equipped with obsolete 7.5cm (3in) tank guns.

Specifications

Crew: 3	Engine: Büssing-NAG L8V
Weight: 9.6 tonnes (8.7 tons)	Speed: 80km/h (50mph)
Length: 5.8m (19ft)	Range: 300km (186 miles)
Width: 2.2m (7ft 2in)	Radio: FuG Spr Ger 'a'
Height: 2.25m (7ft 5in)	

▶ **Panzerkampfwagen IV Ausf E (SdKfz 161)**

3.SS-Panzer-Regiment / I.Abteilung / 1.Kompanie

Early short-barrelled Panzer IVs served with *Totenkopf*'s Panzer troop and the 3rd SS Panzer Regiment in 1942, but they were soon replaced by variants with longer high-velocity 7.5cm (3in) guns.

Specifications

Crew: 5	Speed: 40km/h (25mph)
Weight: 25.9 tonnes (23.5 tons)	Range: 210km (130.5 miles)
Length: 5.92m (19ft 5in)	Radio: FuG5
Width: 2.84m (9ft 4in)	Armament: 1 x 75mm (3in) KwK 37
Height: 2.68m (8ft 9.5in)	L/24 gun; 2 x 7.92mm (0.3in) MG
Engine: Maybach HL120TRM	(one hull-mounted, one coaxial)

▶ **Panzerkampfwagen III Ausf N (SdKfz 141/2)**

3.SS-Panzer-Regiment Totenkopf / II.Battalion / 6.Kompanie

The Panzer III equipped with a short-barrelled 7.5cm (3in) gun was designed to provide close support to medium and heavy (Tiger) companies. There were 155 Ausf Ns in service with the *Wehrmacht* at Kursk.

Specifications

Crew: 5	Engine: Maybach HL120TRM
Weight: 25.4 tonnes (23 tons)	Speed: 40km/h (25mph)
Length: 5.52m (18ft 1in)	Range: 155km (96 miles)
Width: 2.95m (9ft 7in)	Radio: FuG5
Height: 2.5m (8ft 2in)	

Kharkov and Kursk
1943

Early in February 1943, *SS-Panzergrenadier-Division Totenkopf* was transferred back to the Eastern Front as part of Erich von Manstein's Army Group South.

THE DIVISION, AS A PART of SS-*Obergruppenführer* Paul Hausser's *SS-Panzerkorps*, took part in the Third Battle of Kharkov, helping to blunt the Soviet offensive led by General Konev. During this campaign, Theodor Eicke was killed when his plane was shot down.

The *SS-Panzerkorps*, including *Totenkopf*, was then shifted north to take part in Operation *Citadel*, the offensive to reduce the Kursk salient. It was during

REGIMENTAL ORGANIZATION

SS-Pz.Rgt 2
St

I.   II.   s.Pz-Kp
St   St   St

1 2 3   4 5 6   I II III

SS-Panzergrenadier-Division *Totenkopf*, July 1943	Strength
PzKpfw III (long barrel)	63
PzKpfw IV (short barrel)	8
PzKpfw IV (long barrel)	44
PzKpfw VI Tiger	15
Befehls	9

this period that the *3.SS-Panzer-Regiment* received a company of Tiger I heavy tanks *(9.SS-Panzer-Regiment 3)*.

The *Totenkopf* covered the advance on the *SS-Panzerkorps* left flank, with the *Leibstandarte* forming the spearhead. *SS-Panzer-Regiment 3* advanced in a *Panzerkeil* (armoured wedge) across the hot and dusty steppe.

In the afternoon of 12 July, near the village of Andre'evka on the south bank of the Psel, the Soviets launched a counterattack against *Regiment Thule* and the division's *StuG-Abteilung*. The division managed to halt the Soviet assault, destroying many Soviet T-34s, but at the cost of most of the division's remaining operational Panzers.

On 14 July, Hitler called off the operation.

▶ Panzerkampfwagen IV Ausf H (SdKfz 161/2)

3.SS-Panzer-Regiment Totenkopf / I.Abteilung / 2.Kompanie

At the start of the Kursk campaign, the 3rd SS Panzer Regiment had two battalions, each with two medium and one light company. A total of 44 Panzer IVs were on strength.

Specifications

Crew: 5	Speed: 38km/h (23.6mph)
Weight: 27.6 tonnes (25 tons)	Range: 210km (130.5 miles)
Length: 7.02m (23ft 0in)	Radio: FuG5
Width: 2.88m (9ft 5in)	Armament: 1 x 75mm (3in) KwK
Height: 2.68m (8ft 10in)	40/43; 2 x 7.92mm (0.3in) MG
Engine: Maybach HL120TRM	(one hull-mounted, one coaxial)

▶ Panzerkampfwagen V Ausf A (SdKfz 171)

SS-Panzer-Regiment Totenkopf/ I.Abteilung / 3.Kompanie

In July 1944, the *Totenkopf* Division's 1st Panzer Battalion was equipped with four companies of Panzer V Panthers.

Specifications

Crew: 5	Range: 200km (124.3 miles)
Weight: 50.2 tonnes (45.5 tons)	Radio: FuG5
Length: 8.86m (29ft 0in)	Armament: 1 x 75mm (3in)
Width: 3.4m (11ft 2in)	KwK42 L/70; 2 x 7.92mm
Height: 2.98m (9ft 10in)	(0.3in) MG (one hull-mounted,
Engine: Maybach HL230P30	one coaxial)
Speed: 46km/h (28.6mph)	

◀ Mittlerer Kommandopanzerwagen Ausf B (SdKfz 251/6)

1.SS-Panzergrenadier-Regiment Totenkopf / I.Battalion / Stab

In the summer of 1944, the 1st Battalion of *Totenkopf*'s 1st Panzergrenadier Regiment was mounted on half-tracks. The *Kommandopanzerwagen* was a fully equipped command post with both long-range and short-range radios.

Specifications

Crew: 8	Engine: Maybach
Weight: 9.4 tonnes (8.5 tons)	Speed: 53km/h (32.9mph)
Length: 6m (19ft 6in)	Range: 300km (186 miles)
Width: 2.1m (6ft 9in)	Radio: FuG11 plus FuG Tr 100W.
Height: 1.75m (5ft 7in)	Later FuG19 plus FuG12

Retreat from Russia
1943–1944

After Kursk, *Totenkopf* was reassigned along with *Das Reich* to the re-formed Sixth Army commanded by *General der Infanterie* Karl-Adolf Hollidt in the southern Ukraine.

T OTENKOPF WAS INVOLVED in heavy fighting over the next several weeks, as Sixth Army attempted to eliminate the Soviet bridgehead over the Mius River. During the battles of July and August 1943, the division suffered heavy losses, and over the course of the campaign on the Mius Front it suffered more casualties than it had during Operation *Citadel*. By the time the Soviet bridgehead was eliminated, the division had lost 1500 men dead and the Panzer regiment was reduced to a strength of 20 tanks.

The *Totenkopf* was then moved north, back to Kharkov. Along with *Das Reich*, *Totenkopf* took part in the battles to halt Operation *Rumyantsev* and to prevent the Soviet capture of the city. Although the two divisions managed to halt the offensive, inflicting heavy casualties and destroying over 800 tanks, the Soviets outflanked the defenders, forcing them to abandon the city on 23 August.

By early September, the *Totenkopf* had been forced back as far as the the Dnieper. The Soviet Fifth Guards Tank Army had forced a crossing at Kremenchug and threatened to break through the German defensive line. *Totenkopf* was now thrown into action against the bridgehead.

Totenkopf Panzer Division

In October 1943, the division was reorganized and upgraded to become a full Panzer division, and was renamed the 3.*SS-Panzer-Division Totenkopf*. The

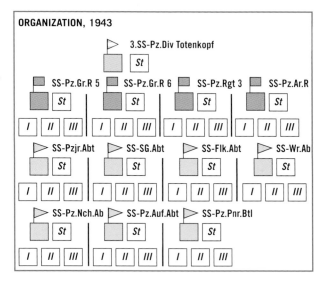

Panzer battalion became a regiment, and the division's two Panzergrenadier regiments were given the honorary titles *Theodor Eicke* and *Thule*. The *Thule* Regiment had been raised in 1942 from the remains of *SS-Infanterie-Regiment 9 Thule*, an independent formation based on the *Totenkopf-Standarte K*, which was merged with the *Totenkopf* Motorcycle Battalion.

After holding the Kremenchug bridgehead for several months, the Soviets broke out, pushing the Germans back towards the Romanian border. By

▶ **2cm Flakvierling 38 auf Zugkraftwagen 8t (SdKfz 7/1)**

3.SS-Panzer-Division Totenkopf / Divisionsstab / Flak-Batterie (Sf)

Initially equipped with single 2cm (0.7in) guns, divisional headquarters later received *Flakvierling* quad guns, which were replaced by 3.7cm (1.5in) guns.

Specifications	
Crew: 7	Engine: Maybach HL62TUK
Weight: 1.16 tonnes (1.06 tons)	6-cylinder (140hp)
Length: 6.55m (21ft 6in)	Speed: 50km/h (31mph)
Width: 2.40m (7ft 10.5in)	Range: 250km (156 miles)
Height: 3.20m (10ft 6in)	Radio: None

November, *Totenkopf* was engaged fighting intense defensive actions against Soviet attacks over the vital town of Krivoi Rog to the west of the Dnieper.

In January 1944, *Totenkopf* was still engaged in heavy defensive fighting alongside the Army's *Grossdeutschland* Division. In February 1944, 56,000 German troops were trapped in the Korsun pocket. *Totenkopf* was sent towards Cherkassy to assist in the relief attempts. The division attacked towards the city of Korsun, attempting to secure a crossing across the Gniloy-Tilkich River. The 1st Panzer Division, fighting alongside the *Totenkopf*, eventually reached the encircled forces, enabling them to break out.

Withdrawn to refit in Romania, the division was ordered to Poland late in July 1944 as part of the German response to the destruction of Army Group Centre in Operation *Bagration*. There it would cover the approaches to Warsaw as part of *SS-Obergruppenführer* Gille's IV SS Panzer Corps. In August, the *Totenkopf*, fighting alongside the 5th SS Panzer Division *Wiking* and the 1st Fallschirm-Panzer Division *Hermann Göring*, virtually annihilated the Soviet III Tank Corps. The Soviets, having pushed forwards more than 482km (300 miles), were exhausted, and the crack German divisions managed to hold the line of the Vistula until December.

▼ **5th Company, 2nd Panzer Battalion** *Totenkopf*

In the fierce fighting around Modlin in August 1944, the terrain suited German armour. *Totenkopf*'s Panzers exploited this to their advantage, engaging Soviet tanks at long range, allowing the superiority of the German sights and the power of the 7.5cm (3in) high-velocity gun to tell. In such combat, Panthers were superior to the T-34, and in well-trained hands the long-barrelled Panzer IVs that equipped the division's 2nd Panzer Battalion were a match for the Soviet tank.

Stab

1.Zug   *2.Zug*   *3.Zug*   *4.Zug*

▶ **Mittlere Schützenpanzerwagen 7.5cm Ausf C (SdKfz 251/9)**

SS-Panzer-Aufklärungs-Abteilung Totenkopf / 1.Aufklärungs-Kompanie (Spw)

Ordinary Panzergrenadier units had towed 7.5cm (3in) infantry guns for close support. Reconnaissance units were issued with self-propelled equipment, which used old 7.5cm (3in) tank guns formerly mounted in Panzer IVs.

Specifications

Crew: 3	Speed: 53km/h (33mph)
Weight: 9.4 tonnes (8.53 tons)	Range: 300km (186 miles)
Length: 5.98m (19ft 7in)	Radio: FuG Spr Ger 'f'
Width: 2.83m (9ft 4in)	Armament: 1 x 75mm (3in) KwK
Height: 2.07m (6ft 10in)	L/24 gun
Engine: Maybach HL42TUKRM	

Specifications

Crew: 5	Speed: 46km/h (28.6mph)
Weight: 50.2 tonnes (45.5 tons)	Range: 200km (124 miles)
Length: 8.86m (29ft 0in)	Radio: FuG5
Width: 3.4m (11ft 2in)	Armament: 1 x 75mm (3in) KwK42 L/70;
Height: 2.98m (9ft 10in)	2 x 7.92mm (0.3in) MG (one hull-mounted,
Engine: Maybach HL230P30	one coaxial)

▲ **Panzerkampfwagen V Ausf A (SdKfz 171)**

SS-Panzer-Regiment Totenkopf/ I.Abteilung / 4.Kompanie

By 1944, the standard Panzer division organization included one battalion of Panthers and one battalion of long-barrelled Panzer IVs .

 # Last stand of the *Waffen-SS*
1944–1945

While the position along the line of the Vistula in Poland might have stabilized at the end of 1944, the rest of the German situation in Europe did not look good.

THE OFFENSIVE IN THE ARDENNES had been pushed back, German armies were retreating in Italy and the Balkans, and Romania and Bulgaria had fallen to the Red Army. In Hungary, the situation was no better. In October 1944, it was clear to the Germans that the Hungarian head of state, Admiral Horthy, was about to abandon his German allies and attempt to negotiate terms with the Soviets. And so *SS-Obersturmbannführer* Otto Skorzeny led a spectacular coup against the Horthy government. A pro-German puppet regime was installed.

This did not halt the Red Army's advance, however, and the Soviets established bridgeheads on the west bank of the Danube. The German defensive

ORGANIZATION
▷ 3.SS-Pz.Pnr.Abt
St

Auf | Sch | Pnr | Pnr

ORGANIZATION
▷ 3.SS-Pz.Auf.Abt
St

St | Spz | Sch | Sch | Sch

positions at Lake Balaton, southwest of Budapest, slowed the Soviet advance for a time. Nonetheless, on 24 December, the Soviets had managed to encircle Budapest, garrisoned by the remnants of 8th SS Cavalry Division *Florian Geyer,* 22nd SS Volunteer Cavalry Division *Maria Theresia* and 18th SS Volunteer Panzergrenadier Division *Horst Wessel.*

The *Führer* decided that Budapest must be relieved. At his personal order, *SS-Gruppenführer* Herbert Gille's IV SS Panzer Corps was selected to lead the assault on the Hungarian capital. *Totenkopf* and *Wiking* were pulled out of the line west of Warsaw and sent by train via Prague, Vienna and Bratislava to western Hungary, where they moved to jumping-off points ready for the drive on Budapest.

Budapest attack

Totenkopf and *Wiking* launched their attack towards Budapest on New Year's Day 1945. The advance stalled in the face of resistance from the Soviet Fourth Guards Army and Sixth Guards Tank Army. By 11 January, fierce Soviet counterattacks had stopped the SS Corps and forced it onto the defensive.

On 8 January, Hitler ordered Sepp Dietrich's Sixth SS Panzer Army to be moved from the Western Front to Hungary. In the meantime, he ordered the

exhausted IV SS Panzer Corps to attack towards Budapest again, without waiting for Dietrich. The second attack began on 18 January. Early success was only temporary, and by 20 January the Soviets had held the German attack.

A Soviet counterattack on 27 January drove the SS divisions back in confusion, although they

▲ **King Tigers in Hungary**

An SS Panzergrenadier shares a cigarette with a Hungarian soldier in a remarkably cheerful scene from Hungary, March 1945.

▶ **Panzerkampfwagen V Ausf G (SdKfz 171)**

SS-Panzer-Regiment Totenkopf/ I.Battalion / 2.Kompanie

The Ausf G was the last variant of the Panther to be mass-produced, entering service in March 1944.

Specifications

Crew: 5	Speed: 46km/h (28.6mph)
Weight: 47.4 tonnes	Range: 200km (124 miles)
(43 tons)	Radio: FuG5
Length: 8.86m (29ft 0in)	Armament: 1 x 75mm (3in)
Width: 3.4m (11ft 2in)	KwK 42 L/70; 2 x 7.92mm
Height: 2.95m (9ft 8in)	(0.3in) MG (one hull-
Engine: Maybach HL230P30	mounted, one coaxial)

managed to re-establish themselves in the Bakony Forest north of Lake Balaton. In these dense woods, *Totenkopf* dug in and awaited the arrival of Sixth SS Panzer Army.

Dietrich's Panzer divisions reached Hungary at the beginning of March 1945. The offensive, codenamed *Spring Awakening (Frühlingserwachen),* was intended to drive the Soviets from the last oilfields in German possession around Lake Balaton, knock them back across the Danube and retake Budapest, which had finally fallen on 11 February.

Final offensive

The offensive opened on 6 March in heavy snow. Despite the appalling conditions, the *Waffen-SS* threw themselves into the battle with their customary determination and elan. However, they ran into trouble almost immediately. On 13 March, the offensive halted due to Soviet resistance and the thaw that turned the roads and surrounding countryside into a quagmire. On 16 March, Marshal Tolbukhin's 3rd Ukrainian Front shifted to the offensive. The

Ninth Guards Tank Army smashed into the *Totenkopf* Division, overwhelmed them and drove into the rear of the IV SS Panzer Corps.

What was left of *Totenkopf* withdrew up the main road to Bratislava and Vienna, with the remnants of Sixth SS Panzer Army. On 3 April, *Totenkopf* halted in the southern suburbs of Vienna and, with the rest of what once had been elite SS divisions, put up largely symbolic resistance to the two Soviet fronts converging on the city.

Final surrender

Meanwhile, the Third US Army was driving towards Regensburg, threatening the rear of Army Group South's position. *Brigadeführer* Becker tried to surrender *Totenkopf* to the Third US Army – which insisted that the division disarmed the camp guards at the Mauthausen concentration camp. This they did, before turning themselves over to the Americans. The SS men were then handed over to the Soviets and transported to detention camps. Those who survived spent many years in Soviet labour camps.

▶ **Jagdpanzer IV (SdKfz 162)**

SS-Panzerjäger-Abteilung Totenkopf / Stab

Nearly 800 Jagdpanzer IVs were built between January and November 1944. The type entered service with tank-destroyer detachments of Panzer divisions in March 1944.

Specifications	
Crew: 4	Engine: Maybach HL120TRM
Weight: Up to 27.6 tonnes (25 tons)	Speed: 38km/h (23.6mph)
Length: 6.85m (22.5ft)	Range: 210km (130.5 miles)
Width: 6.7m (22ft)	Radio: FuG15 and FuG160
Height: 1.85m (6ft)	

▶ **Leichte Schützenpanzerwagen (SdKfz 250/9)**

SS-Panzer-Aufklärungs-Abteilung Totenkopf / 2.Aufklärungs-Kompanie (Spw)

Vastly more capable across country than light armoured cars, the reconnaissance variant of the SdKfz 250 began to replace the SdKfz 222 from 1943. *Totenkopf's* armoured reconnaissance battalion had three half-track companies by late 1944.

Specifications	
Crew: 3	Speed: 60km/h (37mph)
Weight: 6.9 tonnes (6.3 tons)	Range: 320km (199 miles)
Length: 4.56m (14ft 11.5in)	Radio: FuG Spr Ger 'f'
Width: 1.95m (6ft 5in)	Armament: 1 x 20mm (0.7in) KwK 30/38 L/55
Height: 2.16m (7ft 1in)	cannon; 1 x 7.92mm (0.3in) MG (coaxial)
Engine: Maybach HL42TRKM 6-cylinder (100hp)	

4th SS-Polizei-Panzergrenadier-Division

Never one of the first-line SS divisions, the _Polizei_ Division was not officially part of the SS until 1942. It was a product of the expansion of the SS at the outbreak of war in 1939.

FOR SOME TIME BEFORE THE WAR, the _Reichsführer_ together with the head of the _SS-Hauptamt, Obergruppenführer_ Gottlob Berger, who was responsible for recruiting, had been pressing to expand the Armed SS.

In law, the Army had first right to conscript all German nationals, so the SS struggled to find the manpower it needed. The two sources of recruits that were under Himmler's control were the camp guards and the police. The camp guards provided the men for the 3rd SS Division.

The expansion of Nazi control

The other source of at least partially trained manpower under Himmler's control was the police. The _Ordnungspolizei,_ or Order Police, was the uniformed branch of German law enforcement under the Third _Reich_. Prior to the Nazi takeover in 1933,

there was no central police organization in Germany, each of the _Länder_ controlling its own forces. The main branches of the uniformed police usually comprised the _Schutzpolizei_ in the cities and the _Landespolizei_ and the _Gendarmerie_ in rural areas,

Divisional History	Formed
Polizei-Division	1939
SS-Polizei-Division	1942
SS-Polizei-Panzergrenadier-Division	1943
4.SS-Polizei-Panzergrenadier-Division	1943

Commanders

Generalleutnant der Polizei Konrad Hitschler _September 1940_	SS-Brigadeführer Jürgen Wagner _April 1944 – May 1944_
SS-Obergruppenführer Karl von Pfeffer-Wildenbruch _September 1940 – November 1940_	SS-Oberführer Friedrich-Wilhelm Bock _May 1944_
SS-Gruppenführer Arthur Mülverstadt _November 1940 – August 1941_	SS-Brigadeführer Hebert-Ernst Vahl _May 1944 – July 1944_
SS-Obergruppenführer Walter Krüger _August 1941 – December 1941_	SS-Standartenführer Karl Schümers _July 1944 – August 1944_
Generaloberst der Polizei Alfred Wünnenberg _December 1941 – April 1943_	SS-Oberführer Helmuth Dörnder _August 1944_
SS-Brigadeführer Fritz Freitag _April 1943 – June 1943_	SS-Brigadeführer Fritz Schmedes _August 1944 – November 1944_
SS-Brigadeführer Fritz Schmedes _June 1943 – August 1943_	SS-Standartenführer Walter Harzer _November 1944 – March 1945_
SS-Brigadeführer Fritz Freitag _August 1943 – October 1943_	SS-Standartenführer Fritz Göhler _March 1945_
SS-Oberführer Friedrich-Wilhelm Bock _October 1943 – April 1944_	SS-Standartenführer Walter Harzer _March 1945 – May 1945_

INSIGNIA

The _Polizei_ Division used a variant of the Germanic and heraldic Wolf's hook symbol, but unlike the _Totenkopf_ version this was vertical rather than horizontal. In this form it was also known as the _Donnerkeil_ or 'thunderbolt'. The division would not have used the shield until it became a fully integrated SS formation in 1942.

▶ **Mannschafts Kraftwagen Krupp L2H-143 (Kfz 70)**

1.Polizei-Schützen-Regiment / I.Battalion / Infanteriegeschütz-Kompanie

When formed in 1939, the _Polizei_ Division was very much the poor relation of the other SS divisions when it came to equipment, having only minimal supplies of motor transport and with much of its equipment being horse-drawn.

Specifications

Crew: 2	Engine: Krupp 3.3L 4-cylinder (60hp)
Weight: 2.45 tonnes (2.23 tons)	Speed: 70km/h (43mph)
Length: 5.10m (16ft 8in)	Range: 450km (280 miles)
Width: 1.93m (6ft 4in)	Radio: None
Height: 1.96m (6ft 5in)	

although the uniformed police also controlled the fire service and administrative legal officers such as health inspectors and building inspectors.

In 1933, Wilhelm Frick proposed that all German police units should come under the control of the Ministry of the Interior, but unification did not begin until Heinrich Himmler became *Chef der Deutschen Polizei* in 1936.

After Hitler came to power in 1933, Himmler was appointed police chief in Bavaria, a position that he used as a launching platform to eventually bring all German law enforcement agencies, both uniformed and plain-clothed, under SS control. Uniformed police now came under the control of the *Hauptamt Ordnungspolizei*, headed by Kurt Daluege, while the detectives of the *Kriminalpolizei* and the secret police of the *Gestapo* were made part of Heydrich's *Sicherheitspolizei*, or *Sipo*. Although Himmler's aim was to merge the uniformed police with the SS, they remained separate organizations until midway through the war.

On 17 June 1936, the *Reichsführer-SS* had taken control of the unified German police service. Now he used that control to transfer 15,000 members of the uniformed *Ordnungspolizei* into a new division. Raised as the *Polizei-Division* at *Truppenübungsplatz* Wandern, near the Black Forest, the unit was not strictly part of the SS at this stage.

▲ A soldier from the *Polizei* Division braves the harsh northern Russian winter, Leningrad sector, January 1942.

◀ **3.7cm Panzerabwehrkanone (Pak 36)**
Polizei-Panzerabwehr-Abteilung
Although quickly found to be ineffective against modern armour, the 3.7cm (1.5in) Pak 36 remained in use in the *Polizei* Division's Panzerjäger units well into 1943.

Specifications

Crew: 3	Muzzle Velocity: 762m/s (2500fps)
Weight: 0.43 tonnes (0.39 tons)	Range: 600m (656 yards)
Length: 1.67m (5ft 5.5in)	Ammunition: Armour-piercing
Calibre: 37mm (1.5in)	

▶ **Mittlere Nachrichten Kraftwagen (Kfz 15)**
Polizei-Nachrichten-Abteilung
The *Polizei* Signals Battalion was formed in June 1940. By the time the division was in action in the siege of Leningrad over the winter of 1941/42, the battalion had been fully motorized.

Specifications

Crew: 1	Engine: Mercedes-Benz 6-cylinder petrol
Weight: 2.4 tonnes (2.2 tons)	(90hp)
Length: 4.44m (14ft 7in)	Speed: 88km/h (55mph)
Width: 1.68m (5ft 6in)	Range: 400km (250 miles)
Height: 1.73m (5ft 8in)	Radio: Various depending on deployment

Poland and France
1940

The *Polizei* Division was formed in October 1939. It had only just completed its training when orders were given for the division to join Army Group C for the attack in the West.

USED AS OCCUPATION TROOPS in Poland, the *Polizei* Division began to receive more intensive military training in February 1940. However, the men were older, less fit and much less ideologically inspired than other SS units, and the division was only partially equipped – with obsolete and captured weapons.

Attack in the West

On 9 May 1940, all German forces received the codeword *Danzig,* which set in motion one of the most devastating advances in military history. Shortly after 02.30 on 10 May, 64 German troops crossed the Dutch frontier – the spearhead of Germany's invasion of the Low Countries. Some three hours later, glider-borne troops dropped over the Belgian border to capture and demolish the huge fortifications at Eben-Emael. The imposing concrete and steel fortress fell to a crack unit of Fallschirmjäger – paratroops – who landed by glider right on the roof of the fortress.

At 05.45, the 30 infantry divisions of General Fedor von Bock's Army Group B moved out of the Rhineland, heading for the Low Countries. In the centre, the 44 divisions of General Gerd von Runstedt's Army Group A staged through towards the Ardennes, with the lead being taken by seven Panzer divisions under General Ewald von Kleist.

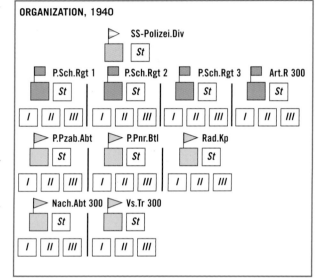

ORGANIZATION, 1940

Army Group C, commanded by General Wilhelm Ritter von Leeb, faced the strongest French defences in the south, its primary task being to pin down the 400,000 French troops manning the Maginot Line.

The bulk of the Armed SS was deployed in this operation. *Leibstandarte* was attached to the right flank of the 227th Infantry Division with von Bock's forces, which also controlled the SS-VT Division. The *Totenkopf* Division was held back as part of von

▶ **3.7cm Fliegerabwehrkanone (Flak 36)**

SS-Polizei-Flak-Abteilung / 2.Batterie

When formed, the *Polizei* Division had no attached Flak unit. By the summer of 1941, however, a Flak battalion was on strength, and by 1942 when the division became an SS unit it had motorized light, medium and heavy batteries.

Specifications

Crew: 5	Muzzle Velocity: 820m/s (2690fps)
Weight: 1.5 tonnes (1.4 tons)	Range: 4800m (5250 yards)
Length: 3.5m (11ft)	Ammunition: High explosive or smoke
Calibre: 37mm (1.5in)	

Rundstedt's reserves, while the *Polizei* Division was assigned to Army Group C, where it would remain largely inactive for more than a month.

On 9/10 June, the *Polizei* Division crossed the Aisne River and the Ardennes Canal with Army Group A. The French counterattacked with armour, and the fighting see-sawed back and forwards for some time, until the French were eventually overcome by the sheer pressure of the German advance. The *Polizei* Division was heavily engaged during this time, and after securing its objectives, was moved on to the old World War I battlefield of the Argonne Forest.

In the Argonne Forest, the division was again involved in heavy fighting, engaged with rearguard units of the retreating French. In the process, the

division captured the small town of Les Islettes. Late in June 1940, the unit was pulled out of combat and placed into reserve.

REGIMENTAL ORGANIZATION

Polizei-Schützen.Rgt 1

▷ 10.5cm leichte Feldhaubitze (leFH18)

Polizei-Artillerie-Regiment / II. (leichte) Bataillon

The *Polizei* Division's artillery regiment was formed in May 1940. It used towed equipment for the entire war, with three light howitzer batteries (later reduced to two) and a single heavy howitzer battery.

Specifications

Crew: 5	Muzzle Velocity: 540m/s (1770fps)
Weight: 1.95 tonnes (1.85 tons)	Range: 12,325m (13,480 yards)
Length: 3.3m (10ft)	Ammunition: High explosive or smoke
Calibre: 105mm (4.3in)	

Operation *Barbarossa*

JUNE–DECEMBER 1941

After almost a year on garrison duties in Burgundy, Paris and elsewhere in occupied France, the *Polizei* Division was ordered to move east to take part in Operation *Barbarossa*.

ON 27 JUNE 1941, the *Polizei* Division was transferred to the Eastern Front and put into Army Group North reserve. Commanded by Field Marshal Ritter von Leeb, the army group was aimed at the Baltic States and Leningrad. Group North consisted of two infantry armies containing 15 infantry divisions between them.

The armoured punch was provided by 4.Panzergruppe, which comprised three Panzer divisions, three motorized infantry divisions and two

infantry divisions. Three infantry divisions were held in support.

The *Polizei* Division saw little action in the opening stages of the campaign, not being called upon to fight for almost two months. In August 1941, the division finally saw action near Luga. It was during heavy fighting for the Luga bridgehead held by a number of Soviet divisions that the *Polizei* Division lost over 2000 soldiers in bloody frontal assaults. The fighting was very difficult, taking place

ORGANIZATION, SS POLIZEI DIVISION, 1942

across swamp and forest land. After a number of bloody assaults, the *Polizei* Division was one of the formations that managed to fight into the northern edge of Luga, where the Germans encircled and destroyed the Soviet defenders. After the battles for Luga, the division was moved to the fighting around Leningrad. From January to March 1942, the division saw action along the Wolchow River and helped in the encirclement and destruction of the Second Soviet Assault Army.

Officially part of the SS

Even though the division was definitely under Himmler's control, it was still known as the Police Division. Its members continued to use police insignia and rank badges until the division came fully under SS administration early in 1941. It was not until January 1942, while its troops were heavily engaged in the fighting around Leningrad, that the division was finally given official *Waffen-SS* status. Its title was changed to the *SS-Polizei-Division* as the formation was absorbed into the *Waffen-SS*, and all of the division's subordinate units received SS rather than police designations.

▶ **Protz Kraftwagen (Kfz 69)**

SS-Polizei-Flak-Abteilung

In 1943, the *Polizei* Division's Flak battalion was fully motorized. The earlier Krupp Protz used to tow light anti-aircraft weapons had been supplanted by variants of the *Wehrmacht*'s standard heavy car.

Specifications

Crew: 1	Engine: Horch 6-cylinder petrol (90hp)
Weight: 2.4 tonnes (2.2 tons)	Speed: 88km/h (55mph)
Length: 4.44m (14 ft 7in)	Range: 400km (250 miles)
Width: 1.68m (5ft 6in)	Radio: None usually fitted
Height: 1.73m (5ft 8in)	

▶ **Leichte Schützenpanzerwagen (SdKfz 250/1)**

4.SS-Aufklärungs-Abteilung / 1.Aufklärungs-Kompanie (Spw)

Originally a bicycle reconnaissance battalion, the *Polizei*'s recce force was converted into a motorcycle unit while in the Balkans in 1944, and by May 1944 it had one company equipped with half-tracks.

Specifications

Crew: 2 plus 4 troops	(100hp)
Weight: 5.9 tonnes (5.38 tons)	Speed: 60km/h (37mph)
Length: 4.61m (15ft 1in)	Range: 300km (186 miles)
Width: 1.95m (6ft 5in)	Radio: FuG Spr Ger 'f'
Height: 1.66m (5ft 5in)	Armament: 1 x 7.92mm (0.3in) MG
Engine: Maybach HL42TRKM 6-cylinder	

▶ **Leichte Personenkraftwagen VW (Kfz 1)**

1.Polizei-Schützen-Regiment

The three infantry regiments of the *Polizei* Division were designated *Schützen* regiments until October 1942, when they were redesignated as *SS-Polizei-Infanterie* regiments. Early in 1943, they became grenadier regiments.

Specifications

Crew: 1	Engine: Volkswagen 998cc petrol (24hp). Later
Weight: 0.64 tonnes (0.58 tons)	Volkswagen 1131cc petrol (25hp)
Length: 3.73m (12ft 3in)	Speed: 100km/h (62mph)
Width: 1.60m (5ft 3in)	Range: 600km (375 miles)
Height: 1.35m (4ft 5in)	Radio: None

Siege of Leningrad
1941–1943

By early December 1941, the German armies that had steamrollered into the Soviet Union in June of that year had all but run out of momentum.

SUPPLY LINES WERE OVERSTRETCHED, the troops were exhausted and the full horrors of the Russian winter were being visited upon German soldiers who, in the main, were still equipped with little more than the summer-weight clothing with which they had begun the campaign. However, on the northern front, it seemed only a matter of time before Leningrad was taken.

Stalin's failure to relieve besieged Leningrad appeared to have doomed the city. Since Hitler had ordered that the cradle of the Bolshevik revolution be levelled, it seemed only a matter of time before it fell.

Its population swollen to over three million by refugees flooding into the city, Leningrad was cut off by Germans to the south and to the north by the Finns, eager to avenge the Winter War.

Communist Party chiefs anxiously calculated their food reserves: on 1 November, they realized there was only enough food for another week. And with winter approaching, there was so little fuel that buildings could not be heated – electricity was rationed to an hour a day.

What followed was the most appalling siege in history, a long-drawn-out agony in which nearly a

Specifications

Crew: 2	Engine: Maybach HL62 6-cylinder (140hp)
Weight: 1.16 tonnes (1.06 tons)	Speed: 50km/h (31mph)
Length: 6.85m (20ft 3in)	Range: 250km (156 miles)
Width: 2.40m (7ft 10.5in)	Radio: None
Height: 2.62m (8ft 7.1in)	

▲ **8.8cm Fliegerabwehrkanone (Flak 18)**

SS-Polizei-Flak-Abteilung / 8.8cm Flak-Batterie (mot)

Flak battalions attached to German divisions had one light (2cm/0.7in) battery, one medium (3.7cm/1.5in) battery, and one heavy battery equipped with four 8.8cm (3.5in) Flak guns towed by SdKfz 7 half-tracks.

million men, women and children died of cold and slow starvation – three times the total war dead suffered by Britain or the United States in the whole of World War II.

For the next two years, the *SS-Polizei-Division* would be engaged on the Leningrad Front. As part of the Eighteenth Army, it would be attached to I Corps until July 1942, then switch between L Corps and LIV Corps until the middle of 1943.

Soviet pressure

In January 1943, the *SS-Polizei-Division*, then situated south of Lake Ladoga, became the subject of fierce Soviet counterattacks that punched a hole in the German defences. The breakthrough occurred south of Schlüsselburg, near the 170th Infantry Division. By early February 1943, the retreating *SS-Polizei-Division* took over its newly assigned position west of Kopino, where it had to repulse a number of fierce Soviet onslaughts.

That month, the division was reduced to a *Kampfgruppe* while the bulk of the division was

transferred westwards to be upgraded to a Panzergrenadier division. The *Kampfgruppe SS-Polizei* was disbanded in May 1944, after serving independently on the Eastern Front since April 1943.

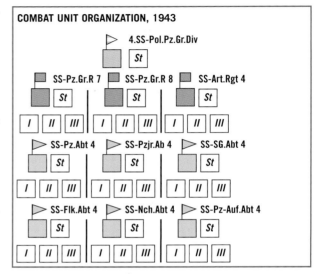

COMBAT UNIT ORGANIZATION, 1943

▷ 4.SS-Pol.Pz.Gr.Div
St

SS-Pz.Gr.R 7 / SS-Pz.Gr.R 8 / SS-Art.Rgt 4
St / St / St
I II III / I II III / I II III

▷ SS-Pz.Abt 4 / ▷ SS-Pzjr.Ab 4 / ▷ SS-SG.Abt 4
St / St / St
I II III / I II III / I II III

▷ SS-Flk.Abt 4 / ▷ SS-Nch.Abt 4 / ▷ SS-Pz-Auf.Abt 4
St / St / St
I II III / I II III / I II III

▶ **Mittlere Lkw Henschel 33D1**

4.SS-Polizei-Panzergrenadier-Division / Versorgungsdienste

Produced from 1933 to 1942, around 22,000 Henschel medium trucks were made for the *Wehrmacht*. The standard cargo/personnel body was most common, but other open and closed bodies were built.

Specifications

Crew: 1	Engine: 10.7 litre (650ci),
Weight: 6.1 tonnes (6 tons)	6-cylinder petrol (100hp)
Length: 7.4m (24ft)	Speed: 60km/h (37mph)
Width: 2.25m (7ft 4in)	Payload: 3 tonnes (2.95 tons)
Height: 3.2m (10ft 6in)	or 18 troops

▶ **Panzerkampfwagen Opel Blitz 3000S**

4.SS-Polizei-Panzergrenadier-Division / Versorgungsdienste

Produced under the Schell Program, which simplified the German automotive industry before the war, the 'S' type Opel Blitz was a commercial 4x2 truck that was used extensively by the supply columns of German divisions.

Specifications

Crew: 1	Engine: Opel 6-cylinder petrol
Weight: 3.29 tonnes (3 tons)	(73.5hp)
Length: 6.02m (19ft 9in)	Speed: 80km/h (50mph)
Width: 2.27m (7ft 5in)	Range: 410km (255 miles)
Height: 2.18m (7ft 2in)	Radio: None

▼ SS-Polizei-Panzerjäger-Abteilung

In 1941 and 1942, the Panzerjäger Battalion of the *Polizei* Division was equipped with a mix of 3.7cm (1.5in) Pak 36 and 5cm (2in) Pak 38 guns. The Pak 36 was the standard German anti-tank gun at the outbreak of war. Light and handy to use in the field, it was a very influential design when first produced between the wars. By World War II, however, its performance was inadequate. It could penetrate up to 38mm (1.5in) of armour at a range of 350m (383 yards).

The 5cm (2in) Pak 38 was more powerful. It was introduced too late to be used in the early campaigns, but on the Eastern Front in 1941 it was the only German anti-tank gun powerful enough to knock out a T-34 tank. With tungsten-cored AP40 projectiles, it could penetrate over 100mm (4in) of armour at 740m (809 yards).

1.*Kompanie*

2.*Kompanie*

3.*Kompanie*

Greece and the Balkans
1943–1944

In April 1943, the division began to upgrade to an armoured infantry formation with the establishment of *Polizei* Panzergrenadier Regiments 1 and 2 at Cracow in Poland.

BOTH REGIMENTS WERE SENT to the Balkans in mid-July 1943, where they were attached to Army Group E. The complete *SS-Polizei-Division* finally arrived in Thessaloniki in December 1943.

After the conquest of Greece in 1941, the country was divided between Germany, Italy and Bulgaria. German forces occupied the strategically important areas, including Athens, Thessaloniki, central Macedonia, and some key Aegean islands.

Responsibility for internal security was initially in the hands of the *Wehrmacht*, which was primarily interested in keeping open lines of communication to Greek ports to supply German troops fighting the British in North Africa. After the fall of Tunisia, German troops were mainly used in anti-partisan operations.

ORGANIZATION
SS-Pol.Inf.Rgt 7
St
| I | II | III | sIG | Flk | Pnr |

ORGANIZATION
1/SS-Pol.Pz.Ab
St
| SG | SG | SG |

▲ **Schwere Kraftrad mit Seitenwagen BMW R75 750-cc**
4.SS-Polizei-Panzergrenadier-Division / Kraftrad-Aufklärungs-Abteilung
In February 1944, the *Polizei* Division was ordered to form a motorcycle battalion in place of its bicycle reconnaissance battalion. While it was being formed, the unit was upgraded to become a full reconnaissance battalion.

Specifications

Crew: 2	Engine: BMW 750cc petrol (26hp)
Weight: 0.67 tonnes (0.61 tons)	Speed: 92km/h (57mph)
Length: 2.4m (7ft 10in)	Range: 340km (211 miles)
Width: 1.73m (5ft 8in)	Radio: None
Height: 1m (3ft 3in)	Armament: 1 x 7.92mm (0.3in) MG (if fitted)

Partisan war

The increasing frequency of attacks by partisans in the Balkans resulted in executions and the slaughter of civilians in reprisal. The 4th SS *Polizei* Panzergrenadier Division saw action in Greece on anti-partisan duties between January and September 1944, before Soviet advances on the Eastern Front threatened to cut off Army Group E in the Balkans. In September and October 1944, the division retreated through Yugoslavia and southern Romania, seeing combat around Belgrade. It continued its anti-partisan duties in the Banat, the region straddling the borders of Serbia, Romania and Hungary.

▶ **2cm Flak 38 auf Fahrgestell Zugkraftwagen 1t (SdKfz 10/5)**
4.SS-Polizei-Panzergrenadier-Division / Stab / Flak-Zug (Sf)
In the summer of 1944, the 4th Division's headquarters was protected by a Flak platoon with four self-propelled 2cm (0.7in) guns. These were just as likely to be used against partisans on the ground as against attacking aircraft.

Specifications

Crew: 7	6-cylinder (100hp)
Weight: 5.5 tonnes (5 tons)	Speed: 65km/h (40mph)
Length: 4.75m (15ft 7in)	Range: 300km (186 miles)
Width: 2.15m (7ft 1in)	Radio: None
Height: 3.20m (10ft 6in)	Armament: Twin 20mm (0.7in)
Engine: Maybach HL42TRKM	Flak 38 L/112.5

▼ 4.SS-Sturmgeschütz-Abteilung, 1.Kompanie

In May 1944, after re-equipping to bring the formation up to Panzergrenadier strength in fact as well as name, the *Polizei* Division had been assigned an armoured detachment for the first time. The 4.*SS-Polizei-Panzer-Abteilung* was a three-battalion unit equipped with *Sturmgeschütz* assault guns rather than tanks. By August 1944, the unit had been redesignated as 4.*SS-Polizei-Sturmgeschütz-Abteilung*.

The 4.*SS-Polizei-Sturmgeschütz-Abteilung* had a staff company, which was equipped with two self-propelled *Flakvierling* anti-tank guns, and three *Sturmgeschütz* companies. The standard table of equipment was for each company to have a staff platoon with two guns and three platoons with four guns each. However, at the time the battalion was established the third company was one gun short with only 13 vehicles.

Stab

1.*Zug*

2.*Zug*

3.*Zug*

▶ Mittlere Zugkraftwagen 8t (SdKfz 7)

4.SS-Polizei-Flak-Abteilung (mot)

The standard tractor for the 8.8cm (3.5in) Flak 18 anti-aircraft gun and the 15cm (5.9in) sFH18 howitzer, the SdKfz 7 was designed by Krauss-Maffei. It was also manufactured by Mercedes, Büssing-NAG and Borgward.

Specifications

Crew: 2	Engine: Maybach HL62
Weight: 1.16 tonnes (1.06 tons)	6-cylinder (140hp)
Length: 6.85m (20ft 3in)	Speed: 50km/h (31mph)
Width: 2.40m (7ft 10.5in)	Range: 250km (156 miles)
Height: 2.62m (8ft 7.1in)	Radio: None

Hungary and Prussia
1945

In January 1945, the Red Army's main priority was to drive the Germans out of Poland, and to take the offensive into Germany's heartlands of Saxony and Prussia.

MARSHAL ZHUKOV AND HIS 1st Belorussian Front was to aim for Poznan, while Marshal Konev would direct his assault towards Breslau to the south. Each massive force comprised over one million men, with over 30,000 guns and 7000 tanks between them. Opposing them was Army Group Centre with only 400,000 men and just over 1000 tanks. The Germans, however, still had some 580,000 troops in East Prussia, which could cause the Soviets considerable problems.

ORGANIZATION
▷ SS-Flk.Abt 4
☐ St
| Bat | Bat | Bat | Bat | Sw |

In January 1945, the *Polizei* Division had been pushed into Slovakia. From there, it was moved north to join the still substantial German forces on the Baltic coast.

Fighting in Prussia

Arriving in Pomerania, as part of *SS-Obergruppenführer* Felix Steiner's Eleventh Panzer Army, the division was pushed into action against the advancing Red Army. After a series of battles, the 4th SS Division was moved to Danzig, where it was

ORGANIZATION
▷ SS-Pz.Auf.Ab 4
☐ St
| Spz | Auf | sch | Ns |

▼ **4.SS-Polizei-Panzerjäger-Abteilung, 1.Kompanie**

For a long period one of the poorest-equipped of the early SS divisions, the *Polizei* Division began to become a formation of real power by the time it was brought up to Panzergrenadier division strength in 1944. The division's Panzerjäger battalion was equipped with two companies of 14 *Jagdpanzers,* together with a motorized company equipped with 17 towed 7.5cm (3in) Pak 40 anti-tank guns. However, by the end of 1944 these were no longer in the division's table of organization.

Stab

1.Zug

2.Zug

3.Zug

trapped when the city was bypassed by Soviet forces. After intense fighting on the Vistula River, the division was shipped across the Hela Peninsula. It was evacuated by sea to Swinemünde in April and fought on the Oder Front north of Berlin. The wounded were sent to Copenhagen along with the division's 1st Medical Company. The division surrendered to US forces in May near Wittenberge-Lenzen.

▲ 15cm Schwere Infanterie Geschütz (sIG33)

7.SS-Polizei-Grenadier-Regiment (mot) / 13.Kompanie

The *Polizei* Division's two grenadier regiments each had a heavy infantry gun company to support each regiment's three infantry battalions.

Specifications	
Crew: 5	Muzzle Velocity: 241m/s (783fps)
Weight: 1.75 tonnes (1.71 tons)	Range: 5504m (6000 yards)
Length: 1.64m (64.57in)	Ammunition: High explosive or smoke
Calibre: 150mm (5.9in)	

▲ 7.5cm Panzerabwehrkanone (Pak 40)

8.SS-Polizei-Grenadier-Regiment / Stab / Panzerjäger-Zug

The HQs of the 7th and 8th SS Grenadier Regiments each had a three-gun anti-tank platoon, as did the heavy companies of the division's six infantry battalions.

Specifications	
Crew: 3	Muzzle Velocity (AP): 990m/s (3248fps)
Weight: 1.5 tonnes (1.37 tons)	Range: AP: 2000m (2190 yards), HE: 7.5km
Length: 3.7m (12ft 1.5in)	(4.66 miles)
Calibre: 75mm (3in)	Ammunition: Armour-piercing, high explosive

▶ Schwere Panzerspähwagen (SdKfz 231)

4.SS-Polizei-Aufklärungs-Abteilung / Spähpanzerwagen-Kompanie

A reconnaissance battalion was raised for the *Polizei* Division when it was upgraded in 1943/44. It had one armoured car company and three light reconnaissance companies equipped with soft-skin vehicles.

Specifications	
Crew: 4	petrol (150hp)
Weight: 9.1 tonnes (8.3 tons)	Speed: 85km/h (52.8mph)
Length: 5.85m (19ft 2in)	Range: 300km (186 miles)
Width: 2.20m (7ft 2.5in)	Radio: FuG Ger 'a'
Height: 2.35m (7ft 8in)	Armament: 1 x 20mm (0.7in)
Engine: Büssing-NAG 8-cylinder	cannon

▶ Sturmgeschütz 40 Ausf G (SdKfz 142/1)

4.SS-Sturmgeschütz-Abteilung / 1.Kompanie

Designed to serve as mobile artillery providing close support to the infantry, the *Sturmgeschütz* evolved into a versatile weapon system able to substitute for tanks or for tank-destroyers.

Specifications	
Crew: 4	Engine: Maybach HL120TRM
Weight: 26.3 tonnes (23.9 tons)	Speed: 40km/h (25mph)
Length: 6.77m (22ft 2in)	Range: 155km (96.3 miles)
Width: 2.95m (9ft 8in)	Radio: FuG15 and FuG16
Height: 2.16m (7ft 0in)	Armament: 1 x 75mm (3in) cannon

Chapter 2

The Expansion of the SS

During the course of World War II, the *Waffen-SS* grew from an elite force of four regiments composed solely of Germans meeting Heinrich Himmler's exacting physical and racial standards to a polyglot force of 900,000 men in 39 divisions, with over half of its troops being either foreign volunteers or conscripts. Even so, at its peak the *Waffen-SS* represented only one-tenth of the strength of the *Wehrmacht* – although it provided a quarter of German Panzer strength.

◀ Warriors of the *Reich*

An SS flamethrower crew prepares for battle. The exceptional physical standards of the early SS divisions could not be maintained in the massive expansion of the *Waffen-SS*, but SS troops remained highly motivated long after other Germans believed the war was lost.

5th SS Panzer Division *Wiking*

The first of the 'international' SS divisions, *Wiking* was one of the most effective fighting formations to have seen combat in World War II.

AFTER THE MAY 1940 *Sieg im Westen,* or Victory in the West, the SS began an active programme to recruit suitably 'Nordic' or 'Germanic' volunteers from northern and western Europe to join a number of *Waffen-SS Freiwilligen* (volunteer) legions. This effort intensified after June 1941, as the SS exhorted volunteers to join the campaign in the Soviet Union.

However, all this was still in the future and standards were still high in September 1940, when Hitler consented to the raising of a new *Waffen-SS* division. Originally to be named *SS-Division Germania,* the backbone of the unit was to be provided by the experienced and combat-tested *Germania* Regiment of the SS-VT Division.

It was hoped that the bulk of its strength would be provided by Dutch, Flemish, Danish and Norwegian volunteers serving in the volunteer *SS-Regiment Westland.* This was a sop to the Army, which had been complaining about the SS poaching the best German recruits. *SS-Infanterie-Regiment* 11, one of the *SS-Totenkopfstandarten,* replaced *Germania* in the

▼ **Eastern Front, early 1943**
Wiking was one of the hardest-fighting, most successful combat units on the Eastern Front, where it served from 1941 to 1945.

INSIGNIA

The sun cross, a cross inside a circle, is one of the oldest mythic symbols. The Nazis used a swastika variant of the sun cross as the *Wiking* insignia.

Insignia varied depending on the background. A dark-painted vehicle necessitated the use of a white shield to make the divisional symbol identifiable.

Commanders

Obergruppenführer Felix Steiner
1940 – January 1943

Obergruppenführer Herbert Gille
January 1943 – August 1944

Oberführer Edmund Deisenhofer
August 1944

Standartenführer Rudulf Mühlenkamp
August 1944 – September 1944

Oberführer Karl Ullrich
September 1944 – May 1945

Divisional History	Formed
Nordische Division (Nr. 5)	1940
SS-Division Germania (mot)	1940
SS-Division Wiking	1941
SS-Panzergrenadier-Division Wiking	1942
5.SS-Panzer-Division Wiking	1943

SS-VT. Further strength was supplied by the transfer of the *SS-Standarte Nordland*. Early 1941 saw the addition of a volunteer unit of Finns, the *Finnisches Freiwilligen-Bataillon der Waffen-SS Nordost*, which had been raised in February 1941.

On 20 December, Hitler ordered that the division should be known as the *SS-Division Wiking*. Commanded by Felix Steiner, one of the most influential officers in the *Waffen-SS, Wiking* was the first 'international' *Waffen-SS* division. It proved to be an excellent fighting unit, and as the *5.SS-Panzer-Division Wiking* it gained a combat reputation second to none. However, in spite of the hopes of the SS to make it a Germanic volunteer formation, Germans always outnumbered Nordic volunteers in its ranks.

▶ **Leichte Spähpanzerwagen (SdKfz 222)**

SS-Aufklärungs-Abteilung Wiking / leichte Spähpanzerwagen-Kompanie

As originally authorized in May 1940, the *Wiking* Division (then known as *Germania*) was to have a single light armoured car company as part of its reconnaissance battalion.

Specifications

Crew: 3	Speed: 85km/h (52.8mph)
Weight: 5.3 tonnes (4.8 tons)	Range: 300km (186 miles)
Length: 4.8m (15ft 8in)	Radio: FuG Spr Ger 'a'
Width: 1.95m (6ft 5in)	Armament: 1 x 20mm (0.7in) KwK 30 L/55
Height: 2.00m (6ft 7in)	cannon; 1 x 7.92mm (0.3in) MG (coaxial)
Engine: Horch 3.5L or 3.8L petrol	

Specifications

Crew: 5	Muzzle Velocity: 520m/s (1706fps)
Weight: 6.3 tonnes (5.7 tons)	Range: 13km (8 miles)
Length: 4.4m (14 ft 5in)	Ammunition: High explosive or smoke
Calibre: 150mm (5.9in)	

▲ **15cm schwere Feldhaubitze (sFH18)**

SS-Artillerie-Regiment Wiking / 4.Bataillon

Wiking was formed with an artillery regiment consisting of three motorized battalions of 10.5cm (4.1in) light field howitzers and a single battalion of 15cm (5.9in) heavy howitzers.

▶ **Panzerfunkwagen 8-Rad (SdKfz 263)**

SS-Nachrichten-Abteilung Wiking

Developed in the 1930s, the *Panzerfunkwagen* was a heavy armoured radio car issued to the radio companies and communications detachments of the signals battalions of Panzer and motorized divisions.

Specifications

Crew: 4	petrol (150hp)
Weight: 9.1 tonnes (8.3 tons)	Speed: 85km/h (52.8mph)
Length: 5.85m (19ft 2in)	Range: 300km (186 miles)
Width: 2.20m (7ft 2.5in)	Radio: FuG Ger 'a'
Height: 2.35m (7ft 8in)	Armament: 1 x 20mm (0.7in)
Engine: Büssing-NAG 8-cylinder	cannon

With Army Group South
SUMMER 1941

Formation of the division began in late 1940, and by the time of the invasion of the Soviet Union in June 1941, *Wiking* was a fully fledged, fully trained SS motorized infantry division.

THE DIVISION FIRST SAW ACTION on 29 June 1941. Assigned to Army Group South, it took part in the fighting for Tarnopol in Galicia. Opposition from isolated pockets of resistance and guerrilla groups aside, the progress of the division's tanks over the roads of the Ukraine from Dubno to the outskirts of Zhitomir was relatively free of problems, as seemingly endless lines of Soviet prisoners captured in the pocket of Lvov were marching towards the rear. Abandoned tanks and guns cluttered the roads.

Across the Dnieper

In August, 1941, the division was at the head of the army group as it fought to establish a bridgehead across the Dnieper River. Continuing the drive, *Wiking* fought its way through Dnepropetrovsk and on to Rostov.

According to one SS man, the fall of Rostov was greeted by its inhabitants with 'tremendous enthusiasm'. As far as the Red Army was concerned, the truth was otherwise. First, the Germans had been slowed by anti-tank obstacles, ditches and minefields. *Wiking* troops faced not Red Army soldiers but fanatical NKVD men, the shock troops of the Communist state. These men fought hand-to-hand in the streets, where they ripped up paving blocks to serve as thick barricades.

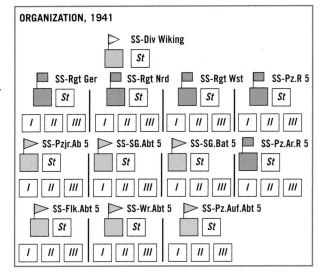

ORGANIZATION, 1941

First reverses

Almost every door concealed booby traps and tripwires. Pillboxes spat fire amid

ORGANIZATION

flamethrowers, grenades, machine guns, rifles and bayonets. The *Wiking* wounded were either

▶ **Mittlere Lkw Opel Blitz 3000S**

Versorgungsdienste Wiking / 30t Kolonne

The motorized transport columns attached to divisional support services were rated by their total load capacity: a 30-tonne (29.4-ton) column controlled two sections each with five medium, or 3-tonne (2.94-ton), trucks.

Specifications	
Crew: 1	Engine: Opel 6-cylinder petrol
Weight: 3.29 tonnes (3 tons)	(73.5hp)
Length: 6.02m (19ft 9in)	Speed: 80km/h (50mph)
Width: 2.27m (7ft 5in)	Range: 410km (255 miles)
Height: 2.18m (7ft 2in)	Radio: None

bayoneted as they lay in the street or were dragged from troop-carriers serving as makeshift ambulances.

Within days, the Soviets had driven the Germans out of the town and they fell back to defensive positions across the Mius, leaving behind piles of dead. Against furious onslaughts, the *Leibstandarte* and the *Wiking* Division held on, but their men knew that the position was hopeless. When the Germans were pushed out of Rostov by the first truly successful Red Army counterattack, *Wiking* moved back to the line of the Mius River, where the division spent the winter months.

 # Advance to the Causasus
MAY–SEPTEMBER 1942

Although it suffered heavy losses in its first year, *Wiking* acquired an excellent reputation, even earning the grudging respect of the Soviets in several battle reports for its pugnacious fighting spirit. Soviet commanders were always concerned to learn that their troops were facing the soldiers of the *Wiking* Division.

WHEN THE GERMANS LAUNCHED their major offensive in the summer of 1942, *Wiking* was again one of the spearhead divisions. Its make-up had changed, however, as individual elements of the *Wiking* Division were added and removed many times in its existence. As a replacement for the disbanded Finnish battalion of the *Nordland* Regiment, the *Estonian Narwa* Regiment was transferred to *Wiking*. The *Nordland* Regiment itself was detached to help establish a new *Waffen-SS* Division, the *Nordland* Division.

Army Group South, renamed Army Group B, was to advance into the bend of the Don River then on to the Volga at Stalingrad. The other claw in a gigantic pincer movement would be a new formation. Army Group A, comprising First Panzer Army, Seventeenth Army and Third Romanian Army, would link up

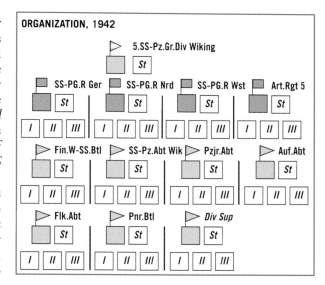

ORGANIZATION, 1942

▶ **Panzerkampfwagen III Ausf J (SdKfz 141)**

5.SS-Panzer-Regiment Wiking / II.Abteilung

In the summer of 1942, the *Wiking* Division added a Panzer battalion to its order of battle. *Wiking* was one of the first divisions to be issued with the long-barrelled Panzer III Ausf J.

Specifications

Crew: 5	Speed: 40km/h (25mph)
Weight: 24 tonnes (21.5 tons)	Range: 155km (96.3 miles)
Length: 6.28m (20ft 7in)	Radio: FuG5
Width: 2.95m (9ft 9in)	Armament: 1 x 50mm (2in) KwK 39
Height: 2.50m (8ft 2in)	L/60 gun; 2 x 7.92mm (0.3in) MG
Engine: Maybach HL120TRM	(one coaxial, one hull-mounted)

with Army Group B somewhere on the steppe west of the Volga, hopefully trapping another vast haul of Soviet prisoners. Army Group A would then lunge south and east to overrun the Soviet oilfields.

Six months after they had endured winter temperatures of -30°C (-22°F), *Wiking* soldiers found themselves leading the First Panzer Army on the Kuban steppe, where the thermometer topped 40°C (104°F) in the shade. Inside the tanks and fighting vehicles, the heat was simply unbearable. The terrain slowed up fighting troops as well as supplies. Roads were rivers of dust, and the rivers were wide, with unpredictable currents.

Nevertheless, the SS *Wiking* Division forced the

▶ 7.5cm Panzerjäger Marder II (SdKfz 131)
SS-Panzerjäger-Abteilung Wiking / Panzerjäger-Kompanie (Sf)
Mounting the powerful Pak 40 anti-tank gun onto a late-model Panzer II chassis produced a highly effective tank-hunter. In October 1942, the division had one self-propelled company and two companies with towed Pak 40s.

Specifications

Crew: 4	Speed: 42km/h (26mph)
Weight: 11.76 tonnes (10.67 tons)	Range: 185km (115 miles)
Length: 5.85m (19ft 2in)	Radio: FuG Spr 'd'
Width: 2.16m (7ft 0in)	Armament: 1 x 76.2mm (3in) FK296
Height: 2.50m (8ft 2in)	anti-tank gun
Engine: Praga EPA or EPA/2	

▶ Mittlere Flammpanzerwagen (SdKfz 251/16)
SS-Pionier-Abteilung Wiking / Panzer-Pionier-Kompanie (Spw)
One of the division's three combat engineer companies was half-track-equipped. Each pioneer company had six flamethrowers, either as individual man-portable equipment or mounted in pairs aboard flamethrower half-tracks.

Specifications

Crew: 5	(0.3in) MG34 or MG42; earlier
Weight: 9.5 tonnes (8.6 tons)	models also carried a single 7mm
Armament: 2 x 14mm (0.6in)	(0.3in) man-portable
Flammenwerfer; 2 x 7.62mm	Flammenwerfer 42

▶ Panzerkampfwagen IV Ausf G (SdKfz 161/1)
5.SS-Panzer-Regiment Wiking / I.Abteilung
While short-barrel Panzer IIIs were taking over the fire-support role, Panzer IVs traded in their short guns for the powerful long-barrelled 7.5cm (3in) KwK40 L/43 gun.

Specifications

Crew: 5	Speed: 40km/h (25mph)
Weight: 25.9 tonnes (23.5 tons)	Range: 210km (130.5 miles)
Length: 6.62m (21ft 8in)	Radio: FuG5
Width: 2.88m (9ft 5in)	Armament: 1 x 75mm (3in) KwK 40/43;
Height: 2.69m (8ft 10in)	2 x 7.92mm (0.3in) MG (one hull-
Engine: Maybach HL120TRM	mounted, one coaxial)

River Kuban in the face of intense Soviet resistance early in August. On 9 August, 1.*Panzerarmee* took Pyatigorsk at the bottom of the first foothills of the Caucasus, and patrols were sent out towards Astrakhan.

Fighting through the steppes

However, this was as far as it went. The *Wiking* Division had fought its way into and through the Caucasus. It would remain in the area until von Kleist's army group was forced to pull back after the fall of Stalingrad early in 1943.

By this time, it had been converted from a motorized infantry division into a Panzergrenadier, or armoured infantry, division.

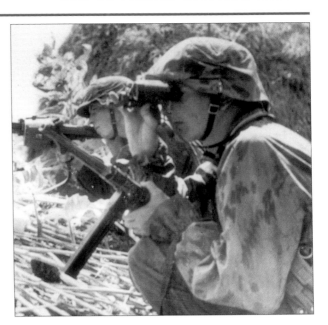

▶ **SS Camouflage**
SS troopers were among the first soldiers to be issued with camouflage smocks and helmet covers as standard combat clothing.

▼ **SS-Panzer-Abteilung Wiking light tank company**
As late as the invasion of the Soviet Union in 1941, the light tank companies of Panzer battalions still had large numbers of Panzer IIs. By the beginning of 1943, however, the few survivors were being used as commander's tanks or for reconnaissance, with the bulk of the company strength being provided by Panzer IIIs with short and long barrels.

Stab

1.*Zug*

2.*Zug*

3.*Zug*

Korsun encirclement
MARCH–DECEMBER 1943

Wiking avoided the cataclysmic battles at Kursk, serving further south with 4.*Panzerarmee* on the Don, fighting a defensive campaign through the summer and autumn of 1943.

IN OCTOBER 1943, the division was again upgraded, being converted from a Panzergrenadier division to a fully armoured Panzer division.

In the summer and autumn of 1943, the division fought in defensive operations in the area of Kharkov and the Dnieper River. By the end of of 1943, *Wiking* was one of six divisions occupying a 96km (60-mile) salient at Korsun, on the east of the Dnieper.

Hitler had the unrealistic belief that the 56,000 men in the salient could thrust in an offensive towards Kiev. He had not reckoned on the Soviets. General Konev's 2nd Ukrainian Front punched through the bridgehead lying between Kremenchug,

ORGANIZATION, 1943

5.SS-Pz.Gr.Div Wiking
St

SS-PG.R Ger | SS-PG.R Nor | SS-PG.R Wst | Art.Rgt 5
St | St | St | St
I II III | I II III | I II III | I II III

SS-Pz.Ab Wik | Flk.Abt | Pzjr.Abt | Auf.Abt
St | St | St | St
I II III | I II III | I II III | I II III

▶ **Panzerkampfwagen III Ausf N (SdKfz 141/2)**

5.SS-Panzer-Regiment Wiking

In July 1943, *Wiking* had eight Panzer III Ausf N tanks on strength. The short-barrelled 7.5cm (3in) gun was used to support other tanks by engaging enemy fortifications and infantry positions with high-explosive rounds.

Specifications

Crew: 5	Engine: Maybach HL120TRM
Weight: 25.4 tonnes (23 tons)	Speed: 40km/h (25mph)
Length: 5.52m (18ft 1in)	Range: 155km (96 miles)
Width: 2.95m (9ft 7in)	Radio: FuG5
Height: 2.5m (8ft 2in)	

▶ **Leichte Feldhaubitze 18/2 auf fahrgestell PzKpfw II (Sf) Wespe (SdKfz 124)**

5.SS-Artillerie-Regiment / I.Abteilung

The *Wiking* Division began to trade in some of its towed artillery pieces for Wespe self-propelled guns in August 1943. Only one battalion was given the new equipment; the other three used towed guns until the end of the war.

Specifications

Crew: 5	Speed: 40km/h (25mph)
Weight: 12.1 tonnes (11 tons)	Range: 220km (136.7 miles)
Length: 4.81m (15ft 10in)	Radio: FuG Spr 1
Width: 2.28m (7ft 6in)	Armament: 1 x LeFH18M L/28 105mm
Height: 2.25m (7ft 4.5in)	(4.1in) howitzer
Engine: Maybach HL62TR	

which lay far to the southwest of Kharkov, and Dnepropetrovsk to the east of Kremenchug. Konev's objective was to form a wedge between First Panzer Army and Eighth Army. The latter was no match for the strong Soviet muscle and was forced to pull back in the face of the steady advance of the 2nd Ukrainian Front.

Kiev

In the north, things were no better, with ever more powerful Soviet forces throwing the Germans out of Kiev on 6 November after they had established a bridgehead there. Soviet pride was further restored with the recapture, after a temporary loss, of the town of Zhitomir on 20 November.

Buildings there were reduced to rubble and the streets were littered with the burnt-out hulks of vehicles. Of considerable compensation were the large supply dumps and foodstuff depots of Fourth

Panzer Army, which the Germans had established in the high summer of triumph two years before.

Encirclement

The men of *Wiking* were assigned to territory where the prospects were bleak for the Germans. Four divisions were encircled in this flat countryside under snow with the temperature in Kirovograd itself at -20°C (-4°F). On 5 January, Konev's 2nd Ukrainian Front launched its attack and took the city. A breakout was eventually achieved by 3rd Panzer Division with fire cover from the artillery; engineers and Panzergrenadiers followed, while the Soviets were pinned down in local fighting.

For all the efforts of the Panzer units and the SS, the truth was that the Soviet advance had become a flood with the great winter offensive dealing the decisive blow.

▶ **Mittlere Schützenpanzerwagen Ausf D (SdKfz 251)**

Panzergrenadier-Regiment Germania / Spw Bataillon

In the summer of 1943, one battalion of the *Germania* Panzergrenadier Regiment was mounted in half-tracks. The *Germania* Regiment, one of the original Armed SS units, was later redesignated as the 9th SS Panzergrenadier Regiment *Germania*.

Specifications

Crew: 2 plus 12 troops	Engine: Maybach HL42TUKRM
Weight: 9.9 tonnes (9 tons)	Speed: 53km/h (33mph)
Length: 5.98m (19ft 7in)	Range: 300km (186 miles)
Width: 2.1m (6ft 11in)	Radio: FuG Spr Ger 1
Height: 1.75m (5ft 8in) or 2.16m	Armament: 1/2 x 7.62mm
(7ft) including MG shield	(0.3in) MG

▶ **Leichte Schützenpanzerwagen (SdKfz 250/9)**

5.SS-Panzer-Aufklärungs-Abteilung / 2.Spähpanzerwagen-Kompanie (Spw)

In 1944, only one of *Wiking's* five reconnaissance companies used armoured cars. The 2nd Armoured Car Company was actually equipped with reconnaissance half-tracks.

Specifications

Crew: 3	Speed: 60km/h (37mph)
Weight: 6.9 tonnes (6.3 tons)	Range: 320km (199 miles)
Length: 4.56m (14ft 11.5in)	Radio: FuG Spr Ger 'f'
Width: 1.95m (6ft 5in)	Armament: 1 x 20mm (0.7in) KwK 30/38
Height: 2.16m (7ft 1in)	L/55 cannon; 1 x 7.92mm (0.3in) MG (coaxial)
Engine: Maybach HL42TRKM 6-cylinder (100hp)	

▼ SS-Panzer-Artillerie-Regiment 5 : I.Bataillon

When formed, the *Wiking* Division's artillery regiment was equipped with towed artillery. By 1943, th 1st Artillery battalion had re-equipped with Wespe self-propelled howitzers.

1.*Batterie*

2.*Batterie*

3.*Batterie*

 # Retreat from Cherkassy

JANUARY 1944

***Wiking's* position in the Korsun salient was perilous. Overwhelming Soviet forces were assembling, clearly ready to pinch off and destroy the German divisions in the area.**

THE CONQUEST OF KIROVOGRAD still left unfinished business for the Soviets. To the north lay the salient around Korsun and Cherkassy, a position that Hitler was determined to hold and which was defended by six-and-a-half divisions with around 56,000 men.

The German positions south of the Korsun bulge took the full bombardment. Fourth Guards, Fifty-Third and Fifth Tank Armies struck at the heart of the German line. From the north of the bulge came the 1st Ukrainian Front. By 28 January, it had met up with Konev's 2nd Ukrainian Front, which had advanced from the south. Men of *5.SS-Panzer-Division Wiking* were among the 56,000 German troops trapped there.

Breakout

Being the only Panzer unit in the pocket, *Wiking* spearheaded the operation to break out of the encirclement. Included under its orders at the time was an independent SS formation of Belgian volunteers, *5.SS-Freiwilligen-Sturmbrigade Wallonien*, which would later become *28.SS-Freiwilligen-Grenadier-Division Wallonien*. The breakout was successful, but casualties were heavy – some 30,000 of the 56,000 German troops escaped. The *Wiking* Division lost all of its armour and much of its equipment in the process.

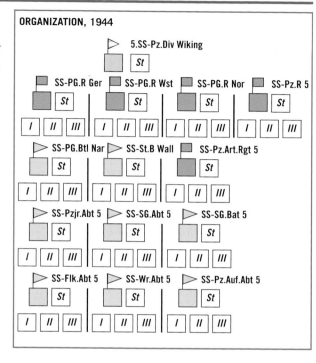

ORGANIZATION, 1944

5.SS-Pz.Div Wiking — St
SS-PG.R Ger — St; SS-PG.R Wst — St; SS-PG.R Nor — St; SS-Pz.R 5 — St
SS-PG.Btl Nar — St; SS-St.B Wall — St; SS-Pz.Art.Rgt 5 — St
SS-Pzjr.Abt 5 — St; SS-SG.Abt 5 — St; SS-SG.Bat 5 — St
SS-Flk.Abt 5 — St; SS-Wr.Abt 5 — St; SS-Pz.Auf.Abt 5 — St

▶ **7.5cm Panzerspähwagen 8-Rad (SdKfz 234/3)**

5.SS-Panzer-Aufklärungs-Abteilung / schwere Zug

The heavy platoon of the Panzer reconnaissance battalion in the last months of the war was equipped with six heavy eight-wheeled armoured cars armed with short-barrelled KwK51 tank guns.

Specifications

Crew: 4	Speed: 80km/h (50mph)
Weight: 11.50 tonnes (10.47 tons)	Range: 900km (559 miles)
Length: 6.0m (19ft 8in)	Radio: FuG Spr Ger 'a'
Width: 2.40m (7ft 10.5in)	Armament: 1 x 75mm (3in) PaK 40 L/46
Height: 2.21m (7ft 4in)	cannon; 1 x 7.92 mm (0.3in) MG
Engine: Tatra 103 12-cylinder (220hp)	

▶ **Panzerkampfwagen IV Ausf H (SdKfz 161/2)**

5.SS-Panzer-Regiment / II.Abteilung / 5.Kompanie

Wiking was equipped with the standard late-war Panzer regiment, comprising one battalion with Panthers and one with Panzer IVs.

Specifications

Crew: 5	Engine: Maybach HL120TRM
Weight: 27.6 tonnes (25 tons)	Speed: 38km/h (23.6mph)
Length: 7.02m (23ft)	Range: 210km (130.5 miles)
Width: 2.88m (9ft 5in)	Radio: FuG5
Height: 2.68m (8ft 10in)	

Specifications

Crew: 5

Weight: 50.2 tonnes (45.5 tons)

Length: 8.86m (29ft)

Width: 3.4m (11ft 2in)

Height: 2.98m (9ft 8in)

Engine: Maybach HL230P30

Speed: 46km/h (29mph)

Range: 200km (124 miles)

Radio: FuG5

▲ Panzerkampfwagen V Ausf G (SdKfz 171)
5.SS-Panzer-Regiment / I.Abteilung / 3.Kompanie

In October 1943, the *Wiking* Division was upgraded to become a full Panzer division. In May 1944, the records of the German high command showed that the 1st Battalion of the 5th Panzer Regiment had completed re-equipping with *Panzerkampfwagen* V Panthers.

▼ 5.SS-Panzer-Regiment, I.Abteilung, 1.Kompanie

In 1943, with the large-scale introduction of the PzKpfw V Panther into service, a major reorganization of German Panzer forces was undertaken. Some Panzer divisions had one tank battalion of three companies, each company being formed of a command troop with two tanks and four platoons each with five tanks. In the summer of 1944, the Panzer divisions were again reorganized. The Panzer regiments in the Type 44 Division now consisted of two battalions, one equipped with Panthers and the second with Panzer IVs. Some companies retained 22 tanks, but in many divisions the number of tanks in a company was reduced from 22 to 17.

Stab

1.Zug

2.Zug

3.Zug

Hungary and Austria
1944–1945

The losses suffered by *Wiking* in the fierce fighting at Korsun and Cherkassy meant that by the spring of 1944 the division was in need of complete rebuilding.

THE REMNANTS OF THE *WIKING* DIVISION fought on as a *Kampfgruppe,* before being transferred to Poland where they would form the nucleus of a new *5.SS-Panzer-Division Wiking.* Because it was out of the line, it missed the massive Soviet summer offensive known as Operation *Bagration.* Perhaps the most powerful military attack in history, *Bagration* smashed the German Eastern Front and virtually destroyed Army Group Centre.

By the time *Wiking* was again in action, the Soviets had pushed all the way to the Vistula River and to Warsaw. Along with the *3.SS-Panzer-Division Totenkopf* and the Army's 19th Panzer Division,

Wiking fought to stem the Soviet advance, stabilizing the front along the line of the Vistula.

As the vast Soviet wave of destruction rolled onwards towards Germany, north of the Carpathians, Hitler found himself obsessed with Hungary. *Wiking* was pulled from Warsaw in December 1944, and transferred south to relieve 60,000 German soldiers and more than 800,000 civilians trapped in the Hungarian capital, Budapest.

Attached to IV SS Panzer Corps, *Wiking* pushed forward for two weeks, but could not penetrate the massed Soviet armies which were besieging the city. Even though units of the Red Army were now in

▲ **Retreat from the East**

Hammered almost into oblivion in the escape from the Cherkassy pocket, the men of the *Wiking* Division were pulled out of the line early in 1944. The division had left most of its equipment behind, so surviving troops were used as a *Kampfgruppe* until more Panzers could be delivered.

sight of the suburbs of the Hungarian capital, IV SS Panzer Corps received orders to shift position to the industrial and farming area of Szekesfehervar in the southwest. This is believed to have been on the personal orders of Hitler himself. It was from here that the next attempt to break the stranglehold on Budapest would be made.

The overall loss of men and materiel to the *Wiking* and *Totenkopf* Divisions was bleeding the *Waffen-SS* formations dry. A slow countermove was set at naught by the strength of enemy fire, and the command post at Szekesfehervar had to be moved back and all resistance collapsed.

The next attack was to be made by Sepp Dietrich's Sixth SS Panzer Army, withdrawn from the fighting in the Ardennes and moved across Europe to

Hungary. On 25 March, the Soviet breakthrough was all but complete, and the next day the Soviets went into the final phase which was the drive into Austria. With the failure of the final attempt to relieve the city, *Wiking* was withdrawn into Austria, where it fought in the final battles to defend Vienna in 1945.

Defence of Vienna

High priority was given to the defence of Vienna by the *Waffen-SS,* although there was nothing that even remotely compared with the defensive systems that had existed at Budapest. Rearguard detachments of Sixth SS Panzer Army, with elements of *Wiking*, *Leibstandarte* and the 17th Infantry Division, set up frequent ambushes, mined roads and blew bridges to hold off the Soviet Army.

▶ **2cm Flak 38 auf Fahrgestell Zugkraftwagen 1t (SdKfz 10/5)**
5.SS-Panzer-Division Wiking / Divisionsstab-Kompanie
Wiking's divisional staff company included Flak, infantry gun and Panzerjäger platoons. The Flak battery was equipped with four self-propelled 2cm (0.7in) anti-aircraft guns.

Specifications

Crew: 7	6-cylinder (100hp)
Weight: 5.5 tonnes (5 tons)	Speed: 65km/h (40mph)
Length: 4.75m (15ft 7in)	Range: 300km (186 miles)
Width: 2.15m (7ft 1in)	Radio: None
Height: 3.20m (10ft 6in)	Armament: Twin 20mm (0.7in)
Engine: Maybach HL42TRKM	Flak 38 L/112.5

Specifications

Crew: 6	Speed: 42km/h (26mph)
Weight: 26.5 tonnes (24 tons)	Range: 215km (133.6 miles)
Length: 7.17m (23ft 6in)	Radio: FuG Spr 1
Width: 2.97m (9ft 8in)	Armament: 1 x 150mm (5.9in) sFH 18/1 L/30; 1 x
Height: 2.81m (9ft 2in)	7.92mm (0.3in) MG
Engine: Maybach HL120TRM (265hp)	

▲ **15cm schwere Panzerhaubitze Hummel (SdKfz 165)**
5.SS-Panzer-Artillerie-Regiment / II.Bataillon / 3.Batterie
The 15cm (5.9in) sFH18 heavy field howitzer mounted in the Hummel could fire a 43.5kg (96lb) shell out to a maximum range of 13,325m (14,572 yards).

However, nothing could stop the Soviet juggernaut, and orders were given for the remnants of the division to retreat towards Graz. On the River Mur, the Soviets were waiting with cavalry and T-34 tanks. Those who survived the onslaught made for the American lines at Rastad, where they surrendered.

▼ 5.SS-Panzerjäger-Abteilung, 1.Kompanie

Anti-tank units in German divisions were equipped at the beginning of the war with a few 3.7cm (1.5in) anti-tank guns, which were of little use against even moderately armed vehicles. By the end of the war, anti-tank guns had grown enormously. These were more versatile, since many were mounted on self-propelled platforms. At the end of the war, *Wiking's* three Panzerjäger companies were all self-propelled. Platforms ranged from the SdKfz 251/22, known as the *Kanonen Spw*, to the long-serving Marder III. The latter was introduced in 1942, and there were more than 350 Marders operational throughout the *Wehrmacht* in February 1945.

Stab

1.Zug

2.Zug

3.Zug

▶ 7.5cm Mittlere Schützenpanzerwagen (SdKfz 251/22)

5.SS-Panzerjäger-Abteilung / 1.Kompanie

Built in large numbers in the last year of the war, the SdKfz 251/22 simply mounted the 7.5cm (3in) Pak 40 onto the loadbed of the *mittlere Schützenpanzerwagen*.

Specifications

Crew: 4 or 5	Engine: Maybach HL42TUKRM
Weight: 8 tonnes (7.28 tons)	6-cylinder petrol (100hp)
Length: 5.98m (19ft 7in)	Speed: 50km/h (31mph)
Width: 2.1m (6ft 11in)	Range: 300km (186 miles)
Height: 2.25m (7ft 4.5in)	Radio: None

6th SS Gebirgs Division *Nord*

Formed in Norway from members of the *Allgemeine-,* or General, SS, the *Nord* Division was the first of the *Waffen-SS Gebirgs,* or mountain, divisions.

IN JUNE 1940, the capitulation of Norway left a large border with Finland and the Soviet Union unguarded. To replace the two Norwegian infantry battalions and the motorized artillery battery that had been deployed in the area, the Germans decided to deploy SS units rather than regular Army formations. The *Totenkopfstandarten* that would provide the manpower for the new force were composed of military-age members of the *Allgemeine-SS*. *SS-Totenkopf-Standarte 9,* commanded by *SS-Obersturmbannführer* Ernst Deutsch, was ordered north, with the first unit – *SS-Bataillon Reitz,*

commanded by *Obersturmbannführer* Wilhelm Reitz – arriving at Kirkenes in the late summer.

In February 1941, two further SS regiments arrived in northern Norway: the 6th and 7th *SS-Totenkopf-Standarten.* Soon afterwards, most of the 6th *Standarte,* reinforced by elements of the 9th, moved forwards to defensive positions at Salla in northern Finland. The German commander in Norway, General von Falkenhorst, was not impressed with the SS men, however. Although well equipped, the *Totenkopf-Standarten* were not made up from highly trained *Waffen-SS* men: the volunteers transferred from the *Allgemeine-SS* lacked the fitness and spirit of the Armed SS men.

Action in Russia

With the attack on Russia in June 1941, the units, now brigaded as *SS-Kampfgruppe Nord,* were launched into battle against veteran Soviet troops on

INSIGNIA

Formed to fight in the harsh terrain north of the Arctic Circle, the *Nord* Division adopted a stylised snowflake as its divisional symbol.

As a mountain division, the shield used on the *Nord* divisional insignia was notched at the top. Panzer division shields were notched at the top right.

Divisional History	Formed
SS-Kampfgruppe Nord	1941
SS-Division Nord (mot)	1941
SS-Gebirgs-Division Nord	1942
6.SS-Gebirgs-Division Nord	1943

Commanders

Brigadeführer Karl Herrmann *February 1941 – May 1941*	Gruppenführer Lothar Debes *January 1943 – June 1943*
Obergruppenführer Karl-Maria Demelhuber *May 1941 – April 1942*	Obergruppenführer Friedrich-Wilhelm Krüger *June 1943 – August 1943*
Obergruppenführer Matthias Kleinheisterkamp *April 1942*	Brigadeführer Gustav Lombard *August 1943 – January 1944*
Oberführer Hans Scheider *April 1942 – June 1942*	Gruppenführer Karl Brenner *January 1944 – April 1945*
Obergruppenführer Matthias Kleinheisterkamp *June 1942 – January 1943*	Standartenführer Franz Schreiber *April 1945 – May 1945*

▶ **Mittlere Lkw Henschel 33D1**

Kampfgruppe Nord / 6.SS-Infanterie-Regiment

As originally created, *Nord* was primarily an infantry formation with minimal motorization. However, by the time the *Kampfgruppe* became a brigade in 1941, its two infantry regiments had been motorized.

Specifications

Crew: 1	Engine: 10.7L (650ci),
Weight: 6.1 tonnes (6 tons)	6-cylinder petrol (100hp)
Length: 7.4m (24ft)	Speed: 60km/h (37mph)
Width: 2.25m (7ft 4in)	Payload: 3 tonnes (2.95 tons)
Height: 3.2m (10ft 6in)	or 18 troops

the Finnish border at Markajärvi-Salla. This was in spite of the fact that the *Kampfgruppe*'s former commander, *Brigadeführer* Hermann, had asked for at least two months' further training to bring the unit up to standard.

The poorly trained SS men made a poor showing in the fighting, suffering 300 killed and more than 400 wounded in two days. *Nord* eventually rallied, however, and took part in the failed drive to interdict

the Murmansk railway at Louhi.

In July and August 1941, units of *Nord* were re-equipped, and their shortcomings were addressed by a period of intensive training. Between July and September *Nord*, now classed a motorized division, was gradually withdrawn from the front and moved 140km (87 miles) south to the Kiestinki–Uhtua area.

▲ **3.7cm Panzerabwehrkanone (Pak 36)**

9.SS-Infanterie-Regiment / 14.leichte Panzerjäger-Kompanie

The only anti-tank assets controlled by *Nord* in 1941 were the single light motorized tank companies assigned to the 6th, 7th and 9th SS Infantry Regiments. These were each equipped with 12 Pak 36 guns.

Specifications

Crew: 3	
Weight: 0.43 tonnes (0.39 tons)	Muzzle Velocity: 762m/s (2500fps)
Length: 1.67m (5ft 5.5in)	Range: 600m (656 yards)
Calibre: 37mm (1.5in)	Ammunition: Armour-piercing

▲ **15cm schwere Infanteriegeschütz (sIG33)**

7.SS-Infanterie-Regiment / 13.Infanteriegeschütz-Kompanie

Each of *Nord*'s three infantry regiments included three infantry battalions. The 13th Company in each regiment was equipped with three light infantry gun platoons and a single heavy platoon with two 15cm (5.9in) sIG33s.

Specifications

Crew: 5	
Weight: 1.75 tonnes (1.71 tons)	Muzzle Velocity: 241m/s (783fps)
Length: 1.64m (64.57in)	Range: 5504m (6000 yards)
Calibre: 150mm (5.9in)	Ammunition: High explosive or smoke

Combat in Soviet Russia
SEPTEMBER 1941 – SEPTEMBER 1944

Although not an *SS-Freiwilligen,* or volunteer, formation in the classic sense, the 6th SS Division did have a significant foreign volunteer component.

IN SEPTEMBER 1941, the *Kampfgruppe* acquired an artillery regiment, and further reinforcements were planned to bring the *Kampfgruppe* up to full divisional status. Hitler directed that 'a new *SS-Gebirgsbrigade* is to be formed by volunteering Norwegians and Finns. An Austrian *SS-Regiment* is to be attached, and the remaining units are to be deployed from *Kampfgruppe Nord*.'

Although the promised Finnish regiment did not appear, the new *SS-Division Nord* did later include the *Freiwilligen-Schikompanie Norwegen*, later enlarged to become the *Schibataillon Norwegen*.

In the meantime, the unit was placed under the temporary command of the veteran Finnish General Siilasvuo – the only time an SS unit was placed under foreign command. As part of the temporary 'Division J', it was assigned to Siilasvuo's III Finnish Army Corps.

Mountain division

In January 1942, it was decided that the *Nord* Division should be redesignated as a mountain division in the near future, and plans were set afoot to create new units for the division. These were assigned

ORGANIZATION, 1941

in June and arrived in September 1942, when the division was redesigned *SS-Gebirgs-Division Nord*.

By now detached from 'Division J', *Nord* was assigned to fight alongside the Army's 7.*Gebirgs-Division* in the new German XVIII *Gebirgs-Armee-Korps*, which had arrived in Finland during the winter of 1941 and spring of 1942. In August 1942, the division returned to Finland.

Nord was deployed to hold the line around the Kiestinki area, where it would remain until autumn of 1944. Early in 1943, the Norwegian Ski Battalion was attached to the division, which became 6.*SS-Gebirgs-Division Nord* on 22 October 1943.

▼ SS-Division *Nord*, Kradschützen-Aufklarungs-Kompanie, schwere Zug

The heavy platoon of the motorcycle reconnaissance company was equipped with heavy machine guns and with two 8.1cm (3.2in) mortars carried by the mortar section.

Stab

1.Gruppe

2.Gruppe

Granatewerfer Gruppe

At the same time, a company raised by the Norwegian police was attached to the ski battalion. Also in October, the division provided a cadre of officers for the newly forming 13.*Waffen-Gebirgs-Division der SS Handschar (kroatische Nr. 1).*

In March 1944, the 2nd Norwegian Police Company, which had been operating with the division, was withdrawn. It was replaced by the 3rd Company of 150 men, assigned to the ski battalion.

On 25 June 1944, after a Soviet assault at Kaprolat, the Norwegian volunteers lost 135 men from a total of 300 in the battalion. The survivors were absorbed by *SS-Polizei-Grenadier-Bataillon (mot) 506.*

▶ Mittlere Nachrichten Kraftwagen (Kfz 15)

SS-Aufklärungs-Abteilung Nord / Kradschützen-Aufklärungs-Kompanie

The headquarters section in each of the motorcycle reconnaissance company's four platoons had two Kfz 15 radio cars.

Specifications

Crew: 1	Engine: Mercedes-Benz 6-cylinder petrol
Weight: 2.4 tonnes (2.2 tons)	(90hp)
Length: 4.44m (14ft 7in)	Speed: 88km/h (55mph)
Width: 1.68m (5ft 6in)	Range: 400km (250 miles)
Height: 1.73m (5ft 8in)	Radio: Various depending on deployment

▶ 21cm Wurfgranate 42

SS-Gebirgs-Infanterie-Regiment Reinhard Heydrich / Nebelwerfer-Batterie

Designed originally as a smoke projector, the *Nebelwerfer* was used almost exclusively as an artillery weapon. It could fire a 10kg (18lb) high-explosive warhead out to a range of nearly 8km (5 miles).

Specifications

Crew: 3	Calibre: 21cm (8.27in)
Weight: 109kg (240lb) overall; 18.27kg	Muzzle Velocity: 320m/s (1050fps)
(40.25lb) propellant	Range: 7850m (8580 yards)
Length: 1.25m (4ft 1in)	Ammunition: High-explosive

▲ 8.8cm Flak 18/Mittlere ZgKw (SdKfz 7)

SS-Gebirgs-Division Nord / Flak-Abteilung / 3.Batterie

Nord's Flak battalion's 1st Battery operated 12 self-propelled 2cm (0.7in) Flak 36 guns; the 2nd Battery had 12 towed 2cm (0.7in) guns (later replaced by 3.7cm/1.5in weapons) and the heavy 3rd Battery was equipped with four towed 8.8cm (3.5in) Flak 18 weapons.

Specifications

Crew: 2	Engine: Maybach HL62 6-cylinder (140hp)
Weight: 1.16 tonnes (1.06 tons)	Speed: 50km/h (31mph)
Length: 6.85m (20ft 3in)	Range: 250km (156 miles)
Width: 2.40m (7ft 10.5in)	Radio: None
Height: 2.62m (8ft 7.1in)	

Arctic operations
JULY 1941 – AUGUST 1944

The border between Russia and Finland offered some of the hardest combat of the war, and after a shaky start the 6th SS Division played a major part in the action north of the Arctic Circle.

FORMED SOON after the creation of the 5th SS Division *Wiking*, the SS *Nord* formation was not to become a division for some time. Constructed around members of the *Totenkopfstandarten* of the *Allgemeine-SS*, *SS-Kampfgruppe Nord* was transferred to Norway for garrison duty.

ORGANIZATION

Trained by the Finns
The *Kampfgruppe* participated in Operation *Silver Fox*, the liberation of part of Soviet-occupied Finland, and the invasion of Soviet Karelia. Routed by the Soviets at Salla in the summer of 1941, it was retrained by the Finns, and operating with the German Army's 7th Mountain Division it performed well for the rest of the war.

ORGANIZATION, 1943

As 6.*SS-Gebirgs-Division Nord*, the formation fought in the Arctic for 1214 consecutive days from 1 July 1941. One of its most effective units was the *SS-Freiwilligen-Schusskompanie Norwegen* – expert skiers from Norway, Sweden and Denmark, who were used on long-range reconnaissance patrols.

▲ **Leichte Pkw Stoewer 40 (Kfz 2)**
SS-Gebirgsjäger-Regiment Reinhard Heydrich / Stab
The motor pool assigned to the divisional staff usually had five light cars like the Stoewer or the VW *Kübel*, five medium cars and an assortment of motorcycles, trucks and specialist communications and maintenance vehicles.

▲ **5cm Panzerabwehrkanone (Pak 38)**
7.SS-Gebirgs-Regiment / Gebirgs-Panzerjäger-Kompanie
The regimental anti-tank companies were reorganized in the summer of 1942, each company receiving a pair of 5cm (2in) Pak 38s to supplement the 3.7cm (1.5in) Pak 36 guns that had been the division's only anti-tank weapons.

Specifications

Crew: 1	Engine: Stoewer AW2 or R180W petrol (50hp)
Weight: 1.81 tonnes (1.65 tons)	Speed: 100km/h (62.5mph)
Length: 3.58m (11ft 9in)	Range: 500km (311 miles)
Width: 1.57m (5ft 2in)	Radio: None
Height: 1.78 (5ft 10in)	

Specifications

Crew: 3	Muzzle Velocity (AP): 835m/s (2900fps)
Weight: 1.2 tonnes (1.13 tons)	Range: AP: 1800m (1968 yards), HE: 2.6km
Length: 3.2m (10ft 5in)	(1.6 miles)
Calibre: 50mm (2in)	Ammunition: Armour-piercing, high explosive

▶ **Panzerjäger 38(t) fur 7.62cm Pak 36(r) (SdKfz 139)**

7.SS-Gebirgs-Regiment / Gebirgs-Panzerjäger-Kompanie

The division received nine Marder tank-hunters in April 1943. Equipped with Soviet guns, they only served in the division for a month.

Specifications

Crew: 4	Speed: 42km/h (26mph)
Weight: 11.76 tonnes (10.67 tons)	Range: 185km (115 miles)
Length: 5.85m (19ft 2in)	Radio: FuG Spr 'd'
Width: 2.16m (7ft 0in)	Armament: 1 x 76.2mm (3in) FK296
Height: 2.50m (8ft 2in)	anti-tank gun
Engine: Praga EPA or EPA/2	

Retreat from the north
SEPTEMBER 1944 – MAY 1945

When the Finns made a separate peace with the Soviets in the autumn of 1944, German forces in Finland were faced with a fighting retreat through what was now hostile territory.

ON 2 SEPTEMBER 1944, the Finns withdrew from the war. The next day, all German units received the message: *Birke anschlagen,* or 'Cut the birch'. The message was a warning to prepare for the evacuation of Finland. Two days later, the message *Birke fällen* ('Birch has fallen') ordered the evacuation to begin.

During August and September, the Germans had activated two temporary units called *Kampfgruppe West* and *Ost* to secure their southern flank. Units

from *Nord,* together with *Divisiongruppe Kräutler,* formed the bulk of thezse two battle groups.

At the end of September, the two *Kampfgruppen* fought several short engagements with their erstwhile Finnish allies, but the retreat was not slowed to any great degree.

Nord reached Norway in October 1944. At the end of the year, it was transferred to Germany, where it took part in Operation *Nordwind*. This was an

▲ **7.5cm Panzerabwehrkanone (Pak 40)**

SS-Panzerjäger-Abteilung Nord

Briefly equipped with self-propelled Marder I tank-hunters, the anti-tank battalion was to have had them replaced by towed Pak 40s in May 1943.

Specifications

Crew: 3	Muzzle Velocity (AP): 990m/s (3248fps)
Weight: 1.5 tonnes (1.37 tons)	Range: AP 2000m (2190 yards), HE: 7.5km
Length: 3.7m (12ft 1.5in)	(4.66 miles)
Calibre: 75mm (3in)	Ammunition: Armour-piercing, high explosive

ORGANIZATION, 1944

6.SS-Gb.Div Nord — St

SS-Gbjr.R 11	SS-Gbjr.R 12	SS-Inf.Rgt 5	SS-Gb.Art.R
St	St	St	St
I II III	I II III	I II III	I II III

SS-PG.Ab 506	SS-Stz.Abt 6	SS-Gb.Pzjr.Ab	SS-SG.Bat
St	St	St	St
I II III	I II III	I II III	I II III

SS-Flk.Abt 6	SS-Gb.Auf.Ab	SS-Skjr.Abt Norge
St	St	St
I II III	I II III	I II III

▲ *Nebelwerfer* artillery

Although not particularly accurate, a battery of *Nebelwerfer* firing salvos of high-explosive rockets was a very effective area weapon against unprotected troops.

abortive attack mounted south of the Ardennes in January 1945, the last major German offensive in the West. Designed to take pressure off the main Ardennes offensive, the action saw *SS-Kampfgruppe Schreiber*, made up from *SS-Gebirgsjäger-Regiment 12*, pass through US VI Corps lines to seize Wingen-sur-Moder. Promised panzer back-up having been diverted elsewhere, the *Kampfgruppe* had to fight its way back to German lines, losing 500 out of 725 men in the process.

Final actions

After a period on the defensive in the Vosges Mountains, *Nord* was transferred to the Saar, where it was employed against Patton's Third Army. In April 1945, *Nord* retreated south to Bavaria, where it surrendered to the Americans in May 1945.

▶ **2cm Flakvierling auf ZgKw 8t (SdKfz 7/1)**

SS-Flak-Abteilung Nord

The *Nord* Flak battalion was equipped with the usual mix of 2cm (0.7in), 3.7cm (1.5in) and 8.8cm (3.5in) towed weapons but by 1944 had also taken on strength two self-propelled light Flak batteries.

Specifications
Crew: 7	Engine: Maybach HL 62 TUK
Weight: 1.16 tonnes	6-cylinder (140hp)
(1.06 tons)	Speed: 50km/h (31mph)
Length: 6.55m (21ft 6in)	Range: 250km (156 miles)
Width: 2.40m (7ft 10.5in)	Radio: None
Height: 3.20m (10ft 6in)	Armament: Quad 20mm
	(0.7in) Flak 38

▶ **Mittlere Lkw Opel Blitz S 3t**

6.SS-Gebirgs-Division Nord

In 1944, as the division retreated through Finland, it was supported by two truck parks, which supplied the division's transport and supply columns. The 120-tonne (109-ton) supply column operated up to 40 medium trucks like this Opel Blitz.

Specifications
Crew: 1	Engine: Opel 6-cylinder petrol
Weight: 3.29 tonnes (3 tons)	(73.5hp)
Length: 6.02m (19ft 9in)	Speed: 80km/h (50mph)
Width: 2.27m (7ft 5in)	Range: 410km (255 miles)
Height: 2.18m (7ft 2in)	Radio: None

7th SS Freiwilligen Gebirgs Division *Prince Eugen*

One of the most effective of all German anti-partisan units, the *Prinz Eugen* Mountain Division was also one of the most feared for its brutal tactics in an already brutal war.

THE *7.SS-FREIWILLIGEN-GEBIRGS-DIVISION* Prinz Eugen was created for partisan operations in the Balkans, and the bulk of its strength consisted of ethnic German *Volksdeutsche* volunteers and conscripts from Romania, Hungary and Yugoslavia.

Formed as a mountain division, *Prinz Eugen* was equipped with obsolete and captured equipment such as Czech-made machine guns and French light tanks. Despite the limited equipment, it was one of the most effective counterinsurgency units the Germans fielded in Yugoslavia during the war, and was greatly feared by the partisans. However, that reputation was gained primarily by brutality and utter ruthlessness.

Volksdeutsche volunteers

The origins of the *Prinz Eugen* Division can be found in Himmler's desire to form entire SS units from the massive manpower resource that was the large *Volksdeutsche* community living outside Germany's borders. Many *Volksdeutsche* were already serving in the *Wehrmacht*, but they had primarily joined as individual volunteers.

Gottlob Berger, head of the SS recruiting office, proposed to form a new SS division early in 1942. It was to be made up of volunteers from the large *Volksdeutsche* community living in Serbia, Croatia and the Banat.

The new *Freiwilligen-Gebirgs-Division* was initially established in March 1942. At its core were two Croatian units, an *SS-Selbstschutz* (a locally recruited SS protection force) and a unit known as the *Einsatz-Staffel Prinz Eugen*.

Commanders

Obergruppenführer Arthur Phleps *January 1942 – May 1943*	Brigadeführer Otto Kumm *January 1944 – January 1945*
Brigadeführer Karl Reichsritter von Oberkamp *May 1943 – January 1944*	Brigadeführer August Schmidthuber *January 1945 – May 1945*

INSIGNIA

Prinz Eugen used an ancient symbol from the Futharc Runic alphabet, modified with extra 'feet' to distinguish it from the symbol used by the 4th Infantry Division.

Divisional History	Formed
SS-Selbstschutz	1941
Einsatz-Staffel Prinz Eugen	1941
Freiwilligen-Gebirgs-Division	1942
SS-Freiwilligen-Division Prinz Eugen	1942
SS-Freiwilligen-Gebirgs-Division Prinz Eugen	1942
7.SS-Freiwilligen-Gebirgs-Division Prinz Eugen	1943

▼ **Mittlere Lkw Henschel 33D1**

7.SS-Division / Versorgungsdienst

As formed, the *Prinz Eugen* Division's supply service was largely horse-drawn, but by March 1943 it was split almost equally between horse-drawn and motorized transport.

Specifications

Crew: 1	Engine: 10.7L (650ci),
Weight: 6.1 tonnes (6 tons)	6-cylinder petrol (100hp)
Length: 7.4m (24ft)	Speed: 60km/h (37mph)
Width: 2.25m (7ft 4in)	Payload: 3 tonnes (2.95 tons)
Height: 3.2m (10ft 6in)	or 18 troops

▶ Panzerkampfwagen B2 740(f)

SS-Panzer-Abteilung Prinz Eugen

Large numbers of Char B tanks were captured in France in 1940.

Specifications	
Crew: 4	Engine: Renault 6-cylinder petrol
Weight: 31 tonnes (30.5 tons)	(307bhp)
Length: 6.37m (20ft 10in)	Speed: 28km/h (17.5mph)
Width: 2.5m (8ft 2in)	Range: 180km (112 miles)
Height: 2.79m (9ft 2in)	Armament: 1 x 75mm (2.95in) cannon

▶ Panzerkampfwagen 35-S 739(f)

SS-Panzer-Abteilung Prinz Eugen

About half of *Prinz Eugen*'s Panzer strength was provided by captured tanks. The Somua S-35 was one of the best of the French tanks pressed into service.

Specifications	
Crew: 3	Engine: SOMUA V-8 petrol engine
Weight: 19.5 tonnes (18.7 tons)	(190bhp)
Length: 5.38m (17ft 8in)	Speed: 40km/h (25mph)
Width: 2.12m (7ft)	Range: 230km (143 miles)
Height: 2.62m (8ft 7in)	Armament: 1 x 47mm (1.8in) cannon

⛨ Anti-partisan operations
1942

Early hopes that there would be a flood of ethnic German volunteers to make up the numbers for the new division proved unrealistic.

THE SS HAD to introduce conscription from among the *Volksdeutsche* community to reach a target divisional strength of 21,500 men for *Prinz Eugen*. This did not please the Pavelic government in Croatia, which felt that its German allies were poaching on national preserves.

Action in Serbia

The new SS division was intended for use in anti-partisan warfare in the Balkans. In October 1942, it saw its first major action in the south of Serbia, in mountainous terrain east of the Ibar River, near the Montenegro border. By now, it had been reclassified as a mountain division, and its designation changed to the *SS-Freiwilligen-Gebirgs-Division Prinz Eugen*.

Late in 1942, *Prinz Eugen* was transferred to the Zagreb–Karlovac area. There it was one of several

ORGANIZATION, 1942

units that were taking part in the massive anti-partisan operation known as Operation *White*. This was one of a series of major anti-partisan operations conducted in the region, whose primary aim was to destroy the Communist resistance movement led by Tito. Some partisans were indeed killed, but for the most part the operation proved to be a failure, since the bulk of Tito's forces managed to evade the German offensive.

In 1942, *Prinz Eugen* was assigned to the *Wehrmacht*'s Army Group E. In May of that year, the division took part in another major anti-partisan campaign, known as Operation *Black*. Later in the year, elements of the division were sent to Bosnia, operating to the north of Sarajevo. After that, the division was deployed around Mostar, and for the next year it would continue to play its part in the fiercely fought, no-quarter-given partisan war.

▲ 3.7cm Panzerabwehrkanone (Pak 36)
13.Waffen-SS-Gebirgsjäger-Regiment / I.Bataillon / schwere Kompanie

The heavy company attached to each Gebirgsjäger battalion had a pioneer platoon, an infantry gun platoon, a mortar platoon and a Panzerjäger platoon that was equipped with two light 3.7cm (1.5in) Pak 36 guns.

Specifications

Crew: 3	Muzzle Velocity: 762m/s (2500fps)
Weight: 0.43 tonnes (0.39 tons)	Range: 600m (656 yards)
Length: 1.67m (5ft 5.5in)	Ammunition: Armour-piercing
Calibre: 37mm (1.5in)	

▲ 15cm schwere Feldhaubitze (sFH18)
7.SS-Gebirgs-Artillerie-Regiment / IV.Abteilung / 1.Batterie

The mountain artillery regiment had a mixed bag of artillery pieces, ranging from light mountain pack howitzers to two batteries of long-range 10cm (3.9in) K18 guns and two batteries of 15cm (5.9in) heavy howitzers.

Specifications

Crew: 5	Muzzle Velocity: 520m/s (1706fps)
Weight: 6.3 tonnes (5.7 tons)	Range: 13km (8 miles)
Length: 4.4m (14 ft 5in)	Ammunition: High explosive or smoke
Calibre: 150mm (5.9in)	

▲ 7.5cm Panzerabwehrkanone (Pak 40)
SS-Panzerjäger-Abteilung Prinz Eugen / 1.Kompanie

In July 1944, the 1st Company of the division's tank-hunter battalion had been re-equipped with towed 7.5cm (3in) Pak 40s. The 2nd Company used 5cm (2in) Pak 38s, and the 3rd Company was a self-propelled Flak unit.

Specifications

Crew: 3	Muzzle Velocity (AP): 990m/s (3248fps)
Weight: 1.5 tonnes (1.37 tons)	Range: AP: 2000m (2190 yards), HE: 7.5km
Length: 3.7m (12ft 1.5in)	(4.66 miles)
Calibre: 75mm (3in)	Ammunition: Armour-piercing, high explosive

▲ 5cm Panzerabwehrkanone (Pak 38)
Panzerjäger-Abteilung Prinz Eugen

In its March 1943 table of organization and equipment, the *Prinz Eugen* Division's tank-hunter battalion consisted of three motorized companies, each equipped with nine 5cm (2in) Pak 38 towed guns.

Specifications

Crew: 3	Muzzle Velocity (AP): 835m/s (2900fps)
Weight: 1.2 tonnes (1.13 tons)	Range: AP: 1800m (1968 yards), HE: 2.6km
Length: 3.2m (10 ft 5in)	(1.6 miles)
Calibre: 50mm (2in)	Ammunition: Armour-piercing, high explosive

▼ **7.SS-Panzer-Abteilung, 2.Panzer-Kompanie**

Captured armour was mainly used for training or for occupation duties. However, the inability of German industry to provide an adequate supply of tanks meant that such vehicles were pressed into operational use in areas where they were unlikely to meet first-line Allied armour. *Prinz Eugen*'s Panzer battalion had two companies, the first being equipped with German tanks. The 2nd Company was exclusively equipped with foreign, mostly French, tanks.

Target Tito
1943–1944

In the summer of 1943, the *Prinz Eugen* Division was sent to the Dalmatian coast, where in September it disarmed Italian units in the region after the Badoglio government signed an armistice with the Allies.

*P*RINZ *E*UGEN WAS THEN USED to occupy former Italian positions on Brac, Hvar and Korcula Islands and on the Peljesac Peninsula.

In August 1943, *Prinz Eugen* came under the control of the *Wehrmacht*'s XV.*Gebirgs-Korps* (XV Mountain Corps), part of the Second Panzer Army under Army Group F.

In November 1943, *Prinz Eugen* was transferred to V.*SS-Gebirgs-Korps*. In December, the *Prinz Eugen*

Division fought with the mountain corps from the area northwest of Sarajevo south to Gorazde.

On 21 September 1944, the former divisional commander, *SS-Obergruppenführer* and General of the *Waffen-SS* Arthur Phleps, was killed en route from Montenegro to Transylvania, where he was to form a front against the Red Army. In October 1943, *Prinz Eugen* officially became the *7.SS-Freiwilligen-Gebirgs-Division Prinz Eugen*. In December 1943, the 7th SS Division once more moved inland, where actions against Tito's forces, as before, proved to be less than effective.

Partisan battles

In January 1944, the 7th SS Division was transferred to the area around Split and Dubrovnik for training, recuperation and re-equipment. In March, it was back in Bosnia, where it again took up the fight against Tito's partisans, with a major battle being fought at Drvar in May.

The goal of this operation was to kill or capture Tito himself on Drvar Island. *Prinz Eugen* played a supporting role; the actual snatch was to be made by the *SS-Fallschirmjäger-Bataillon* 500 and the 1st *Brandenburg* Regiment. However, the assault missed Tito.

After Drvar, the 7th SS Division was sent on further anti-partisan operations. In May, the division saw action in Operation *Waldrausch*, then took part in Operation *Freie Jagd* in June and July; between 12 and 30 August, it was part of Operation *Rübezahl*, which was designed to prevent partisan forces from moving into Montenegro.

COMBAT UNITS ORGANIZATION, 1944

7.SS-Fre.Gb.Div Prinz Eugen — St

SS-Fr.Gbjr.R 13 — St — I II III
SS-Fr.Gbjr.R 14 — St — I II III
SS-Fr.Gb.Art.Rgt 7 — St — I II III

SS-Fr.Gb.Au.A — St — I II III
SS-Pz.Abt — St — I II III
SS-Gb.Pnr.B — St — I II III
SS-Pzjr.A — St — I II III

SS-Gb.Flk.A — St — I II III
SS-Rad.Btl — St — I II III
SS-Kav.Abt — St — I II III

▶ **Panzerkampfwagen II Ausf F (SdKfz 121)**

7.SS-Freiwilligen-Gebirgs-Division Prince Eugen / Divisionsstab / Panzer-Aufklärungs-Zug

In July 1944, the divisional HQ had one Panzer reconnaissance platoon equipped with old Panzer II light tanks.

Specifications

Crew: 4	Speed: 40km/h (25mph)
Weight: 21.8 tonnes (19.8 tons)	Range: 165km (102 miles)
Length: 5.38m (17ft 7in)	Radio: FuG5
Width: 2.91m (9ft 5in)	Armament: 1 x 20mm (0.7in) cannon;
Height: 2.44m (8ft)	1 x 7.92mm (0.3in) MG
Engine: Maybach HL120TR	

▶ **Leichte Schützenpanzerwagen (SdKfz 250/1)**

7.SS-Freiwilligen-Gebirgs-Division Prince Eugen / Divisionsstab / Spw Aufklärungs-Zug

Alongside the Panzer IIs, the HQ reconnaissance element included a platoon of light reconnaissance SdKfz 250 half-tracks.

Specifications

Crew: 2 plus 4 troops	(100hp)
Weight: 5.9 tonnes (5.38 tons)	Speed: 60km/h (37mph)
Length: 4.61m (15ft 1in)	Range: 300km (186 miles)
Width: 1.95m (6ft 5in)	Radio: FuG Spr Ger 'f'
Height: 1.66m (5ft 5in)	Armament: 1 x 7.92mm (0.3in) MG
Engine: Maybach HL42TRKM 6-cylinder	

▶ **Leichte Schützenpanzerwagen (SdKfz 250/9)**

7.SS Aufklärungs-Abteilung / Stab-Kompanie

Prinz Eugen's reconnaissance assets in August 1944 ranged from horse cavalry and bicycle-mounted troops to modern half-track reconnaissance vehicles like the SdKfz 250/9, four of which were used by the reconnaissance battalion staff.

Specifications

Crew: 3	(100hp)
Weight: 6.9 tonnes (6.3 tons)	Speed: 60km/h (37mph)
Length: 4.56m (14ft 11.5in)	Range: 320km (199 miles)
Width: 1.95m (6ft 5in)	Radio: FuG Spr Ger 'f'
Height: 2.16m (7ft 1in)	Armament: 1 x 20mm (0.7in) KwK 30/38 L/55
Engine: Maybach HL42TRKM 6-cylinder	cannon; 1 x 7.92mm (0.3in) MG (coaxial)

Retreat from Bosnia
1944–1945

The battle against the partisans came to an end only when Soviet advances threatened to cut off German forces in the Balkans, and the *Wehrmacht* had to retreat into Croatia and Hungary.

THE RED ARMY'S SUMMER OFFENSIVE was unleashed in June 1944, and the Soviet steamroller threatened to smash through the Axis forces without stopping. In August, *Prinz Eugen* was transferred north to Bulgaria, where it suffered great losses fighting against the Red Army.

Holding the corridor

The Soviet advance threatened to cut off *Heeresgruppe* E in Greece, so in September *Prinz Eugen* and other *Waffen-SS* units were moved south to Macedonia. Linking up with 13.*Waffen-Gebirgs-Division der SS Handschar (kroatische Nr. 1)*, the remnants of the 23.*Waffen-Gebirgs-Division der SS Kama (kroatische Nr. 2)* and 21.*Waffen-Gebirgs-Division der SS Skanderbeg (albanische Nr. 1)*, *Prinz Eugen* created the Vardar corridor in Macedonia, allowing the retreat north of 350,000 German soldiers from occupation duties in the Aegean and Greek regions. While

fighting on the flanks of the Vardar corridor, they were subordinated to *Armeekorps Müller*, part of *Generaloberst* Alexander Löhr's *Heeresgruppe* E.

Once again, the 7th SS Division was badly mauled, but the operation succeeded in its main aim. Even though the Red Army had captured Belgrade, the corridor had been held open long enough for the bulk of the trapped German troops to escape. Now the *Prinz Eugen* Division was free to retreat itself, moving from Cacak to Brcko and over the Drina. In November, the division absorbed the remnants of the

▼ **Leichte Pkw VW (Kfz 1)**

13.Waffen-SS-Gebirgsjäger-Regiment / Stab-Kompanie

Cars had all but replaced motorcycles in staff units by 1944, although solo motorbikes were still used as messengers. The ubiquitous VW *Kübel* was also used as a reconnaissance vehicle.

Specifications

Crew: 1	Engine: Volkswagen 998cc petrol (24hp). Later
Weight: 0.64 tonnes (0.58 tons)	Volkswagen 1131cc petrol (25hp)
Length: 3.73m (12ft 3in)	Speed: 100km/h (62mph)
Width: 1.60m (5ft 3in)	Range: 600km (375 miles)
Height: 1.35m (4ft 5in)	Radio: None

DIVISIONAL SUPPORT ORGANIZATION, 1945

disbanded *Skanderbeg* Division.

Final battles

In January 1945, the division fought partisans near Otok, and later was sent to the area of Vukovar, where it fought again against advancing Soviet forces and Tito's partisans. From February 1945 to April 1945, the division was in action against the partisans and the Soviets, retreating from Bosnia through Croatia to defensive positions south of Karlovac.

The division began its final retreat on 10 May 1945, heading towards Celje in Slovenia. Even though the war had officially ended, the division did not surrender to Yugoslav forces on 11 May.

The *Prinz Eugen* SS Division was accused by the Yugoslavs of committing some of the worst atrocities of World War II. In the vicious action against the partisans, the division murdered unarmed civilians, burned and looted entire villages and tortured and massacred men, women and children.

▲ **Sturmbannführer, *Prinz Eugen* Division**

A *Sturmbannführer* (major) from the *Prinz Eugen* Division poses proudly for a portrait photograph, his sleeve demonstrating his divisional identity. Despite the large numbers of *Volksdeutsche* in the division, most officers were German.

▼ **7.5cm Sturmgeschütz 40 Ausf G (SdKfz 142/1)**

SS-Panzerjäger-Abteilung Prinz Eugen / Sturmgeschütz-Kompanie

Before the division suffered heavy losses in the autumn of 1944, one company of the tank-destroyer battalion was issued with 12 assault guns to be used as tank-hunters.

Specifications

Crew: 4	Engine: Maybach HL120TRM
Weight: 26.3 tonnes (24 tons)	Speed: 40km/h (25mph)
Length: 6.77m (22ft 2in)	Range: 155km (96 miles)
Width: 2.95m (9ft 7in)	Radio: FuG15 and FuG16
Height: 2.16m (7ft)	

8th SS Kavallerie Division
Florian Geyer

Cavalry had always been highly regarded by the German armed forces, so it is no surprise that with the expansion of the Armed SS Himmler's private army also formed cavalry units.

THE *FLORIAN GEYER* Division was one of several SS units that started out as purely German, but which during the course of the war increasingly numbered ethnic-Germans, or *Volksdeutsche*, among its units. It was named after Florian Geyer (1490–1525), a Franconian knight. Geyer was a supporter of Martin Luther (1483–1546), and led the German Peasants' War of 1522–1525.

SS cavalry units

The origins of the *Florian Geyer* Division date back to the original SS cavalry units. The cavalry components of the *SS-Totenkopf-Standarten*, or regiments, were formed in the winter of 1939. As part of the *Allegemeine-*, or General, *SS*, their primary mission was to teach horse-handling, although they had an important secondary role in policing.

In the summer of 1941, the *Totenkopf* cavalry detachments were combined as an *SS-Kavallerie-Regiment* under the aegis of the *Kommandostab-Reichsführer-SS* (RFSS). The cavalry so gathered were

INSIGNIA

Many divisions adopted symbols indicative of the formation's origins. The *Florian Geyer* Division used a horse's head to indicate its cavalry history.

Commanders

Brigadeführer Gustav Lombard *March 1942 – April 1942*	Gruppenführer Bruno Streckenbach *September 1943 – October 1943*
Gruppenführer Hermann Fegelein *April 1942 – August 1942*	Gruppenführer Hermann Fegelein *October 1943 – January 1944*
Obergruppenführer Willi Bittrich *August 1942 – February 1943*	Gruppenführer Bruno Streckenbach *January 1944 – April 1944*
Brigadeführer Fritz Freitag *February 1943 – April 1943*	Brigadeführer Gustav Lombard *April 1944 – July 1944*
Brigadeführer Gustav Lombard *April 1943 – May 1943*	Brigadeführer Joachim Rumohr *July 1944 – February 1945*
Gruppenführer Hermann Fegelein *May 1943 – September 1943*	

Divisional History	Formed
SS-Kavallerie-Brigade	1941
SS-Kavallerie-Division	1942
8.SS-Kavallerie-Division	1943
8.SS-Kavallerie-Division Florian Geyer	1944

▲ **SS cavalry**
This rare colour photograph shows men of the *SS-Kavallerie-Brigade* on the Eastern Front in the summer of 1942.

formed into an official unit in August 1941, known variously as the *SS-Kavallerie-Brigade* or the *SS-Reiter-Brigade*. It was commanded by Hermann Fegelein, and it was often referred to as the *Fegelein* Brigade or *Kampfgruppe Fegelein*.

Hermann Fegelein

Fegelein began his career in Middle Franconia as a groom and then became a jockey. A chance contact with a horse-fancier who was a Nazi led him into the National Socialist Party. Fegelein's knowledge of horses led the *Waffen-SS* to select him as the commanding officer of the *SS-Kavallerie* units, and he became commander of the new brigade on its formation in 1941.

He was wounded in September 1943 south of Kharkov and posted to the Führer's HQ as Himmler's official SS liaison officer.

Specifications

Crew: 3	Muzzle Velocity: 762m/s (2500fps)
Weight: 0.43 tonnes (0.39 tons)	Range: 600m (656 yards)
Length: 1.67m (5ft 5.5in)	Ammunition: Armour-piercing
Calibre: 37mm (1.5in)	

▼ Leichte Panzerspähwagen (SdKfz 222)
8.Panzer-Aufklärungs-Abteilung

The Cavalry Division's reconnaissance unit was originally a bicycle battalion, but early in 1944 this was converted into an armoured car unit equipped with 18 SdKfz 222 light armoured cars.

▲ 3.7cm Panzerabwehrkanone (Pak 36)
4.Bataillon / Panzerabwehr-Zug

As formed, the SS Cavalry Brigade was known as the *SS-Totenkopf-Reiterstandarte*. It consisted of 12 squadrons organized into four battalions plus attached horse artillery batteries.

Specifications

Crew: 3
Weight: 5.3 tonnes (4.8 tons)
Length: 4.8m (15ft 8in)
Width: 1.95m (6ft 5in)
Height: 2.00m (6ft 7in)
Engine: Horch 3.5L or 3.8L petrol
Speed: 85km/h (52.8mph)
Range: 300km (186 miles)
Radio: FuG Spr Ger 'a'
Armament: 1 x 20mm (0.7in) KwK 30 L/55 cannon;
1 x 7.92mm (0.3in) MG (coaxial)

▶ Leichte Panzerspähwagen (Fu) (SdKfz 223)
8.Panzer-Aufklärungs-Abteilung

Manufactured until 1944, the SdKfz 223 was designed to provide a communications capability for armoured reconnaissance units. The FuG10 radio had a range of 40km (25 miles) reduced to 10km (6.2 miles) for voice telephony.

Specifications

Crew: 4	Engine: Horch 3.5L
Weight: 4.7 tonnes (4.3 tons)	Speed: 85km/h (53mph)
Length: 4.83m (15ft 8in)	Range: 310km (192 miles)
Width: 1.99m (6ft 5in)	Radio: FuG Spr Ger 'a' plus FuG7 or FuG12
Height: 1.78m (5ft 8in)	

Combat operations in Russia
1941–1942

The SS Cavalry Brigade operated largely in the front line of the central and southern sectors of the Eastern Front, although its duties also included mounting rear area security patrols.

IN JUNE 1942, the *SS-Kavallerie-Brigade* was upgraded to divisional status with the addition of 9000 Hungarian *Volksdeutsche* volunteers. One month later, the division went into action with the Ninth Army, part of Army Group Centre. It was used to destroy pockets of Soviet resistance around the Vyazma-Bryansk-Rzhev salient. It continued to fight under Ninth Army control until December 1942, when most of the division was sent south to Army Group South. In the Don Basin, it was assigned to the Second Panzer Army as *Kampfgruppe Fegelein*.

In January 1943, the division's reserve and training battalion had been ordered to Warsaw, where it took part in the suppression of the Ghetto uprising. On 18 January, the Jews of the Warsaw Ghetto rose in rebellion as the Germans began deporting the inhabitants, who were ultimately destined for the extermination camps.

Jewish insurgent groups took control of the Ghetto, building dozens of fighting posts and killing Jews they considered to be Nazi collaborators, including Jewish police officers and *Gestapo* agents.

Specifications

Crew: 2	Engine: Maybach HL62 6-cylinder (140hp)
Weight: 1.16 tonnes (1.06 tons)	Speed: 50km/h (31mph)
Length: 6.85m (20ft 3in)	Range: 250km (156 miles)
Width: 2.40m (7ft 10.5in)	Radio: None
Height: 2.62m (8ft 7.1in)	

▲ **Mittlere Zugraftwagen 8t / 8.8cm Flak 18 (SdKfz 7)**
8.SS-Flak-Abteilung / schwere Batterie

Florian Geyer had been operating with a heavy Flak battery since the days of the SS Cavalry Brigade in 1941. The battery was equipped with four towed Flak 18 guns, the famous 'Eighty-Eight' that could also be used as an anti-tank gun.

▶ **Mittlere Zugkraftwagen 8t 3.7cm Flak 36 Sf (SdKfz 7/2)**
SS-Flak-Abteilung

In the summer of 1942, the SS Cavalry Division's Flak battalion had two self-propelled batteries with 2cm (0.7in) and 3.7cm (1.5in) guns. Later in the war, these were replaced by motorized units with towed guns.

Specifications

Crew: 7	Engine: Maybach HL62TUK
Weight: 1.16 tonnes	6-cylinder (140hp)
(1.06 tons)	Speed: 50km/h (31mph)
Length: 6.55m (21ft 6in)	Range: 250km (156 miles)
Width: 2.40m (7ft 10.5in)	Armament: Twin 37mm (1.5in)
Height: 3.20m (10ft 6in)	Flak 36/37/43 L/89

▲ 7.5cm Panzerabwehrkanone (Pak 40)

15.Waffen-SS-Kavallerie-Regiment / schwere Schwadrone / Pzjr.Zug

The heavy squadrons of the division's four cavalry regiments each had an anti-tank platoon equipped with three towed Pak 40s.

Specifications

Crew: 3	Muzzle Velocity (AP): 990m/s (3248fps)
Weight: 1.5 tonnes (1.37 tons)	Range: AP: 2000m (2190 yards), HE: 7.5km
Length: 3.7m (12ft 1.5in)	(4.66 miles)
Calibre: 75mm (3in)	Ammunition: Armour-piercing, high explosive

Suppression of the Warsaw Ghetto

Over the next three months, the Ghetto fought off increasingly heavy German attacks as SS troops, *Ordnungspolizei*, *Sicherheitsdienst* units, Army troops and Ukrainian, Latvian and Lithuanian auxiliaries sought to end the stalemate. The final battle began on 19 April as the Germans used smoke grenades and gas to force the Jews from their bunkers. The uprising ended on 16 May 1943. Most of the 50,000 survivors of the Ghetto were sent to the death camp at Treblinka, northeast of Warsaw.

In January and February 1943, the rest of the division was again under the control of Ninth Army, where it saw extensive combat south of Orel. In March, it was part of XLVII Armoured Corps. In April 1943, it was moved to Bobruysk for refitting. The Cavalry Division's primary mission was now security, its units being increasingly used behind the front lines to mop up bypassed Soviet units.

In May 1943, the *SS-Kavallerie-Division* began the anti-partisan campaign that it would fight until the end of the war. Successful in this brutal form of combat, the division was transferred to Army Group South in July 1943. It was ordered to Croatia, where it would be used for combat against Tito's Communist partisans.

Czechoslovakia and Poland
1943–1944

As a mounted formation, the division was effective against the partisans, having the advantage over them on foot and able to operate more rapidly over terrain impassable to vehicles.

THE DIVISION SAW A CONSIDERABLE amount of action at Bespalowka and Bol-Gomolscha before being withdrawn to Croatia for rest and refitting. On 23 October, the unit was redesignated as *8.SS-Kavallerie-Division*. At the end of the year, the division had over 9300 men on strength, the bulk being Hungarian *Volksdeutsche*.

In January and February 1944, the division continued anti-partisan operations. In March, the divisional units were dispersed, being used for anti-partisan operations in the Balkans, Hungary and Poland. On 12 March, the division received the honour title 'Florian Geyer', becoming the *8.SS-Kavallerie-Division Florian Geyer*.

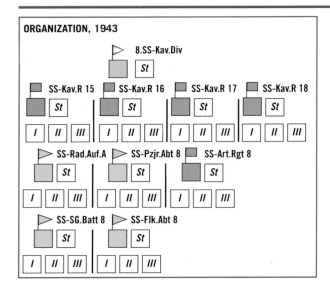

ORGANIZATION, 1943

Budapest. In April, one of the division's regiments – *SS-Kavallerie-Regiment* 17 – was dispatched to Kisber, Hungary, for rest and refitting. From there, the unit would form the nucleus of *22.SS-Freiwilligen-Kavallerie-Division Maria Theresia*, made up largely of Hungarian *Volksdeutsche* troops.

While it operated in small groups against Yugoslav partisans, the 8th SS Cavalry Division nevertheless retained its supporting arms. These included artillery assets of 32 10.5cm (4.1in) field howitzers and four 15cm (5.9in) howitzers; Flak units with 2cm (0.7in) and 3.7cm (1.5in) guns; as well as 35 7.5cm (3in) and 8.8cm (3.5in) anti-tank guns. Infantry weapons included 30 8.1cm (3.2in) mortars, four Soviet 12cm (4.7in) mortars, 213 light machine guns and 42 heavy machine guns. The two SS cavalry divisions operated together in the defensive battles in the difficult terrain of Transylvania. The SS probably intended to organize them into a cavalry corps, but due to the continuous combat they experienced this was never accomplished and they came under the control of the IX SS Mountain Corps.

On 19 March, elements of the *Florian Geyer* Division became part of *Kampfgruppe Streckenbach* under *SS-Gruppenführer* Bruno Streckenbach. The unit was transferred north from Osijek, Yugoslavia, to

▶ 7.5cm Pak 40 auf PzJäg 38 (t) Marder III
8.SS-Panzerjäger-Abteilung / Panzerjäger-Kompanie (Sf)

When fighting on the Eastern Front, the Cavalry Division's tank-hunting battalion had one self-propelled company equipped with Marders. These were replaced by towed guns when the division switched to anti-partisan operations.

Specifications

Crew: 4	Speed: 35km/h (22mph)
Weight: 10.8 tonnes (9.8 tons)	Range: 240km (150 miles)
Length: 5.77m (19ft 11in)	Radio: FuG Spr Ger 1
Width: 2.16m (7ft 1in)	Armament: 1 x 75mm (3in) Pak 40/3 L/46
Height: 2.51m (8ft 3in)	anti-tank gun; 1 x 7.92mm (0.3in) MG
Engine: Praga EPA 6-cylinder (140hp)	

▶ Sturmgeschütz 7.5cm Sturmkanone 40 Ausf F8 (SdKfz 142/1)
8.SS-Sturmgeschütz-Abteilung / 1.Kompanie

In October 1943, the divison had a single assault gun battalion assigned. In June 1944, this was absorbed by the division's *Panzerjäger-Abteilung*.

Specifications

Crew: 4	Engine: Maybach HL120TRM petrol (300hp)
Weight: 25.6 tonnes (23.3 tons)	Speed: 40km/h (25mph)
Length: 6.77m (22ft 2in)	Range: 210km (87 miles)
Width: 2.92m (9ft 7in)	Radio: FuG15 or FuG16
Height: 2.15m (7ft)	Armament: 1 x 75mm (3in) StuK 40

▶ **Anti-partisan cavalry**
Both the German Army and the SS used cavalry in the partisan war, such troops
being particularly effective in difficult terrain.

The reverses in the Balkans in the summer of 1944 convinced Hungary that the Axis had lost the war. In October 1944, the government of Admiral Horthy decided to follow the examples of Romania and Bulgaria and sought to come to terms with the Soviets. To stop the Hungarian defection, Hitler ordered that Hungary be occupied, and an SS team led by *Obersturmbannführer* Otto Skorzeny kidnapped Horthy's son to force the admiral to resign in favour of a pro-German government.

But the Red Army was little more than 100km (62 miles) from Budapest. On 20 October, it captured Debrecen in eastern Hungary and attacked towards Budapest on 29 October. Soviet tanks were in Vecses and Kispest by 3 November. However, the Soviet advance was slowed by dogged German resistance as reinforcements were rushed to Hungary.

In November, the 8th SS Division was moved north to became part of the Budapest garrison. By December, the Red Army had reached the shores of Lake Balaton. By Christmas Eve, Budapest had been surrounded by 250,000 Soviet troops of the 2nd and 3rd Ukrainian Fronts. In the ensuing siege, 800,000 civilians were trapped in the city.

▶ **Schwere Panzerspähwagen 8-Rad (SdKfz 231/1)**
6.Panzer-Aufklärungs-Abteilung
In March 1944, the division's bicycle reconnaissance battalion was fully motorized
and restructured as an armoured reconnaissance battalion with five companies.
The armoured car platoon was enlarged to full company size.

Specifications

Crew: 4	Engine: Büssing-NAG 8-cylinder
Weight: 9.1 tonnes (8.3 tons)	petrol (150hp)
Length: 5.85m (19ft 2in)	Speed: 85km/h (52.8mph)
Width: 2.20m (7ft 2.5in)	Range: 300km (186 miles)
Height: 2.35m (7ft 8in)	Radio: FuG Ger 'a'
	Armament: 1 x 20mm (0.7in) cannon

Destroyed in Hungary
1945

During the fighting for Budapest, the SS units in the city were pulled back to Buda on the west bank of the Danube. Their only hope was a planned relief effort, which never came.

AFTER SEVERAL WEEKS OF BITTER fighting, the Buda pocket had been reduced to a semi-circle about 1000m (1093 yards) across. On 11 February 1945, the remnants of the division attempted a last-ditch breakout along with what was left of the *22.SS-Freiwilligen-Kavallerie-Division Maria Theresia*, and the *33.Waffen-Kavallerie-Division der SS*. Budapest fell on 12 February.

▼ 8.Flak-Abteilung / 2.Batterie

Much harder-hitting and with a longer range than the 2cm (0.7in) Flak guns with which most German units had started the war, the 3.7cm (1.5in) Flak 36/37 had a maximum effective vertical range of 4800m (15,748ft) but was generally used against low-flying targets. It could also be effective against soft-skin vehicles and light armour, and was also lethal against the kind of improvised fortifications encountered in the partisan war. Initially towed by the Kfz 69 Krupp Protze, by the later years of the war these pre-war light trucks were being replaced by variants of the German Army's standard heavy car chassis, the *schwere Einheits Personenkraftwagen*.

ORGANIZATION

▷ Pz.Auf.Abt 8

St

Spz | Auf | sch

▲ **Winter positions**

Hungarian defence minister Marshal Karoly Beregfy visits the *Florian Geyer* Division in its defensive positions at Budapest late in 1944. By Christmas, the German garrison of the city had been cut off by the Red Army, and the 8th SS Cavalry Division was fighting for its existence.

The division was annihilated. Only 170 survivors managed to reach the German lines. The 8th SS Division's commander, *SS-Brigadeführer* Joachim Rumohr, commited suicide, while the members of the formation who got away were transferred to the newly forming 37th SS Cavalry Division. However, this unit never reached full strength.

Fegelein executed

Hermann Fegelein, the unit's original commander, did not long survive the division he had founded. Having become one of Hitler's inner circle, he had married Margarete Braun, Eva Braun's sister, on 3 June 1944. Fegelein was in the *Führerbunker* in Berlin in the last days of the *Reich*.

As Berlin fell to the Soviets, Fegelein tried to escape from the city with a mistress, who may have been an Allied spy. Captured by the *Gestapo*, he was shot for desertion on 29 April 1945.

▲ **10.5cm leichte Feldhaubitze leFH18**

8.SS-Artillerie-Regiment / I.Abteilung / 1.Batterie

Florian Geyer's artillery regiment had three battalions, each equipped with three batteries of 10.5cm (4.1in) howitzers. The division had no heavy artillery from the summer of 1944.

Specifications

Crew: 5	Muzzle Velocity: 540m/s (1770fps)
Weight: 1.95 tonnes (1.85 tons)	Range: 12,325m (13,480 yards)
Length: 3.3m (10ft)	Ammunition: High explosive or smoke
Calibre: 105mm (4.1in)	

▶ **Mittlere Lkw Opel Blitz 3.6-3600S**

8.SS Kavallerie Division Florian Geyer / Versorgungstruppe

For much of the war, the 8th Cavalry Division utilized horse-drawn transport, but by 1944 the divisional supply unit had three 120-tonne (118-ton) capacity transport companies each with 40 or more medium cargo-carrying trucks.

Specifications

Crew: 1	Engine: Opel 6-cylinder petrol
Weight: 3.29 tonnes (3 tons)	(73.5hp)
Length: 6.02m (19ft 9in)	Speed: 80km/h (50mph)
Width: 2.27m (7ft 5in)	Range: 410km (255 miles)
Height: 2.18m (7ft 2in)	Radio: None

▶ **Leichte Personenkraftwagen VW Kübel (Kfz 1)**

8.SS-Kavallerie-Division Florian Geyer / Stab

Light cars with standard military bodies were known as *Kübelwagen*, or bucket vehicles. This was not because of their shape, but because the vehicles were fitted with three or four bucket seats.

Specifications

Crew: 1	Engine: Volkswagen 998cc petrol (24hp). Later
Weight: 0.64 tonnes (0.58 tons)	Volkswagen 1131cc petrol (25hp)
Length: 3.73m (12ft 3in)	Speed: 100km/h (62mph)
Width: 1.60m (5ft 3in)	Range: 600km (375 miles)
Height: 1.35m (4ft 5in)	Radio: None

9th SS Panzer Division *Hohenstaufen*

The second major expansion of the *Waffen-SS* was planned towards the end of 1942, and early in 1943 orders were issued for the formation of new Panzergrenadier divisions.

THE SUCCESS OF HIS TROOPS in Russia prompted *Reichsführer-SS* Heinrich Himmler to expand the *Waffen-SS* still further. Four new divisions were authorized, three of them armoured. These were to become the 9.*SS-Panzer-Division Hohenstaufen*, the 10.*SS-Panzer-Division Frundsberg*, the 11.*SS Freiwilligen-Panzergrenadier-Division Nordland* and the 12.*SS-Panzer-Division Hitlerjugend*. All began forming in 1943, but none were ready to take part in the summer offensive that year.

The division that was later to be called *Hohenstaufen* was ordered to be formed in January 1943. Divisional cadres were established in Berlin Lichterfelde, and elements of the division began to be gathered later that month. The ninth division to be formed by the *Waffen-SS*, it was initially known as *SS-Panzergrenadier-Division 9*.

On 8 February 1943, the first elements of the division began to be assembled in France at the *Truppenübungsplatz* Mailly-le-Camp, east of Paris. Much of the first batch of personnel had been sent from the LSSAH Replacement Battalion in Berlin Lichterfelde. In the same month, *SS-Brigadeführer*

INSIGNIA

The insignia for the 9th SS Panzer Division incorporated a sword and the letter 'H', standing for the division's honour title of 'Hohenstaufen'.

Commanders

Brigadeführer Willi Bittrich *February 1943 – June 1944*	Oberführer Friedrich-Wilhelm Bock *July 1944 – August 1944*
Oberführer Thomas Müller *June 1944 – July 1944*	Standartenführer Walter Harzer *August 1944 – October 1944*
Brigadeführer Sylvester Stadler *July 1944*	Brigadeführer Sylvester Stadler *October 1944 – May 1945*

und Generalmajor der Waffen-SS Wilhelm 'Willi' Bittrich arrived to take command of the division.

Conscripts

By now, the SS could no longer sustain itself on volunteers alone, and conscripts provided up to 70 per cent of two of the new divisions, the 9th and the 10th. Nevertheless, they had been given full SS-style training, and they fought at least as well as the original divisions. By accepting conscripts, the SS

▲ **BMW R75 schweres Kraftrad 750cc mit Seitenwagen**
SS-Division Hohenstaufen / 9.Stabs-Begleit-Kompanie / Kraftrad-Zug
The divisional staff of the *Hohenstaufen* Division had a mapping detachment, a military police detachment and an escort company that had a self-propelled Flak platoon and a motorcycle platoon.

Specifications

Crew: 2	Engine: BMW 750cc petrol (26hp)
Weight: 0.67 tonnes (0.61 tons)	Speed: 92km/h (57mph)
Length: 2.4m (7ft 10in)	Range: 340km (211 miles)
Width: 1.73m (5ft 8in)	Radio: None
Height: 1m (3ft 3in)	Armament: 1 x 7.92mm (0.3in) MG (if fitted)

▲ **Intense training**
The new SS divisions formed in 1943 underwent a long period of assembling and training. The 9th and 10th Divisions received additional specialist training in anti-airborne operations, which called for very fast and aggressive reaction to enemy parachute assaults.

solved at least part of its manpower problem. However, the recruits were very young, most being around 18 years of age.

The division was given the name *Hohenstaufen*, after the family that ruled the Holy Roman Empire in the twelfth and thirteenth centuries. Most of 1943 was spent in training. In addition to standard combat training, *Hohenstaufen* also received specialized instruction in countering airborne attacks, which would prove extremely useful at Arnhem a year later.

In October, the division was redesignated as a Panzer division, and a battalion of Panthers was attached. The same month IV SS Panzer Corps had been formed with SS Panzer Division *Hohenstaufen* and SS Panzergrenadier Division *Reichsfuhrer-SS*.

Early in 1944, the division was transferred to the south of France as part of II SS Panzer Corps. In March, disaster threatened in the East when the First Panzer Army was trapped in a Russian encirclement at Tarnopol. By the middle of the month, the Soviets were at the Polish border and Hitler ordered four of

Divisional History	Formed
SS-Panzergrenadier-Division 9	1943
SS-Panzergrenadier-Division Hohenstaufen	1943
SS-Panzer-Division Hohenstaufen	1943
9.SS-Panzer-Division Hohenstaufen	1943

his Panzer divisions, including the *Waffen-SS* Divisions *Hohenstaufen* and *Frundsberg*, to the Eastern Front.

Into combat

In the spring of 1944, the SS Panzer arm was a shadow of the powerful force that had spearheaded Operation *Citadel*. However, the 9th and 10th Divisions had now completed their training and went into action at Tarnopol in April 1944.

On 5 April, Fourth Panzer Army attacked the Soviets, with II SS Panzer Corps on the flank of the offensive. *Hohenstaufen* smashed through the First Soviet Tank Army. On the 9th, the division's forward tanks broke through to the German First Panzer Army, allowing it to retreat to safety.

▶ **Mittlere Schutzenpanzerfwagen I Ausf C (SdKfz 251/1)**

20.SS-Panzergrenadier-Regiment / III.Bataillon (mot)

Most of *Hohenstaufen*'s Panzergrenadiers were truck-mounted, but the 3rd Battalion of the 20th Regiment had three half-track Panzergrendier companies and a single heavy half-track Panzergrenadier company.

Specifications	
Crew: 2 plus 12 troops	Engine: Maybach HL42TUKRM
Weight: 9.9 tonnes (9 tons)	Speed: 53km/h (33mph)
Length: 5.98m (19ft 7in)	Range: 300km (186 miles)
Width: 2.1m (6ft 11in)	Radio: FuG Spr Ger 1
Height: 1.75m (5ft 8in) or 2.16m	Armament: 1/2 x 7.62mm
(7ft) including MG shield if fitted	(0.3in) MG

▶ **Schwere Panzerspähwagen 8-Rad (SdKfz 231)**

9.SS-Panzer-Aufklärungs-Abteilung / Stab / Panzerspähwagen-Zug

The headquarters staff company of the reconnaissance battalion had an armoured car platoon equipped with three support cars with short-barrelled 7.5cm (3in) guns and 13 reconnaissance cars with 2cm (0.7in) weapons.

Specifications	
Crew: 4	petrol (150hp)
Weight: 9.1 tonnes (8.3 tons)	Speed: 85km/h (52.8mph)
Length: 5.85m (19ft 2in)	Range: 300km (186 miles)
Width: 2.20m (7ft 2.5in)	Radio: FuG Ger 'a'
Height: 2.35m (7ft 8in)	Armament: 1 x 20mm (0.7in)
Engine: Büssing-NAG 8-cylinder	cannon

Normandy

JUNE–AUGUST 1944

The Allied landings in Normandy came as a surprise to the Germans, who expected the invasion to take place farther to the north, in the Pas-de-Calais.

WITHIN DAYS OF THE INVASION, *Oberkommando der Wehrmacht* (OKW) realized that this was indeed the real thing and that it was in danger of losing control of the battlefield to the enemy unless reinforcements could be brought to the front as soon as possible. To that end, the 9th SS Panzer Division *Hohenstaufen* and the 10th SS Panzer Division *Frundsberg* were immediately ordered from Poland to Normandy, but they did not arrive until almost the end of the month.

On reaching Normandy on 25 June, both *Hohenstaufen* and *Frundsberg* were fed into the line between Caen and Villers-Bocage. Their arrival was timely, coinciding as it did with Montgomery's

Operation *Epsom* (his attempt to take Caen). What initially seemed to be good Allied progress deteriorated quickly into a vicious battle for every metre of ground as the German defenders fought tenaciously to blunt the advance. The Germans counterattacked on 27 June, but their assault was stopped in its tracks by the 11th Armoured Division,

9.SS-Panzer-Division *Hohenstaufen*	Strength
Panzer strength 1944	
PzKpfw IV	46
PzKpfw V	79
StuG III	40

▶ **15cm schwere Panzerhaubitze (Sf) Hummel (SdKfz 165)**

9.SS-Artillerie-Regiment / I.Abteilung (Sf) / 1.Batterie

The 1st Battalion of *Hohenstaufen*'s artillery regiment was equipped with self-propelled guns. The 1st Battery of the battalion had six 15cm (5.9in) Hummel self-propelled howitzers.

Specifications

Crew: 6	Speed: 42km/h (26mph)
Weight: 26.5 tonnes (24 tons)	Range: 215km (133.6 miles)
Length: 7.17m (23ft 6in)	Radio: FuG Spr 1
Width: 2.97m (9ft 8in)	Armament: 1 x 150mm (5.9in) sFH
Height: 2.81m (9ft 2in)	18/1 L/30; 1 x 7.92mm (0.3in) MG
Engine: Maybach HL120TRM (265hp)	

▶ **Leichte Schutzenpanzerwagen (SdKfz 250/1)**

9.SS-Panzer-Aufklärungs-Abteilung / 1.Panzer-Aufklärungs-Kompanie / Stab

In 1944, *Hohenstaufen*'s reconnaissance battalion had one armoured car company and three companies equipped with armoured half-tracks. The 3rd Company had a staff platoon, a Panzerjäger platoon, a mortar platoon and a pioneer platoon.

Specifications

Crew: 2 plus 4 troops	Engine: Maybach HL42TRKM 6-cylinder
Weight: 5.9 tonnes (5.38 tons)	(100hp)
Length: 4.61m (15ft 1in)	Speed: 60km/h (37mph)
Width: 1.95m (6ft 5in)	Range: 300km (186 miles)
Height: 1.66m (5ft 5in)	Radio: FuG Spr Ger 'f'

which then followed through to cross the Odon River on the following day and capture the crucial Hill 112 on 29 June.

In reply, *SS-Obergruppenführer* Paul Hausser launched a major counterattack using both *Hohenstaufen* and *Frundsberg*, but the *Waffen-SS* divisions were beaten back. Fortunately for the Germans, the Allies had expected an even heavier attack and had withdrawn the 11th Armoured Division back across the Odon.

The American breakout at St Lô and Allied advances in the Caen sector threatened to trap the entire German army in a pocket around Falaise. The only possible escape lay through a narrow gap between Falaise and Argentan, and the II SS Panzer Corps – the *Hohenstaufen* and *Das Reich* Divisions – managed to get through to safety.

Hohenstaufen fought continuously and without replacements in Normandy from its arrival there in late June until its withdrawal on 21 August. Retreating northwards through France, the division provided a battalion to defend the line along the

ORGANIZATION, 1944

River Meuse. Moving up to Rouen, it skirted south of Brussels, crossed the Dutch border and arrived at the Veluwe area, north of Arnhem, on 7 September.

On 10 September, the remnants of the division – only 2500 men – were ordered back to Germany to be rebuilt. The men were on the point of leaving when the British airborne forces landed in the outskirts of Arnhem and near Nijmegen.

▶ **7.5cm Sturmgeschütz 40 Ausf G (SdKfz 142/1)**

9.SS-Panzer-Regiment / II.Abteilung / 8.Kompanie

The 2nd Battalion of the *Hohenstaufen*'s Panzer regiment was equipped with two companies of Panzer IVs and two companies of assault guns, which had been exchanged for tanks by June of 1944.

Specifications

Crew: 4	Engine: Maybach HL120TRM
Weight: 26.3 tonnes (23.9 tons)	Speed: 40km/h (25mph)
Length: 6.77m (22ft 2in)	Range: 155km (96.3 miles)
Width: 2.95m (9ft 8in)	Radio: FuG15 and FuG16
Height: 2.16m (7ft 0in)	

Arnhem, the Bulge and Budapest
SEPTEMBER 1944 – APRIL 1945

The men of *Hohenstaufen* were on the point of leaving for the *Reich* by rail on 17 September when paratroopers of the British 1st Airborne Division landed in the outskirts of Arnhem.

OPERATION *MARKET GARDEN*, a massive Allied air assault, was intended to seize a corridor of territory up to the mouths of the Rhine. It would isolate the V2 launching sites and the ports of

Antwerp, Amsterdam and Rotterdam. From there, it should have been possible to liberate northern Holland and leave the North German Plain vulnerable to an Allied offensive.

Generalfeldmarschall Walter Model ordered the understrength *Hohenstaufen* to form a battle group, *SS-Kampfgruppe Harzer*. It was ordered to make a reconnaissance in the direction of Arnhem and Nijmegen, and then to secure the Arnhem bridge and destroy the British paratroopers who had landed to the west of Arnhem at Oosterbeek.

On 20 September, *Hohenstaufen's Aufklärungs-Abteilung* crossed the bridge at Arnhem, driving off the British paratroopers who had held the northern end for four days. Other elements of the division had managed to prevent the British Guards Armoured Division from driving north from Eindhoven.

Battle of the Bulge

Hohenstaufen played a major part in the Battle of the Bulge. The Ardennes offensive was launched on 16 December 1944, and *Hohenstaufen* was assigned to the II SS Panzer Corps alongside 2nd SS Panzer Division *Das Reich* and the 560th Infantry Division.

By 18 December, *Hohenstaufen* and *Das Reich* were fighting in the dense forests between Malmedy and St Vith. St Vith eventually fell to a simultaneous attack by the LXVI Corps and *Hohenstaufen* and the *Führerbegleitbrigade* attacking from the north.

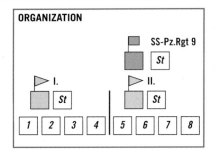

However, Hitler's gamble was doomed from the beginning, and the last German offensive in the West failed. By the middle of January 1945, *Hohenstaufen* had suffered serious losses at Houffalize and had been transferred to the OKW reserve.

On 3 March, the division was moved by rail to Hungary, where the last major German offensive of the war was under way. *Hohenstaufen* suffered severe

▼ 9.SS-Panzer-Regiment / I.Abteilung / 1.Kompanie

After suffering heavy losses in Normandy, the 9th SS Panzer Division's 1st Panzer Battalion was reorganized with four companies, each equipped with 14 *Panzerkampfwagen* V Panther tanks. These were to be handed over to the *Frundsberg* Division in September 1944 while *Hohenstaufen's* personnel were sent from Holland back to Germany to form the nucleus of a completely reconstructed division. After the battles at Arnhem, the reconstruction plans were reinstituted, and by December 1944 the four Panther companies had been re-equipped. More Panthers were en route at that time, intended to bring each company up to full strength.

Stab

1.Zug

2.Zug

3.Zug

losses in fighting to the west of Budapest. By the middle of March, the *Hohenstaufen* Division had nearly reached the Danube, but as overwhelming Soviet superiority in numbers came into play the offensive ground to a halt. Remnants of the division were formed into two battle groups, which fought their way back to Austria. In Vienna, the division was attached to Sixth SS Panzer Army. However, the attempt to defend Vienna failed, and on 13 April the SS abandoned the city, retreating westwards. What was left of *Hohenstaufen* continued to fight until the division surrendered to US forces at Steyr in May.

▶ **Panzerkampfwagen IV Ausf H (SdKfz 161/2)**

9.SS-Panzer-Regiment / II.Abteilung / 5.Kompanie

At the time of the Ardennes offensive in December 1944, *Hohenstaufen*'s 5th and 6th Panzer Companies were equipped with a total of 32 Panzer IVs.

Specifications

Crew: 5	Speed: 38km/h (23.6mph)
Weight: 27.6 tonnes (25 tons)	Range: 210km (130.5 miles)
Length: 7.02m (23ft 0in)	Radio: FuG5
Width: 2.88m (9ft 5in)	Armament: 1 x 75mm (3in) KwK
Height: 2.68m (8ft 10in)	40/43; 2 x 7.92mm (0.3in) MG
Engine: Maybach HL120TRM	(one hull-mounted, one coaxial)

▶ **Panzerkampfwagen V Ausf A (SdKfz 171)**

9.SS-Panzer-Regiment / I.Abteilung / Stab

The B13 on the turret of this Panther would normally indicate that it is the tank of the 2nd Battalion's ordnance officer, but in fact it belonged to the 1st Battalion.

Specifications

Crew: 5	Speed: 46km/h (28.6mph)
Weight: 50.2 tonnes	Range: 200km (124 miles)
(45.5 tons)	Radio: FuG5
Length: 8.86m (29ft 0in)	Armament: 1 x 75mm (3in)
Width: 3.4m (11ft 2in)	KwK42 L/70; 2 x 7.92mm
Height: 2.98m (9ft 10in)	(0.3in) MG (one hull-
Engine: Maybach HL230P30	mounted, one coaxial)

▶ **3.7cm Flak 43 auf Fgstl PzKpfw IV Sf (SdKfz 161/3)**

9.SS-Panzer-Regiment / Stab / Flak-Zug

Issued to to the anti-aircraft platoons of Panzer regiments in Panzer divisions, the *Möbelwagen*, or moving van, was seen as a temporary defensive measure. A twin gun mounted on a Panther chassis, intended to replace this design, never entered production.

Specifications

Crew: 6	Engine: Maybach HL120TRM
Weight: 26.5 tonnes (24 tons)	Speed: 38km/h (23.6mph)
Length: 5.92m (19.4ft)	Range: 200km (124.3 miles)
Width: 2.95m (9.7ft)	Radio: FuG5 and FuG2
Height: 2.73m (9ft)	

10th SS Panzer Division *Frundsberg*

Often regarded as a twin of the 9th SS Panzer Division *Hohenstaufen*, the 10th SS Panzer Division *Frundsberg* trained and fought alongside its sister division until the end of 1944.

FORMED AT THE SAME TIME as the 9th SS Division *Hohenstaufen*, the tenth SS division to be created served alongside its sister division for much of the war. The division's first year closely paralleled that of *Hohenstaufen*. Authorized early in 1943, the division was largely manned by conscripts, many of whom had been serving with the *Reich* Labour Service. The division spent the rest of the year assembling its constituent units and in training. It was briefly known as the *Karl der Grosse* Panzergrenadier Division. Under the orders of Army Group D, the incomplete formation was moved to various locations in southern and western France.

Named for knight

On 3 October 1943, the division was redesignated as the *SS-Panzer-Division Frundsberg*, taking its definitive title of 10.*SS-Panzer-Division Frundsberg* three weeks later. The division was named after Georg von Frundsberg, a south German knight who fought for the imperial Habsburg dynasty of Austria in the sixteenth century and who was instrumental in creating the Landsknechts, the archetypal German mercenary soldiers of the period.

At the same time, the formation of a new corps, the VII SS Panzer Corps, was ordered. *Frundsberg* was assigned to the corps along with another new formation, the 17th SS Panzergrenadier Division *Gotz von Berlichingen*. *Frundsberg* had given up part of its artillery and the motorcycle companies from its

Panzergrenadier regiments to provide a nucleus for the new division.

In March 1944, although neither formation was fully worked up, the incomplete *Frundsberg* Division was sent with the *Hohenstaufen* Division to join II *SS-Panzerkorps*. They were part of a major reinforcement of the Eastern Front, where Army Group Centre was under severe pressure as a result of advances made by the Soviet winter offensive, which had been launched at the beginning of the year.

INSIGNIA

A Germanic letter 'F', for the 10th SS Division's honour title of 'Frundsberg', was superimposed onto an oak leaf in the division's insignia.

Divisional History	Formed
SS-Panzergrenadier-Division 10	1943
SS-Panzergrenadier-Division 10 Karl der Grosse	1943
SS-Panzer-Division Frundsberg	1943
10.SS-Panzer-Division Frundsberg	1943

Commanders

Standartenführer Michael Lippert
January 1943 – February 1943

Gruppenführer Lothar Debes
February 1943 – November 1943

Gruppenführer Karl Fischer von Treuenfeld
November 1943 – April 1944

Gruppenführer Heinz Harmel
April 1944 – April 1945

Obersturmbannführer Franz Roestel
April 1945 – May 1945

▶ **Leichte Schützenpanzerwagen (SdKfz 250/10)**

10.SS-Aufklärungs-Abteilung / 3.Panzerspähwagen.Kompanie / 1.Zug

The SdKfz 250/10, armed with a 3.7cm (1.5in) Pak 35/36, was issued to platoon leaders of half-track-mounted reconnaissance platoons. The vehicle had a crew of four and carried 216 rounds of 3.7cm (1.5in) ammunition.

Specifications	
Crew: 4	Engine: Maybach HL42TRKM (100hp)
Weight: 6.3 tonnes (5.67 tons)	Speed: 60km/h (37.3mph)
Length: 4.56m (14ft 11.5in)	Range: 320km (199 miles)
Width: 1.95m (6ft 5in)	Radio: FuG Spr Ger 1
Height: 1.97m (6ft 6in)	Armament: 1x 37mm (1.5in) Pak 35/36

The Soviets had pushed almost as far as the Polish border, in the process encircling the First Panzer Army around Tarnopol. Among the trapped German units were the 1st SS Panzer Division *Leibstandarte SS Adolf Hitler* and a battle group from 2nd SS Panzer Division *Das Reich*.

Even though its Panzer regiments had not yet received the Panzer V Panthers with which their first battalions were to be equipped, the division joined Army Group North Ukraine with the rest of II SS Panzer Corps. The division made its combat debut early in April, and after fighting fiercely broke through the Soviet encirclement of First Panzer Army on 6 April at Buczacz, linking up with the beleaguered *Waffen-SS* divisions the same day.

The Soviets continued to press forward, and the *Frundsberg* Division remained in the line, seeing heavy combat on the Strypa River Line and counterattacking the Red Army in the area around Tarnopol and Kovel. Fought to a standstill by the Soviet 1st Ukrainian Front, the division then spent some weeks embroiled in static defensive actions on the Bug River.

Sent to Normandy

On 6 June 1944, the Western Allies invaded Normandy. On 12 June, II SS Panzer Corps was withdrawn from the Russian Front and rushed westwards as the German High Command sought to reinforce the Normandy battle front.

▶ **10.5cm leFH18 auf PzKpfw II Wespe (SdKfz 124)**
10.SS-Panzer-Artillerie-Regiment / I. (Sf) Abteilung / 2.Batterie

Two batteries of the division's 1st (Self-Propelled) Artillery Battalion were equipped with 10.5cm (4.1in) Wespe SP field howitzers. Most were lost in Normandy, and the division was not brought up to full strength until early 1945.

Specifications

Crew: 5	Speed: 40km/h (25mph)
Weight: 12.1 tonnes (11 tons)	Range: 220km (136.7 miles)
Length: 4.81m (15ft 10in)	Radio: FuG Spr 1
Width: 2.28m (7ft 6in)	Armament: 1 x 105mm (4.1in) LeFH 18M
Height: 2.25m (7ft 4.5in)	L/28 howitzer
Engine: Maybach HL62TR	

Specifications

Crew: 5	Height: 2.98m (9ft 10in)
Weight: 50.2 tonnes	Engine: Maybach HL230P30
(45.5 tons)	Speed: 46km/h (28.6mph)
Length: 8.86m (29ft 0in)	Range: 200km (124 miles)
Width: 3.4m (11ft 2in)	Radio: FuG5

▲ **Panzerkampfwagen V Ausf A (SdKfz 171)**
10.SS-Panzer-Regiment / II.Abteilung / 5.Kompanie

The division's 2nd Battalion was equipped with Panther tanks from June 1944, and was engaged in fighting against the British near Caen and then around Falaise. This profile dates from December 1944, when the division was stationed in Alsace.

Normandy and Arnhem
JUNE–SEPTEMBER 1944

Frundsberg was rushed across Europe with the rest of II SS Panzer Corps in only six days, the entire movement requiring the use of 67 trains to complete.

ONCE IN FRANCE, however, they were delayed by constant Allied air attacks. The 9th and 10th SS Divisions took longer to cross France than they had taken in getting to France from the Russian border. As a result, the Allies were too firmly established for an attack against the beachhead to be feasible, so the divisions were thrown into the battle for Caen.

Defending Caen, the corps immediately encountered Montgomery's *Epsom* offensive, and in a week of heavy fighting stopped the 51st Highland Division in its thrust towards the Orne River. The II *SS-Panzerkorps* suffered more than 1200 casualties; by 30 June divisional manpower was down to less than 16,000 men. The combat around Caen continued for the first three weeks in July. By 18 July, the *Frundsberg* Division had lost more than 2200 men dead or wounded. Yet, in spite of their best efforts, the British were unable to drive back the German defenders. Montgomery even used heavy bombers to blast the German positions, but the attack ground to a halt with heavy Allied losses.

The battle in Normandy ended on 21 August with the remaining divisional remnants fleeing eastwards towards the Seine. Many of the divisions were sent back to Germany for rest and refit, with the exception

ORGANIZATION, 1943

of II *SS-Panzerkorps* under Wilhelm Bittrich. This was sent to Holland for refitting, ready to take on General Patton's forces, whom the Germans thought would launch a new offensive. However, the next confrontation would come sooner than the *Hohenstaufen* and *Frundsberg* Divisions expected – right on their very doorstep, at Arnhem.

Arnhem

On paper, two SS Panzer divisions should have been enough to annihilate the lightly armed airborne

▶ **Mittlere Schützenpanzerwagen Ausf C (SdKfz 251/9)**

21.SS-Panzergrenadier-Regiment / I.Bataillon / 1.Kompanie

In June 1944, *Frundsberg*'s two Panzergrenadier regiments each had one battalion equipped with half-tracks. The first three companies of each battalion had a pair of SdKfz 251 half-tracks with short-barrelled 7.5cm (3in) KwK 37 cannon. The vehicles were attached to the company staff and were designed to provide close-range fire support to the infantry-carrying half-tracks.

Specifications	
Crew: 3	Speed: 53km/h (33mph)
Weight: 9.4 tonnes (8.53 tons)	Range: 300km (186 miles)
Length: 5.98m (19ft 7in)	Radio: FuG Spr Ger 'f'
Width: 2.83m (9ft 4in)	Armament: 1 x 75mm (3in) KwK
Height: 2.07m (6ft 10in)	L/24 gun
Engine: Maybach HL42TUKRM	

forces in very short order. However, this was less than a month since a large chunk of the German Army had been annihilated in the Falaise pocket, from which the *Hohenstaufen* and *Frundsberg* Divisions had escaped by the skin of their teeth.

Vastly understrength, with their equipment replacement programme barely under way, the two SS divisions nevertheless provided a solid core on which the Germans could base their defence of the Rhine bridges.

▲ **Assault guns**

Although designed as an artillery piece, the *Sturmgewehr* was often used as a relatively inexpensive tank substitute in the Panzer regiments of some Panzer divisions in the last two years of the war.

The presence of these two battle-hardened units was decisive in defeating Montgomery's drive on the Rhine. Neither division acted as a unit: the *Kampfgruppen* operated independently with only the lightest of direction from Bittrich's II Panzer Corps.

▶ **7.5cm Sturmgeschütz 40 Ausf G (SdKfz 142/1)**

10.SS-Panzer-Regiment / II.Abteilung / 8.Kompanie

In May 1944, the 2nd Battalion of the 10th Panzer Regiment was a mixed unit. The 5th and 6th Companies operated long-barrel Panzer IVs; the 7th and 8th Companies were equipped with assault guns.

Specifications

Crew: 4	Speed: 40km/h (25mph)
Weight: 26.3 tonnes (23.9 tons)	Range: 155km (96.3 miles)
Length: 6.77m (22ft 2in)	Radio: FuG15 and FuG16
Width: 2.95m (9ft 8in)	Armament: 1 x 75mm (3in) StuG L/48
Height: 2.16m (7ft 0in)	cannon
Engine: Maybach HL120TRM	

Defence of the Reich

JANUARY–APRIL 1945

On 18 November, the *Frundsberg* Division, now reduced to a battle group after its losses in Normandy and at Arnhem, was withdrawn to Aachen in Germany for rest and refit.

D URING DECEMBER, its strength was built up once again to around 15,500 men – about 75 per cent of establishment. In December 1944 and January 1945, it saw action around Linnich and Geilenkirchen, and Julich northeast of Aachen. In January, it was attached to Army Group *Niederrheim*, and was earmarked for use in the reserve forces for Operation *Nordwind*.

On 24 January, *Frundsberg* crossed the Moder River and captured the high ground commanding the area between Hagenau and Kaltenhaus. Despite being at near full strength after its recent refit, the division met such fierce resistance that its advance faltered, and the following day orders arrived withdrawing it from the line for immediate transfer to the Eastern Front.

Eastern Front 1945
On 10 February 1945, the division was committed to a German counteroffensive codenamed Operation *Sonnenwende* as part of III SS Panzer Corps. For the next month, it was engaged with the advancing Soviets at Stargard and Fürstenwalde, before being pulled back across the Oder into Stettin for a rest.

In mid-April, *Frundsberg* was encircled by Soviet forces near Spremberg. Despite its perilous position, Hitler ordered the division to close a gap in the

10.SS-Panzer-Regiment, Feb 1945	Strength
PzKpfw IV (long gun, side armour)	38
PzKpfw V Panther	53
FlakPanzer IV (3.7cm/1.5in)	8

German lines by immediately attacking. Heinz Harmel, the divisional commander, realized that the attack would be suicide. He decided instead to break out and head for the last major German troop concentration south of Berlin.

The breakout came at the cost of further fragmentation of the division. Some units managed to form a line of defences near Dresden. Harmel was dismissed for refusing to obey orders.

The end
Now under the control of the Fourth Panzer Army of Army Group Centre, the pitiful remnants of the division were led by *SS-Obersturmbannführer* Franz Röstel in combat against the advancing Soviets, but to little effect.

The division fell back to the Elbe near Dresden and headed south. After claiming a few Soviet T-34 tanks on 7 May, the last few Panzers of the *Frundsberg* Division were destroyed by their own crews to prevent their being captured and used against them.

The *Frundsberg* Division moved west to avoid capture by Soviet forces. Some Frundsbergers managed to reach the relative safety of US captors; the remainder of the division surrendered to the advancing Red Army at the town of Teplitz-Schönau (Teplice in the modern Czech Republic).

ORGANIZATION, 1945

10.SS-Pz.Div Frundsberg

St

SS-Pz.Rgt 10   SS-Pz.Gr.R 21   SS-Pz.Gr.R 22   SS-Pz.Art.R

St   St   St   St

I   II   III   I   II   III   I   II   III   I   II   III

SS-Flk.Abt 10   SS-SG.Abt 10   SS-Pzjr.Ab 10   SS-Krd.R 10

St   St   St   St

I   II   III   I   II   III   I   II   III   I   II   III

ORGANIZATION, 1945

SS-Pz.Rgt 10

St

I.   II.

St   St

1   2   3   4   5   6   7   8

▶ Panzerkampfwagen IV Ausf G (SdKfz 161/1 or 161/2)

10.SS-Panzer-Regiment / II.Abteilung / 5.Kompanie

Before the invasion of Normandy, *Frundsberg*'s Panzer regiment was equipped with the standard Panzer inventory of the time with four companies of Panthers and four of Panzer IVs.

Specifications

Crew: 5	Speed: 40km/h (25mph)
Weight: 25.9 tonnes (23.5 tons)	Range: 210km (130.5 miles)
Length: 6.62m (21ft 8in)	Radio: FuG5
Width: 2.88m (9ft 5in)	Armament: 1 x 75mm (3in) KwK 40/43;
Height: 2.69m (8ft 10in)	2 x 7.92mm (0.3in) MG (one hull-
Engine: Maybach HL120TRM	mounted, one coaxial)

▶ Panzerkampfwagen IV Ausf H (SdKfz 161/2)

10.SS-Panzer-Regiment / I.Abteilung / 3.Kompanie

After being shattered in Normandy, the 10th Panzer Regiment was organized as a single battalion with two companies of Panthers and two companies of Panzer IVs. The 2nd Battalion was eventually rebuilt in January 1945.

Specifications

Crew: 5	Speed: 38km/h (23.6mph)
Weight: 27.6 tonnes (25 tons)	Range: 210km (130.5 miles)
Length: 7.02m (23ft 0in)	Radio: FuG5
Width: 2.88m (9ft 5in)	Armament: 1 x 75mm (3in) KwK 40/43;
Height: 2.68m (8ft 10in)	2 x 7.92mm (0.3in) MG (one hull-
Engine: Maybach HL120TRM	mounted, one coaxial)

Specifications

Crew: 5	Speed: 46km/h (28.6mph)
Weight: 50.2 tonnes (45.5 tons)	Range: 200km (124 miles)
Length: 8.86m (29ft 0in)	Radio: FuG5
Width: 3.4m (11ft 2in)	Armament: 1 x 75mm (3in) KwK42 L/70; 2 x
Height: 2.98m (9ft 10in)	7.92mm (0.3in) MG (one hull-mounted,
Engine: Maybach HL230P30	one coaxial)

▲ Panzerkampfwagen V Ausf A (SdKfz 171)

10.SS-Panzer-Regiment / I.Abteilung / 2.Kompanie

In January 1945, *Frundsberg* began to receive new armour as the division was built up to full strength at Aachen. Twenty-five Panthers were delivered in the second week of that month.

11th SS Panzergrenadier Division *Nordland*

Based on the 5th SS Division *Wiking*, the *Nordland* Division was to be a Germanic formation, manned by Scandinavian and other suitably 'Nordic' volunteers.

T HE 11TH SS PANZERGRENADIER Division had its origins in an OKW order to activate a new SS Panzer corps in early 1943. This new corps was to be designated III.*(Germanische) SS-Panzerkorps*, and to as great an extent as possible it was to be made up of Germanic volunteers. It was to include the 5th SS Panzergrenadier Division *Wiking*, together with a new German-Scandinavian division yet to be formed. The corps headquarters was activated on 30 March 1943, but it proved impossible to withdraw *Wiking* from the Eastern Front and the plan to field the new corps was delayed.

However, plans to create the new SS volunteer division went ahead. *Reichsführer-SS* Heinrich Himmler wanted to give the new division the name *Waräger* in reference to the Swedish Viking Varangian Guard, which saw service as the bodyguard of the Byzantine emperors in the dark ages. Hitler, more practical than his mystical SS henchman, considered the name too obscure. Deciding that the name of the veteran volunteer regiment *Nordland* deserved to be honoured, he ordered the division to be so named in July 1943.

Nordland was to differ from the prototype volunteer division *Wiking* in its make-up. Much had been made of the multi-national nature of the elite

INSIGNIA

The divisional insignia, the so-called *Sonnenrad*, or Sunwheel variant of the swastika, had been used by the Thule Society, which was an important influence on the early National Socialists.

Commanders

Brigadeführer Franz Augsberger *March 1943 – May 1943*	Brigadeführer Joachim Ziegler *July 1944 – April 1945*
Brigadeführer Fritz Scholz *May 1943 – July 1944*	Brigadeführer Gustav Krukenberg *April 1945 – May 1945*

▲ ***Nordland* reconnaissance**

An SdKfz 232 heavy armoured radio car of the 11th SS Panzergrenadier Division *Nordland* is identified by the *Sonnenrad*, or sunwheel symbol, it carries on the front hood, next to the vehicle's blacked-out headlamp.

Specifications

Crew: 5	Muzzle Velocity: 540m/s (1770fps)
Weight: 1.95 tonnes (1.85 tons)	Range: 12,325m (13,480 yards)
Length: 3.3m (10ft)	Ammunition: High explosive or smoke
Calibre: 105mm (4.3in)	

◀ **10.5cm leichte Feldhaubitze (leFH18)**

11.SS-Artillerie-Regiment / II.Abteilung / 4.Batterie

The bulk of *Nordland*'s artillery strength was provided by the 10.5cm (4.1in) light field howitzer. A capable enough weapon, it was not all that light; in fact, it was heavier and less accurate than its Soviet equivalents.

Wiking Division by Nazi propaganda organs, but in truth the bulk of its strength and nearly all of its senior NCOs and officers were German. In the new division, the Germans hoped to utilize a far greater proportion of foreign volunteers, especially in the more senior ranks.

A large part of the division's manpower was provided by the remnants of the various Germanic legions, most of which were being disbanded at this time. As a result, nationalities represented in *Nordland* had the widest range to be found in any *Waffen-SS* division. By the spring of 1945, units from Denmark, Norway, Sweden, Switzerland, France, the Netherlands, Estonia, Finland, and even a handful of British volunteers, had been attached.

First action

The principle combat units were made up of veterans of the *Legion Norwegien* and the *Freikorps Danmark*. The ranks were filled out with *Volksdeutsche* and with *Reichdeutsche*. The first division commander was *SS-Brigadeführer und Generalmajor der Waffen-SS* Fritz

Divisional History	Formed
Kampfverband Waräger	Feb 1943
Germanische-Freiwilligen-Division	Feb 1943
SS-Panzergrenadier-Division 11	Apr 1943
11.SS-Freiwilligen-Panzergrenadier-Division Nordland	July 1943
11.SS-Panzergrenadier-Division Nordland	Nov 1943

Scholz, who had been commander of the *Nordland* Regiment of *Wiking*.

After completing training, *Nordland* and III. *(Germanische) SS-Panzerkorps* were posted to Croatia to gain combat experience in the war against Tito's Communist partisans. Going into action on 28 August, *Nordland* fought several vicious actions against an equally cut-throat enemy. Just before *Nordland* was reassigned, on 12 November 1943, it was upgraded to full Panzergrenadier status. Along with III.*(Germanische) SS-Panzerkorps*, *Nordland* transferred to the Eastern Front; it was fully deployed with Army Group North by 22 December 1943.

▶ **Panzerkampfwagen III Ausf E (SdKfz 141)**

SS-Panzer-Abteilung Nordland / 2.Kompanie

As formed in 1943, the *Nordland* Division was to have a Panzer battalion of four companies. However, by May 1944 in the Baltic the division was equipped with three StuG companies in place of Panzer IIIs and IVs.

Specifications	
Crew: 5	Speed: 40km/h (25mph)
Weight: 21.8 tonnes (19.8 tons)	Range: 210km (130.5 miles)
Length: 5.38m (17ft 7in)	Radio: FuG5
Width: 2.91m (9ft 5in)	Armament: 1 x 50mm (2in) gun;
Height: 2.44m (8ft)	2 x 7.92mm (0.3in) MG (one
Engine: Maybach HL120TRM	hull-mounted, one coaxial)

▶ **Sturmgeschütz III Ausf D**

SS-Sturmgeschütz-Abteilung Nordland

The short-barrelled StuG III Ausf D was still in use when the *Nordland* Division formed in 1943, but was soon replaced by long-barrelled variants.

Specifications	
Crew: 4	Speed: 40km/h (25mph)
Weight: 19.6 tonnes (17.9 tons)	Range: 160km (99.4 miles)
Length: 5.38m (17ft 8in)	Radio: FuG15 or FuG16
Width: 2.92m (9ft 7in)	Armament: 1 x 75mm (3in)
Height: 1.95m (6ft 5in)	StuK 37 L/24 gun
Engine: Maybach HL120TR (300hp)	

With Army Group North
1944

The *Nordland* Division was sent to the Eastern Front at a critical time. The initiative had been seized by the Red Army, and the new formation was almost immediately fighting for its life.

THE DIVISION ARRIVED IN THE LENINGRAD sector to take part in the unsuccessful German attempt to fight off a massive Soviet breakout from the Oranienbaum pocket, a breakout that succeeded in relieving the 900-day siege of Leningrad. Over the next three months of continuous combat, the Germans were driven back over the Narva. In fact, so many volunteer units saw action at Narva that it became known as the 'Battle of the European SS'.

Although the Germans had been forced to retreat, the long period of combat had also exhausted the Soviets. The impetus had run out of the Red Army's advance and the battle for Narva became a battle of snipers. During this period, the battered 1st Battalions of both the *Norge* and *Danmark* Panzergrenadier Regiments were withdrawn to Germany for rest and rebuilding. They would never again be assigned to *Nordland*. In December 1944, after being brought up to strength, both battalions were assigned to the 5th SS Panzer Division *Wiking*. Early in 1945, the battalions were transferred south for the failed attempt to relieve Budapest.

Back on the Baltic Front, Soviet pressure began to increase in early June 1944, and it soon became apparent that a major Soviet thrust was in the making. Then, on 22 June, the third anniversary of Operation *Barbarossa*, the Soviets launched Operation *Bagration* against Army Group Centre. This was the long-awaited Soviet summer offensive, and it tore a 400km- (248-mile) wide gap in the German lines, annihilating the entire German army group in the process.

The Tannenberg Line

The rapid Soviet advance threatened to isolate the hundreds of thousands of German troops in the Baltic States. To avoid being cut off, the Germans began planning for the withdrawal from the Narva bridgehead to the Tannenberg Line. Through July and August, the troops of III.*(Germanische) SS-Panzerkorps* took part in some of the most vicious fighting ever seen on the Eastern Front.

The Tannenberg Line anchored on three strategic hills that protected the rear side of the town of Narva.

▲ **2cm Flak (Sf) auf Fahrgestell leichte Zugkraftwagen 1t (SdKfz 10/4)**

SS-Panzergrenadier-Division Nordland / Stab-Begleit-Kompanie

The divisional headquarters was protected from air attack by a Flak battery equipped with four self-propelled 2cm (0.7in) guns. The four batteries of the division's Flak battalion used heavier, towed weapons.

Specifications

Crew: 7	6-cylinder (100hp)
Weight: 5.5 tonnes (5 tons)	Speed: 65km/h (40mph)
Length: 4.75m (15ft 7in)	Range: 300km (186 miles)
Width: 2.15m (7ft 1in)	Radio: None
Height: 3.20m (10ft 6in)	Armament: Twin 20mm (0.7in)
Engine: Maybach HL42TRKM	Flak 38 L/112.5

From 27 July, *Nordland* fought alongside *Sturmbrigade Langemarck* and *Kampfgruppe Strachwitz* from the *Grossdeutschland* Division to keep control of Orphanage Hill.

Despite the death of the *Nordland's* commander, *SS-Gruppenführer* Fritz Scholz, who was killed in the fighting, and the subsequent deaths of the commanders of the *Norge* and *Danmark* Regiments, the division held on to Orphanage Hill, destroying 113 tanks on 29 July.

On 14 September 1944, the German forces in Estonia were ordered to fall back into Latvia. By the morning of the 22nd, *Nordland* had taken up position 30km (18.6 miles) to the northeast of Riga, the Latvian capital. By the evening, *Nordland* had been relocated to the southeast of the city. Its arrival prevented the encirclement of the German Eighteenth Army by Soviet forces.

ORGANIZATION, 1944

▲ **7.5cm Panzerabwehrkanone (Pak 40)**

11.SS-Panzerjäger-Abteilung

One company of the division's Panzerjäger battalion used the powerful Pak 40; the other companies were equipped with self-propelled weapons. The heavy companies of the *Nordland's* three Panzergrenadier battalions each had three Pak 40s.

Specifications

Crew: 3	Muzzle Velocity (AP): 990m/s (3248fps)
Weight: 1.5 tonnes (1.37 tons)	Range: AP: 2000m (2190 yards), HE: 7.5km
Length: 3.7m (12ft 1.5in)	(4.66 miles)
Calibre: 75mm (3in)	Ammunition: Armour-piercing, high explosive

▶ **Leichte Panzerspähwagen (SdKfz 222)**

11.SS-Aufklärungs-Abteilung / 1.leichte Spähpanzerwagen-Kompanie

Most of the *Nordland* Division's reconnaissance companies were motorized units, equipped with soft-skin cars and motorcycles. However, one company of the reconnaissance battalion was equipped with armoured cars.

Specifications

Crew: 3	Speed: 85km/h (52.8mph)
Weight: 5.3 tonnes (4.8 tons)	Range: 300km (186 miles)
Length: 4.8m (15ft 8in)	Radio: FuG Spr Ger 'a'
Width: 1.95m (6ft 5in)	Armament: 1 x 20mm (0.7in) KwK 30 L/55
Height: 2.00m (6ft 7in)	cannon; 1 x 7.92mm (0.3in) MG (coaxial)
Engine: Horch 3.5L or 3.8L petrol	

As the Red Army moved forward, *Nordland* slowly pulled back into the Courland pocket, fighting doggedly all the way, from where it was evacuated to Germany in early 1945. At this time III.*(Germanische) SS-Panzerkorps* included *Kampfgruppen* from the 27.*SS-Freiwilligen-Grenadier-Division Langemarck*, 28.*SS-Freiwilligen-Panzergrenadier-Division Wallonien*, elements of 10.*SS-Panzer-Division Frundsberg*, and 11.*SS-Freiwilligen-Panzergrenadier-Division Nordland*; it was subordinated to the newly created 11th Panzer Army, commanded by *SS-Obergruppenführer* Steiner.

Steiner launched Operation *Sonnenwende* to destroy a Soviet salient and to relieve the troops besieged in the town of Arnswalde. However, the assault had ground to a halt by 21 February. Clearly, nothing more could be achieved against an increasingly powerful enemy without extremely high casualties, so Steiner ordered a general withdrawal back to the north bank of the Ihna.

ORGANIZATION

East Prussia and Berlin

MARCH–APRIL 1945

The Soviet offensive of 1 March pushed the *Nordland* Division back to Berlin, along with the rest of the remnants of the III (Germanic) SS Panzer Corps.

IN A DESPERATE FIGHTING withdrawal, the SS Panzer Corps inflicted heavy casualties on the Soviets, but they could not stop the Red Army. By 4 March, the division was at Altdamm, the last defensive position east of the Oder itself. Over the next two weeks, *Nordland* doggedly held its position, inflicting severe casualties on the enemy but suffering equally high losses in the process. On 19 March, after the *Danmark* and *Norge* Regiments had been all but destroyed, the battered division fell back behind the Oder. It was ordered back to the Schwedt–Bad Freinwalde area to be refitted as best as could be managed at this late stage of the war.

On 16 April, *Nordland* was ordered back into the line east of Berlin. The division was still far from being at full strength, and apart from a small number of French and Spanish volunteers most of the division's reinforcements had little combat experience. Back in combat on 17 April, *Nordland* had been driven back into Berlin by the 20th. Two days later, on 22 April, the remnants of the *Nordland* Division were fighting around the Tiergarten in the centre of the city. By the end of April, any divisional organization had ceased to exist.

Last defence of Berlin

What little remained of the *Norge* and *Danmark* Regiments, with elements of the division's pioneer battalion, tried to defend the bridges across the Spree. After this futile attempt, the few survivors were pushed back into the Government District, and on 26 April they were fighting around the *Reichstag*.

At 20:00 on 30 April, the *Norge* and *Danmark* *Kampfgruppe* commander, *SS-Sturmbannführer* Ternedde, was given the news of Hitler's death. Ternedde was given orders to take the survivors and break out of the ruined city. In the event, very few of

them made it to safety. Several small groups managed to reach the American forces at Charlottenburg, but many more did not, among them the 3rd (Swedish) Company of the reconnaissance battalion, who fought a desperate and ultimately useless battle to escape the surrounding Red Army.

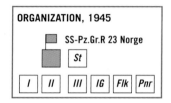

ORGANIZATION, 1945

SS-Pz.Gr.R 23 Norge

St

| I | II | III | IG | Flk | Pnr |

ORGANIZATION

SS-Auf.Btl 11

St

| 1 | 2 | 3 | 4 | 5 |

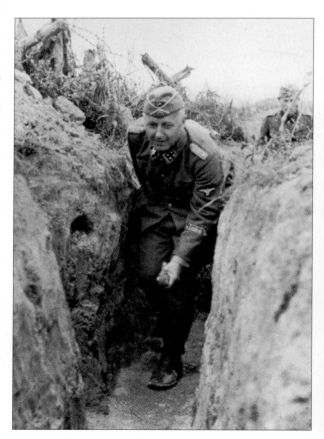

▶ **On the Narva Front**
A Norwegian *Oberstürmbannführer* of the *Nordland* Division still wears the cuff title of his former unit, the *Legion Norwegen*.

By 1 May, the Soviet Army had overcome the last defenders of the *Reichstag*. Organized resistance in the ruined city no longer existed. As dusk descended on 2 May, the few survivors of *Nordland* and the rest of the exhausted Berlin garrison, some 130,000, marched into Soviet captivity. The few survivors of *Nordland* who surrendered to the Soviets were never to be seen again. Those who broke out westwards and reached the Americans or the British were handed over to their respective countries and tried as traitors. Most were imprisoned for varying lengths of time; a few were executed.

When infantry vehicles carried identification numbers, they usually meant the same as they did on Panzers – in this case 1st Battalion, 1st Company, 7th vehicle of a Panzergrenadier regiment.

▶ Mittlere Schützenpanzerwagen (SdKfz 251/22)

24.SS-Panzergrenadier-Regiment Danmark / III.Bataillon / 13.Kompanie

Towards the end of 1944, the 3rd Battalion of the *Danmark* Panzergrenadier Regiment was equipped with half-tracks. The battalion's heavy company had a platoon of three 7.5cm (3in) Pak 40 anti-tank guns

Specifications

Crew: 4 or 5	Speed: 50km/h (31mph)
Weight: 8 tonnes (7.28 tons)	Range: 300km (186 miles)
Length: 5.98m (19ft 7in)	Radio: None
Width: 2.1m (6ft 11in)	Armament: 1 x 75mm (3in) PaK 40
Height: 2.25m (7ft 4.5in)	L/46 anti-tank gun; 1 x 7.92mm
Engine: Maybach HL42TUKRM	(0.3in) MG (rear-mounted)
6-cylinder petrol (100hp)	

▶ 15cm schwere Infanterie Geschütz auf Selbsfahrlafette 38(t) Ausf K Grille (SdKfz 138/1)

23.SS-Panzergrenadier-Regiment Norge / 17.Kompanie (sIG Sf)

The self-propelled infantry gun companies of the *Norge* and *Danmark* Regiments were each equipped with a battery of six Grille vehicles.

Specifications

Crew: 5	Engine: Praga EPA/2
Weight: 12.7 tonnes (11.5 tons)	Speed: 35km/h (21.7mph)
Length: 4.61m (15ft 1in)	Range: 185km (115 miles)
Width: 2.16m (7ft 0in)	Radio: FuG16
Height: 2.40m (7ft 10.5in)	Armament: 1 x 150mm (5.9in) sIG 33 gun

▶ Mittlere Schützenpanzerwagen (SdKfz 251/1)

24.SS-Panzergrenadier-Regiment Danmark / I.Battalion / 1.Kompanie

The late-war Ausf D variant of the *mittlere Schützenpanzerwagen* had a simplified armoured body that cost less to manufacture than earlier models.

Specifications

Crew: 2 plus 12 troops	Engine: Maybach
Weight: 9.9 tonnes (9 tons)	HL42TUKRM
Length: 5.98m (19ft 7in)	Speed: 53km/h (33mph)
Width: 2.1m (6ft 11in)	Range: 300km (186 miles)
Height: 1.75m (5ft 8in) or	Radio: FuG Spr Ger 1
2.16m (7ft) including MG	Armament: 1/2 x 7.62mm
shield if fitted	(0.3in) MG

12th SS Panzer Division *Hitlerjugend*

Known as 'Hitler's Baby Division' to the Allies in Normandy, the 12th SS Division drew most of its personnel from the school-age boys of the Hitler Youth.

INSIGNIA
The *Hitlerjugend* Division honoured its close association with the *Leibstandarte* by adopting a variant of that division's 'Key' insignia.

Divisional History	Formed
SS-Panzergrenadier-Division Hitlerjugend	1943
SS-Panzer-Division Hitlerjugend	1943
12.SS-Panzer-Division Hitlerjugend	1943

Commanders

Brigadeführer Fritz Witt
June 1943 – June 1944

Brigadeführer Kurt Meyer
June 1944 – September 1944

Obersturmbannführer Hubert Meyer
September 1944 – October 1944

Brigadeführer Fritz Kraemer
October 1944 – November 1944

Brigadeführer Hugo Kraas
November 1944 – May 1945

◄ **Normandy, June 1944**
The *Hitlerjugend* Division fought with unparalleled ferocity in the battles against the British at Caen, suffering huge losses in the process.

IN A DWINDLING SUPPLY of manpower, the existence of an entire generation of ideologically pure boys, raised as Nazis, eager to fight for the Fatherland and even die for the *Führer*, could not be ignored.

The first thousand-bomber raid hit Cologne in May 1942. In that month, *Reich* Youth Leader Artur Axmann persuaded Hitler to set up pre-military training camps that all boys between the ages of 16 and 18 were obliged to attend. In turn, the SS persuaded the HJ, or *Hitlerjugend*, to reserve to them exclusively one-fifth of the product of these camps.

In this preparation for combat, especially in the camps run by the SS, German adolescents received training heavily laced with brainwashing. War was taught as a struggle of competing ideologies, culminating in victory or annihilation. The type of soldier produced under this 'fight or die' indoctrination largely explains the continuing Nazi war effort, when most outsiders and an increasing number of insiders knew the cause was lost.

During the three weeks of mandatory war training, the boys learned how to handle German infantry weapons, including pistols, machineguns, hand grenades and *Panzerfaust* anti-tank weapons.

Indoctrination

The Army high command and the SS were in constant competition for the best recruits. Both organizations assigned veterans to HJ administrative posts primarily as a means of recruitment. They regaled their wide-eyed audiences with the perils and thrills of combat. They reinforced the will to fight the 'Bolshevik hordes' and the 'Jew-backed Western powers'. These Pied Pipers did all they could to produce cannon fodder for the *Reich* war machine.

The results were impressive. Army leaders were the first to acknowledge the achievements of the HJ in preparing recruits for the battlefield. Departing from traditional methods, the *Hitlerjugend* tailored paramilitary training to the particular needs and potential of 16- and 17-year-olds. With the exception of a few coarse SS veterans, there were no hard-bitten drill sergeant types in the training camps. Most cadre members were sensitive young soldiers, most of whom had been in the *Hitlerjugend* themselves not too many years before. German youth was, in effect, training itself.

The camps also served to eliminate class distinctions. Boys from town and city, volunteer and conscript, were thrown in together. The soldiers that were turned out fought with greater professional skill, resourcefulness and independent initiative than their enemy counterparts. Between the spring of 1942 and 1945, every German volunteer and draftee filtered

through the HJ training schemes before he donned field grey or SS camouflage. But although he was better trained than his opponent, he was also more prone to embrace the barbarity of battle.

Hitler Youth Division

The natural progression to giving the HJ more military training was the formation of the 12th SS Panzer Division *Hitlerjugend*. A recruitment drive began, drawing principally on 17-year-old volunteers. However, boys of 16 and under eagerly joined. During July and August 1943, some 10,000 recruits arrived at the new division's training camp in Beverloo, Belgium.

▶ **Mittlere Funkpanzerwagen Ausf C (SdKfz 251/3)**
2.SS-Panzergrenadier-Regiment Hitlerjugend / Stab
The radio variant of the SdKfz 251 was originally equipped with frame antennae as seen here, but from 1942 these began to be replaced by less conspicuous pole antennae. However, frame-equipped vehicles were still in service in 1944.

Specifications

Crew: 2 plus 12 troops	Engine: Maybach HL42TUKRM
Weight: 9.9 tonnes (9 tons)	Speed: 53km/h (33mph)
Length: 5.98m (19ft 7in)	Range: 300km (186 miles)
Width: 2.1m (6ft 11in)	Radio: FuG Spr Ger 1
Height: 1.75m (5ft 8in) or 2.16m	Armament: 1/2 x 7.62mm
(7ft) including MG shield if fitted	(0.3in) MG

Specifications

Crew: 5	Speed: 46km/h (28.6mph)
Weight: 50.2 tonnes (45.5 tons)	Range: 200km (124 miles)
Length: 8.86m (29ft 0in)	Radio: FuG5
Width: 3.4m (11ft 2in)	Armament: 1 x 75mm (3in) KwK42 L/70;
Height: 2.98m (9ft 10in)	2 x 7.92mm (0.3in) MG (one hull-mounted,
Engine: Maybach HL230P30	one coaxial)

▲ **Panzerkampfwagen V Ausf A (SdKfz 171)**
12.SS-Panzer-Regiment / I.Abteilung / 1.Kompanie
Before its losses in Normandy, the *Hitlerjugend*'s Panzer regiment was equipped with one battalion totalling 66 Panthers and one battalion with 96 Panzer IVs. After Normandy, it was reduced to a single battalion regiment.

⚡ Normandy

JUNE–JULY 1944

Nobody could question the determination of the ideologically trained teenagers who volunteered for the *Hitlerjugend* Division, but fighting spirit was no substitute for experience.

To PROVIDE THE HJ DIVISION with a cadre of experienced soldiers and officers, *Waffen-SS* veterans were drafted into the formation from the Eastern Front. Many were from the elite *Leibstandarte-SS Adolf Hitler*. The *Wehrmacht* assigned 50 officers with combat experience who had also been Hitler Youth leaders as officers for the division. The remaining shortfall of squad and section leaders was filled with Hitler Youth members who had demonstrated leadership aptitude during HJ paramilitary training.

By the spring of 1944, training was complete. The *Hitlerjugend* Panzer Division, now fully trained and equipped, conducted divisional manoeuvres observed by General Heinz Guderian and Field Marshal Gerd von Rundstedt. Both senior officers admired the enthusiasm and expressed their approval of the proficiency achieved by the young troops in such a short time.

The division was transferred to Hasselt, Belgium, in anticipation of the Allied invasion of northern France, where it subsequently fought with fanaticism

ORGANIZATION, 1943

ORGANIZATION, MAY 1944

▶ **Panzerkampfwagen IV Ausf H (SdKfz 161/2)**

12.SS-Panzer-Regiment / II.Abteilung / 5.Kompanie

The Ausf H variant of the Panzer IV differed from earlier models mainly in having thicker armour and an upgraded transmission system.

Specifications

Crew: 5	Speed: 38km/h (23.6mph)
Weight: 27.6 tonnes (25 tons)	Range: 210km (130.5 miles)
Length: 7.02m (23ft 0in)	Radio: FuG5
Width: 2.88m (9ft 5in)	Armament: 1 x 75mm (3in) KwK
Height: 2.68m (8ft 10in)	40/43; 2 x 7.92mm (0.3in) MG
Engine: Maybach HL120TRM	(one hull-mounted, one coaxial)

and bravery against the numerically superior Allies. On the morning of 6 June 1944, the Allied powers landed on the coast of Normandy. The Western Front now officially existed.

As can be imagined, great confusion existed in both the Allied and German military commands. At 14:30 on 6 June 1944, the SS Panzer Division *Hitlerjugend* was ordered to proceed to Caen. This was in close proximity to the British and Canadian landing sites of Juno and Sword beaches.

Slaughter in Normandy

As soon as the *Hitlerjugend* Division arrived in the area, they came under heavy and relentless Allied air attacks. As a result, the division did not make it to its assigned attack positions until 22:00 that night, by which time the Allies had a firm foothold on the Normandy coast.

Although the HJ troops were fanatical in their determination and tenacity to fight to the death, it did not take long for the division to suffer

horrendous casualties. In their first engagement with the Canadians, the HJ Division destroyed 28 tanks while sustaining only six casualties. Such a favourable exchange rate would not last. They fought with incredible determination, playing no small part in preventing the British from achieving their early targets in Normandy. However, the odds were against them. In just over one month of combat, the HJ Panzer Division lost more than 60 per cent of its strength, 20 per cent being killed and the remainder being either wounded or posted missing.

After the British and Canadian forces eventually captured Caen, *Hitlerjugend* was one of 24 German divisions encircled in the Falaise pocket. It was ordered to hold open the northern edge of the pocket so that the trapped divisions could escape as best they could. The remnants of the 12th SS Panzer Division escaped the encirclement, as did about 20,000 other Germans, but more than 50,000 more German troops were trapped in the Falaise pocket and surrendered to the Allies.

▶ Flakpanzer 38(t) Ausf L (SdKfz 140)

12.SS-Panzer-Regiment / I.Abteilung / Stab-Kompanie / Flak-Zug

In June 1944, the 12th SS Panzer Regiment had 12 self-propelled 2cm (0.7in) Flak guns mounted on the chassis of the Panzer 38(t). The single light AA gun proved relatively ineffective against fast, low-flying fighter bombers.

Specifications

Crew: 5	Engine: Praga AC 6-cylinder petrol
Weight: 9.8 tonnes (9.3 tons)	Speed: 42km/h (26mph)
Length: 4.61m (15ft 2in)	Range: 210km (130 miles)
Width: 2.13m (7ft)	Radio: None
Height: 2.25m (7ft 5in)	

▶ 2cm vierling Flakpanzer IV Wirbelwind

12.SS-Panzer-Regiment / Stab / Flak-Zug

The *Wirbelwind* was an attempt to increase the anti-aircraft firepower of Panzer divisions. However, even with four 2cm (0.7in) cannon, it was still less effective than a single 3.7cm (1.5in) weapon, and production ceased in autumn 1944.

Specifications

Crew: 5	Engine: Maybach HL120TRM
Weight: 24.3 tonnes (22 tons)	Speed: 38km/h (23.6mph)
Length: 5.92m (19ft 4in)	Range: 200km (124 miles)
Width: 2.9m (9ft 5in)	Radio: FuG2 and FuG5
Height: 2.76m (9ft)	Armament: 4 x 2cm (1.8in) cannon

Ardennes: Wacht am Rhein

SEPTEMBER–DECEMBER 1944

After a short time to rest and refit, the division was at the front again. This time, the *Hitlerjugend* was covering the German withdrawal from France.

ON 6 SEPTEMBER, near the Franco–Belgian border, *SS-Oberführer* Kurt Meyer was captured by the Americans as the rest of the division fought with the advancing US troops trying to enter Belgium.

In November, the division was transferred to Bremen, Germany. Replacement tanks and other equipment arrived, together with additional manpower, most being former *Kriegsmarine* and *Luftwaffe* personnel. *SS-Standarten-führer* Hugo

Kraas became commander of the division, taking over from *SS-Obersturmbannführer* Hubert Meyer, and the formation was assigned to the Sixth SS Panzer Army.

On 16 December 1944, the HJ Division took an active role in the Ardennes offensive. Starting in the northern sector, the division was allocated to the right flank of the Sixth Panzer Army to provide protection as it punched forward towards Malmedy, driving deep into the thinly held Allied lines. However, stiff

▲ **Panzer IV/70 (SdKfz 162/1)**

12.Panzerjäger-Abteilung / 1.Kompanie

In Normandy, the *Hitlerjugend* tank-hunter battalion had two companies of the tank-destroyer variant of the Panzer IV. Fitted with a 7.5cm (3in) Pak 39 gun, the vehicles were later replaced with the Panzer IV/70 series.

Specifications

Crew: 4	Speed: 35km/h (21.7mph)
Weight: 25.8 tonnes (23.48 tons)	Range: 210km (130.5 miles)
Length: 8.50m (27ft 10.5in)	Radio: FuG5
Width: 3.17m (10ft 5in)	Armament: 1 x 75mm (3in) PaK 42 L/70 anti-
Height: 2.85m (9ft 4in)	tank gun; 1 x 7.92mm (0.3in) MG
Engine: Maybach HL120TRM (300hp)	

▶ **Panzerkampfwagen VI Ausf E (SdKfz 181)**

Kampfgruppe Wünsche / 101.schwere SS-Panzer-Abteilung / 1.Kompanie

The *Wünsche* battle group formed in mid-July 1944. It included units from the *Hitlerjugend* and *LSSAH* Divisions as well as the Tiger tanks of the 101st SS Heavy Panzer Battalion.

Specifications

Crew: 5	Speed: 38km/h (23.6mph)
Weight: 62.8 tonnes (57 tons)	Range: 140km (87 miles)
Length: 8.45m (27ft 8in)	Radio: FuG5
Width: 3.7m (12ft 1in)	Armament: 1 x 88mm (3.5in) KwK
Height: 2.93m (9ft 7in)	36 L/56; 2 x 7.92mm (0.3in) MG
Engine: Maybach HL210P45 (700hp)	(one hull-mounted, one coaxial)

American resistance forced the division to swing left and follow the path of the *Leibstandarte*.

By New Year's Day 1945, the HJ Division was one of the many German units forming a ring around Bastogne. But initial successes had been countered by superior Allied resources, and the German front was under heavy pressure from the flanks of the salient. In particular, the *Wehrmacht* had no answer to the overwhelming Allied air superiority, and the troops, including those of the *Hitlerjugend* Division, were eventually forced to withdraw. By 18 January, the German armies had returned to the positions they had held before the offensive had begun.

ORGANIZATION

SS-Pzjr.Abt 12

St

1 2 Pzjr

▼ **25.Panzergrenadier-Regiment, III.Bataillon, 1.Kompanie**

The late-war armoured infantry company was mostly equipped with variants of the SdKfz 251. These were fitted with either short or long barrel 7.5cm (3in) Pak 40s. Two of the heavy platoon vehicles carried mortars.

Stab

1.*Zug*

2.*Zug*

3.*Zug*

schwere Zug

Weapon Specifications

Crew: 7	Shell weight (HE): 9.24kg (20.34lb)
Weight: 5.1 tonnes (4.9 tons)	Muzzle Velocity (HE): 820m/s (2690fps)
Barrel length: 4.93m (16ft 2in)	Range (aerial, HE): 8000m (26,245ft)
Calibre: 88mm (3.45in)	Ammunition: Armour-piercing, high explosive

▲ **Mittlere Zugkraftwagen 8t / 8.8cm Flak 18 (SdKfz 7)**
12.SS-Flak-Abteilung (mot) / 1.Kompanie

The *Hitlerjugend* Division had more heavy Flak guns than many German Army divisions. Typically, it would deploy two batteries of six 8.8cm (3.5in) guns rather than the single battery of four guns more usually found.

Germany and Hungary
JANUARY–MAY 1945

The final German offensive in the West was followed by another, equally futile, offensive in the East, in which the Sixth SS Panzer Army would play a major part.

THERE WOULD BE NO TIME TO REST because on 20 January the entire Sixth Panzer Army was ordered to the East. The plan was to attack Soviet elements who had surrounded Budapest and had trapped 45,000 men of the IX.*SS-Gebirgskorps* there. Before the end of the month, the division was transferred by rail to Hungary. While the HJ Division was in transit, the IV.*SS-Panzerkorps* launched several ill-fated relief operations. Being in Army Group South, HJ was one of the first units to arrive. In early

February, before the attack was launched, HJ and elements of the *Leibstandarte* attacked and successfully destroyed a Soviet bridgehead that had been established on the River Danube at Gran, the German name for Esztergom in Hungary.

Last battles
The division was next to take part in Operation *Frühlingserwachen* (Spring Awakening), the operation to retake the Hungarian oilfields. Hitler, desperate to

▶ **LeFH18/2 auf PzKpfw II (SdKfz 124)**
12.SS-Artillerie-Regiment / I.Abteilung / 1.Batterie
From the original formation of the division one battalion of the 12th Artillery Regiment was equipped with self propelled guns. Two out of three batteries operated with the Wespe 10.5cm (4.1in) howitzer.

Specifications

Crew: 5	Speed: 40km/h (25mph)
Weight: 12.1 tonnes (11 tons)	Range: 220km (136.7 miles)
Length: 4.81m (15ft 10in)	Radio: FuG Spr 1
Width: 2.28m (7ft 6in)	Armament: 1 x LeFH 18M L/28 105mm
Height: 2.25m (7ft 4.5in)	(4.1in) howitzer
Engine: Maybach HL62TR	

keep the operation a secret, had ordered that no reconnaissance of the battlefield would be allowed before the attack began.

The attack got under way on 6 March 1945 in atrocious conditions. The spring thaw meant that the German assault was confined to a few narrow roads, and after initial successes, the offensive was aborted after a Soviet counterattack threatened to encircle the German forces.

Hitler lost faith in the *Waffen-SS* and ordered that the honorary cuffbands issued to the divisions involved in the attack be returned. Outraged at the order, army commander Sepp Dietrich refused to pass it on to his men.

By the middle of March, the 12th SS Division was on the retreat heading for Austria. By 13 April, the

12.SS-Panzer-Division *Hitlerjugend*	Strength
August 1944:	
PzKpfw IV	37
PzKpfw V	41
January 1945:	
PzKpfw IV	19
PzKpfw V	36

division had reached Linz. On 8 May, the division crossed the demarcation line between the Western and Eastern Allies near the town of Enns and entered American captivity. Defiant until the end, the HJ refused to comply with the American order that its vehicles carry white flags as a token of surrender.

Specifications

Crew: 3

Weight: 9.4 tonnes (8.53 tons)

Length: 5.98m (19ft 7in)

Width: 2.83m (9ft 4in)

Height: 2.07m (6ft 10in)

Engine: Maybach HL42TUKRM

Speed: 53km/h (33mph)

Range: 300km (186 miles)

Radio: FuG Spr Ger 'f'

Armament: 1 x 75mm (3in) KwK L/24 gun

▲ **Mittlere Schützenpanzerwagen (7.5cm) Ausf D (SdKfz 251/9)**

25.Panzergrenadier-Regiment / III.Bataillon / 11.Kompanie

A fully armoured Panzergrenadier company typically operated with 17 or more SdKfz 251 armoured half-tracks. Two of the vehicles would be armed with short-barrelled 7.5cm (3in) KwK37 tank guns, originally fitted to Panzer IVs.

▶ **Leichte Schützenpanzerwagen (SdKfz 250/9)**

12.SS-Panzer-Aufklärungs-Abteilung / 2.(Spw) Aufklärungs-Kompanie

Three out of the division's four reconnaissance companies were issued with half-tracks. By 1944, the SdKfz 250 fitted with a 2cm (0.7in) turret had all but replaced the SdKfz 222 light armoured car in such units.

Specifications

Crew: 3

Weight: 6.9 tonnes (6.3 tons)

Length: 4.56m (14ft 11.5in)

Width: 1.95m (6ft 5in)

Height: 2.16m (7ft 1in)

Engine: Maybach HL42TRKM 6-cylinder (100hp)

Speed: 60km/h (37mph)

Range: 320km (199 miles)

Radio: FuG Spr Ger 'f'

Armament: 1 x 20mm (0.7in) KwK 30/38 L/55 cannon; 1 x 7.92mm (0.3in) MG (coaxial)

Chapter 3

Volunteer Divisions

The change in the nature of the *Waffen-SS*, which first became apparent with the expansion of the organisation in the first years of the war, became even more obvious with the formation of large numbers of new divisions from 1943 onwards. Many of the new formations were manned partly or entirely by foreign volunteers – a distinction which was marked by the use of *Freiwilligen,* or 'Volunteer', in the divisional titles.

◀ **SS in Normandy**
Waffen-SS divisions played a major part in the German defence of Normandy, where these men are working on a Panzer IV. For the most part, the divisions involved were Germanic formations of the 'old' SS. Elsewhere, however, the SS was opening its ranks to a wide variety of nationalities.

13th Waffen Gebirgs Division der SS *Handschar*

The formation of the 13th SS Division marked a major departure from the Nazi state's original policy of using only German or Germanic volunteers in the SS.

REICHSFÜHRER-SS Heinrich Himmler was fascinated by Islam. He believed that Muslims would make excellent shock troops, since he understood their faith offered them a place in paradise if they gave their lives against an enemy. He also supported the crackpot Nazi theory that Croatians were not Slavs, but were descended from the Aryan Goths.

As a result of his beliefs, Himmler advocated the formation of a European Muslim division, which was approved by Hitler on 13 February 1943. The idea was resented by Croatian dictator Ante Pavelic, who felt that the SS was poaching on his preserves, but there was little that his government could do.

When the Independent State of Croatia proclaimed its existence on 10 April 1941, part of the

territory it claimed was the former Austro-Hungarian province of Bosnia–Herzegovina. The province was a volatile ethnic and religious mix, including large numbers of Catholic Croats, Orthodox Serbs and Bosnian Muslims. It was these Muslim inhabitants of Bosnia–Herzegovina that Himmler and the *Waffen-SS* would target in their recruitment of a Croatian SS division. Grudging approval was given by the Croatian leader, Ante Pavelic, on 5 March 1943.

Muslim division forms

The division began forming on 5 March 1943, and reached its full strength of at least 20,000 men by July. Muslims already serving in the Croatian Army were keen on serving in the new division, and the

Divisional History	Formed
Kroatische SS-Freiwilligen-Division	1943
Kroatische SS-Freiwilligen-Gebirgs-Division	1943
SS-Freiwilligen Bosnien-Herzegowina Gebirgs-Division (Kroatien)	1943
13.SS-Freiwilligen-bosn.herzegow. Gebirgs-Division (Kroatien)	1943
13.Waffen-Gebirgs-Division der SS Handschar (kroatische Nr. 1)	1944

Commanders

Oberführer Herbert von Obwurzer
April 1943 – August 1943

Gruppenführer Karl-Gustav Sauberzweig
August 1943 – June 1944

Brigadeführer Desiderius Hampel
June 1944 – May 1945

▶ **Leichte Panzerspähwagen (MG) (SdKfz 221)**

SS Aufklarungs Abteilung 13

In September 1944 a number of *Handschar's* units, including its reconnaissance battalion, were detached from the division to serve as Corps troops for the II SS Cavalry Corps.

Specifications

Crew: 2
Weight: 4 tonnes (3.61 tons)
Length: 4.80m (15ft 8in)
Width: 1.95m (6ft 5in)
Height: 1.70m (5ft 7in)
Engine: Horch 3.5L petrol (75hp)
Speed: 90km/h (56mph)
Range: 320km (199 miles)
Radio: None
Armament: 1 x 7.92mm (0.3in) MG

▲ **5cm Panzerabwehrkanone (Pak 38)**

13.SS-Panzerjäger-Bataillon (mot)

For the first year of its existence, *Handschar*'s tank-hunting battalion was equipped exclusively with towed Pak 36 5cm (2in) guns. By the summer of 1944, however, these had been replaced by assault guns and 7.5cm (3in) Pak 40s.

Specifications	
Crew: 3	Muzzle Velocity (AP): 835m/s (2900fps)
Weight: 1.2 tonnes (1.13 tons)	Range: AP: 1800m (1968 yards), HE: 2.6km
Length: 3.2m (10ft 5in)	(1.6 miles)
Calibre: 50mm (2in)	Ammunition: Armour-piercing, high explosive

▲ **15cm schwere Felfhaubitze (sFH18)**

13.SS-Gebirgs-Artillerie-Regiment / IV.Abteilung / 2.Batterie

Although three of the four battalions attached to the *Handschar* Division's artillery regiment were equipped with lightweight mountain artillery, the fourth battalion operated one battery of long-range guns and two batteries of heavy howitzers.

Specifications	
Crew: 5	Muzzle Velocity: 520m/s (1706fps)
Weight: 6.3 tonnes (5.7 tons)	Range: 13km (8 miles)
Length: 4.4m (14 ft 5in)	Ammunition: High explosive or smoke
Calibre: 150mm (5.9in)	

Croats had to take measures to prevent men from deserting to serve the Germans.

Not all were Muslim volunteers, however. Several thousand *Volksdeutsche* and Catholic Croats were included, and initial Muslim enthusiasm quickly fell off, so numbers had to be made up by conscription.

Croats and Bosnians

Originally known as the *Kroatische SS-Freiwilligen-Division*, it was turned into a mountain unit and became known as the *Kroatische SS-Freiwilligen-Gebirgs-Division*. In an attempt to appease the Bosnian members of the formation, who for historical, religious and ethnic reasons did not get on with the Croats, it was renamed 13.*SS-Freiwilligen-bosn.herzogow. Gebirgs-Division (Kroatien)*, before eventually receiving its final name of 13.*Waffen-Gebirgs-Division der SS Handschar (kroatische Nr. 1)* in May of 1944. The name comes from the Croat word for a curved scimitar-like sword traditionally associated with Bosnia, the *Handzar*, which is spelled *Handschar* in German.

The division wore regular SS issue uniforms. The divisional collar patch showed an arm holding a *Handschar* over a swastika. A red and white Croatian shield was worn on the left arm, and the divisional headgear was a traditional Muslim fez. Non-Muslims wore standard SS mountain caps.

 # Partisan war

1944–1945

The division departed for training at Villefranche-de-Rouergue in Aveyron, in occupied France, being fully transferred by September 1943.

WHILE AT VILLEFRANCHE, it became the only SS division to mutiny, the rising being incited by Communists who had infiltrated the recruitment process. Several German officers were killed during the mutiny, though most of the troops did not take part. Fourteen soldiers were executed as mutineers.

By February 1944, after further training at Neuhammer in Germany, the division was declared operational. It was transferred back to Bosnia for active service against the partisans. Its area of operations was northeastern Bosnia and western Serbia. In a bitter irony, its operations against Bosnian and Serb partisans saw many of the division's members who came from villages and towns in the area fighting against former neighbours.

Guerrilla warfare

The division participated in several anti-partisan campaigns, including Operations *Wegweiser*, *Save*, *Osterei*, *Maibaum* and *Maiglockchen*. Some successes were achieved, and overall the *Handschar* proved itself a competent anti-guerrilla unit, as long as its men were fighting their hereditary enemies. Atrocities were committed, but atrocity was standard in the Balkans, and the *Handschar* was no worse than many other SS divisions, and less brutal than some.

In more conventional action against the Soviets, the *Handschar* Division was far less effective. With the penetration of the Red Army up to the Croatian borders in late 1944, the division was transferred to southern Hungary, and became involved in front-line fighting. Desertions plagued the division from this point on, as many of the Muslims decided to return to Bosnia to protect their homes and families. A number of the deserters switched sides and joined Tito's partisan forces.

The 9000 German personnel of the 13.*Waffen-Gebirgs-Division der SS Handschar* were deployed as an SS battle group, known as *Kampfgruppe Henke*.

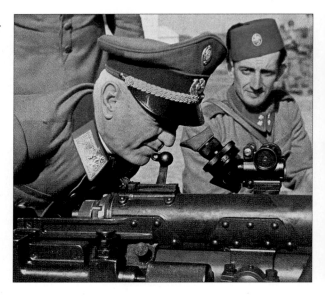

▲ Weapons inspection

The commander of the Croatian Army inspects the weapons of a Bosnian Muslim unit. When the SS began raising similar formations, it allowed Muslim members of the divisions to retain the traditional fez as headgear.

This force fought in southern Hungary, entering combat with the Soviets near the Yugoslav border. On 7 May 1945, the remnants of the division surrendered to the British in Austria. All remaining Muslim volunteers were handed over to Tito's forces after the capitulation and most were executed at Maibor on the Drava.

COMBAT UNIT ORGANIZATION, 1944

13.Waf.Gb.Div der SS Handschar — St

SS-W.Gb.R 27 — St — I II III
SS-W.Gb.R 28 — St — I II III
SS-W.Art.R 13 — St — I II III

SS-Pzjr.A 13 — St — I II III
SS-Auf.Ab 13 — St — I II III
W.Flk.Abt 13 — St — I II III

Kt SS-Rad.B — St — I II III
Kt SS-Krd.B — St — I II III

SUPPORT UNIT ORGANIZATION, 1944

13.Waf.Gb.Div der SS Handschar — St

SS-Div.Ns.Tr — St — I II III
SS-Div.Ns.Fü 13 — St — I II III

Vs.Rgt.St 13 — St — I II III
SS-V.Btl 13 — St — I II III
SS-Wir.B 13 — St — I II III
SS-San.Ab — St — I II III

SS-Gb.Vet.Kp — St — I II III
Divstp 13 — St — I II III

▲ 3.7cm Fliegerabwerkanonen (Flak 36/37)
13.SS-Flak-Abteilung / 2.Batterie

The 3.7cm (1.5in) Flak 36/37 was an effective low-level anti-aircraft weapon, but it was also extremely useful in engaging ground targets and improvised partisan positions in the mountainous terrain of Bosnia.

Specifications

Crew: 5	Muzzle Velocity: 820m/s (2690fps)
Weight: 1.5 tonnes (1.4 tons)	Range: 4800m (5249 yards)
Length: 3.5m (11ft)	Ammunition: High explosive or smoke
Calibre: 37mm (1.5in)	

▲ 3.7cm Panzerabwehrkanone (Pak 36)
1.SS-Freiwilligen-Gebirgsjäger-Regiment (kroat) / I.Gebirgs-Bataillon

The heavy support company in each mountain battalion had a single anti-tank platoon that was armed with three Pak 36 guns.

Specifications

Crew: 3	Muzzle Velocity: 762m/s (2500fps)
Weight: 0.43 tonnes (0.39 tons)	Range: 600m (656 yards)
Length: 1.67m (5ft 5.5in)	Ammunition: Armour-piercing
Calibre: 37mm (1.5in)	

Specifications

Crew: 1	Engine: Horch 3.5L or 3.8L V8 petrol
Weight: 1.89 tonnes (1.72 tons)	(82 or 92hp)
Length: 5.05m (16ft 7in)	Speed: 120km/h (74mph)
Width: 1.79m (5ft 10in)	Range: 400km (248 miles)
Height: 1.69m (5ft 6.5in)	Radio: None

▲ Sanitätswagen Phänomen Granit 1500A (Kfz 31)
Waffen-Gebirgs-Division der SS Handschar / 13.Krankenkraftwagen-Zug

The *Handschar* Division's medical detachment had two ambulance platoons and a stretcher-bearer company to service two medical companies.

▶ Mittlere Personenkraftwagen Mercedes 340 (Kfz 15)
Waffen-Gebirgs-Division der SS Handschar / Stab

Used as a staff and communications vehicle, the Mercedes 340 had a long wheelbase chassis that impaired its cross-country ability.

Specifications

Crew: 1	Engine: Mercedes-Benz 6-cylinder petrol
Weight: 2.4 tonnes (2.2 tons)	(90hp)
Length: 4.44m (14ft 7in)	Speed: 88km/h (55mph)
Width: 1.68m (5ft 6in)	Range: 400km (248 miles)
Height: 1.73m (5ft 8in)	Radio: Various depending on deployment

14th Waffen Grenadier Division der SS

Following the German defeats at Stalingrad and Kursk, *Reichsführer-SS* Heinrich Himmler began to reappraise the SS attitude towards the 'subhuman' Slavs of Eastern Europe.

THE 14TH WAFFEN GRENADIER DIVISION DER SS was formed in Galicia in mid-1943. The region of Galicia, covering southeastern Poland and western Ukraine, was colonized by German settlers in the fourteenth century. It had became a province of Maria-Theresa's Austro-Hungarian Empire by the 1770s, with the provincial capital at Lemberg (Lvov). Although the population was considered Germanic, or *Volksdeutsche*, by the Nazis, the main cultural influence in the region was in fact Ukrainian, as were most of the troops in the division.

What was to become the 14.*Waffen-Grenadier-Division der SS (ukrainische Nr. 1)* was authorized as the *SS-Freiwilligen-Division Galizien* in April 1943, the name being changed briefly to *SS-Schützen-Division Galizien*. The western Ukraine's historical name of Galicia was applied to the new division, possibly to avoid alerting Hitler to the fact that the SS was forming a division which included large numbers of the despised Slavs.

Training of the troops began at the *Truppenübungsplatz der SS* Heidelager in Debica in September 1943 before the division was moved to Silesia in April 1944 for further training. The recruits were mainly *Volksdeutsche* and Ukrainians from the area around Lemberg. On 22 October 1943, the division's name was changed back to *SS-Freiwilligen-Division Galizien*.

Inauspicious combat debut

The *Galizien* Division was sent to the front at Brody in the Ukraine in June 1944. Inadequately armed, poorly trained, and with troops lacking in motivation, it was no match for the powerful Soviet assault that was launched as part of the Red Army's massive summer offensive. The division was quickly encircled and smashed, with only about 3000 of its 15,000 members managing to reach the German lines and safety.

The formation was soon rebuilt as the 14.*Waffen-Grenadier-Division der SS*. After the completion of basic training at *Truppenübungsplatz* Neuhammer in Silesia, it was sent into Slovakia at the end of August

Commanders

Gruppenführer Walther Schimana *June 1943 – November 1943*	Brigadeführer Nikolaus Heilmann *July 1944 – September 1944*
Brigadeführer Fritz Freitag *November 1943 – April 1944*	Brigadeführer Fritz Freitag *September 1944 – April 1945*
Brigadeführer Sylvester Stadler *April 1944 – July 1944*	Brigadeführer Pavlo Shandruk *April 1945 – May 1945*

1944, where it was used to help suppress the Slovak National Uprising. From there, the division was deployed into northern Yugoslavia to fight partisans.

In January 1945, the division was again redesignated, now becoming known as the 14.*Waffen-Grenadier-Division der SS (ukrainische Nr. 1)*. In January 1945, it was transferred to Pressburg (now Bratislava in Slovakia), where it took part in anti-partisan operations in the *Untersteiermark* (the area which is today known as Slovenia).

In April 1945, the formation was officially transferred to the newly forming Ukrainian National Army as the 1.*Ukrainische Division der Ukrainischen National-Armee*. Although still strong numerically, the division was short of weaponry and supplies. Retreating into the Austrian Alps north of Klagenfurt, the division surrendered to the Americans between the towns of Tamsweg and Judenberg at the beginning of May.

Divisional History	Formed
SS-Freiwilligen-Division Galizien	1943
SS-Schützen-Division Galizien	1943
SS-Freiwilligen-Division Galizien	1943
14.Galizische SS-Freiwilligen-Division	1944
14.Waffen-Grenadier-Division der SS (ukrainische Nr. 1)	1945
1.Ukrainische Division der Ukrainischen National-Armee	1945

▲ 10.5cm leichte Feldhaubitze (leFH18)

SS-Artillerie-Regiment Galizische / III.Abteilung

Although poorly equipped by late-war SS standards, the Galician Division had a standard infantry division's complement of artillery, with three battalions each equipped with a dozen light field howitzers.

Specifications

Crew: 5	Muzzle Velocity: 540m/s (1770fps)
Weight: 1.95 tonnes (1.85 tons)	Range: 12,325m (13,480 yards)
Length: 3.3m (10ft)	Ammunition: High explosive or smoke
Calibre: 105mm (4.1in)	

COMBAT UNIT ORGANIZATION

Specifications

Crew: 1 + maintenance section
Weight: 9 tonnes (8.85 tons)
Length: 7.4m (24ft 5in)
Width: 2.5m (8ft 2in)
Height: 3m (9ft 9in)
Engine: 6-cylinder petrol (90bhp)
Speed: 45km/h (28mph)
Range: not known
Payload: printing equipment

▲ Henschel/Magirus 33 G1 (Kfz 72)

14.Waffen-Grenadier-Division der SS / Stab

Medium 6x4 van-bodied trucks were used as command posts by divisional headquarters, and were also used by mapping and printing sections.

▼ Mittlere Landkraftwagen 3t Opel Blitz 3.6 36S

14.SS-Division / Versorgungsdienst

The 14th Division's supply service had two supply companies, capable of lifting 60 tonnes (59 tons) and 90 tonnes (88 tons). A 60-tonne company was divided into four sections, each of which had five medium trucks at full strength.

Specifications

Crew: 1
Weight: 3.29 tonnes (3 tons)
Length: 6.02m (19ft 9in)
Width: 2.27m (7ft 5in)
Height: 2.18m (7ft 2in)
Engine: Opel 6-cylinder petrol (73.5hp)
Speed: 80km/h (50mph)
Range: 410km (255 miles)
Radio: None

15th Waffen Grenadier Division der SS

Early in 1943, the *Lettische SS-Freiwilligen-Legion* was formed from several SS-linked Latvian internal security units, known as *Schutzmannschaft* Battalions.

THE ORIGINS OF THE 15. *Waffen-Grenadier-Division der SS (lettische Nr. 1)* date back to 1943, when the *Lettische SS-Freiwilligen-Legion* was enlarged and upgraded to divisional status. The legion had been formed in the spring of 1943, with the raising of three infantry regiments. Along with the 2nd Latvian SS Volunteer Brigade (formerly the Latvian SS Volunteer Brigade), the Latvian Volunteer Legion served under the VI SS Volunteer Corps. In November 1943, the legion saw action at Novo-Sokolniki, northern Russia, as part of the Sixteenth Army with Army Group North.

The legion was taken out of combat in October 1943 to become the kernel of a new volunteer division, the 1st Division of the SS Latvian Legion (renamed 15. *Lettische SS-Freiwilligen-Division*). The

Divisional History	Formed
Lettische SS-Freiwilligen-Division	1943
15.Lettische SS-Freiwilligen-Division	1943
15.Waffen-Grenadier-Division der SS (lettische Nr. 1)	1944

division later became the 15. *Waffen-Grenadier Division der SS (lettische Nr. 1)* and was assigned to the XLIII Corps of the German Sixteenth Army.

The Soviet winter offensive that was launched at the end of December 1943 continued until February 1944. The fighting was furious, and both sides suffered heavy casualties. The 15. *Lettische SS-Freiwilligen-Division* was assigned to the VI SS Corps, where it fought alongside the 19th Latvian SS Division, which had been formed around the 2nd Latvian SS Volunteer Brigade. In March 1944, both Latvian divisions fought to control strategic points

Commanders

Brigadeführer Peter Hansen
February 1943 – May 1943

Gruppenführer Carl Graf von Pückler-Burghauss
May 1943 – February 1944

Brigadeführer Nikolas Heilmann
February 1944 – July 1944

Brigadeführer Herbert von Obwurzer
July 1944 – January 1945

Oberführer Arthur Ax
January 1945 – February 1945

Oberführer Karl Burk
February 1945 – May 1945

INSIGNIA

The divisional insignia of the 15th SS Division was a simple letter 'L' for Latvia, with the Roman numeral 'I' to indicate that this was the 1st Latvian Division.

▲ **15cm schwere Infanterie Geschütz (sIG33)**

32.SS-Freiwilligen-Regiment (lettische Nr. 3) / 13.Kompanie

The 13th Company of each of the three Latvian volunteer regiments in the 15th Division was an infantry gun unit. It was equipped with two heavy sIG33s in addition to six of the lighter 7.5cm (3in) *leichte Infanterie Geschütze*.

Specifications

Crew: 5

Weight: 1.75 tonnes (1.71 tons)

Length: 1.64m (64.57in)

Calibre: 150mm (5.9in)

Muzzle Velocity: 241m/s (783fps)

Range: 5504m (6000 yards)

Ammunition: High explosive or smoke

COMBAT UNIT ORGANIZATION, 1944

along the Velikiye River. Although the corps faced 11 Soviet divisions, the Soviet offensive was contained at great cost.

The launch of the Soviet offensive in June 1944 saw the 15th SS Division forced back from its defensive positions on the River Sanukha. A month later, the Latvian division was fighting yet another attack, near Ostrova in Estonia. The power of the offensive meant that the Latvians could pull back only at the cost of two regiments all but wiped out.

Surviving infantrymen and the divisional artillery were transferred to the 19th SS Division while NCO and officer cadres were shipped to the *Truppenübungsplatz der SS* West Prussia. In September, conscripts from Latvia and engineers from the SS Training and Replacement Battalions at Dresden were used to reform the 15.*Waffen-Grenadier-Division der SS (lettische Nr. 1)*.

Premature action

In January 1945, although training was far from complete, the division was ordered to positions along the Oder–Vistula Canal. By end of February, the Red Army had broken through to the Baltic at Kolberg, cutting off large German forces, including the 15th SS Division. As part of *Kampfgruppe Tettau*, the division broke through the Soviet lines to reach German-held territory, its 33rd Grenadier Regiment acting as rearguard.

Survivors were sent to Neubrandenburg, north of Berlin, for refitting. As the Soviets pushed on towards the German capital, a battle group drawn from the 32nd and 33rd Regiments was dispatched towards Berlin to help in the defence of the city. On 24 April, after fighting off Soviet attacks in the south of the

▲ **Baltic SS**

A Latvian SS man fires a flare from a Walther LP signal gun. The 15th SS Division to which he belonged fought long and hard against the Soviets.

city, the *Kampfgruppe* began to withdraw westwards to surrender to the Americans. A week later, the remainder of the division also moved west from Neubrandenburg and reached the American lines near Schwerin, where it too surrendered.

▶ **Mittlere LKW Opel Blitz 3.6-6700A**

15.SS-Flak-Abteilung

Although officially a towed gun, the 2cm (0.7in) Flak 38 was small enough and light enough to be mounted on and operated from the bed of a truck, giving divisions a field-expedient self-propelled capability.

Specifications

Crew: 1	(73.5hp)
Weight: 3.29 tonnes (3 tons)	Speed: 80km/h (50mph)
Length: 6.02m (19ft 9in)	Range: 410km (255 miles)
Width: 2.27m (7ft 5in)	Radio: None
Height: 2.18m (7ft 2in)	Armament: Twin 20mm (0.7in)
Engine: Opel 6-cylinder petrol	Flak 38 cannon

16th SS Panzergrenadier Division *Reichsführer-SS*

The 16th SS Panzergrenadier Division *Reichsführer-SS* began its war service as the *Begleit-Bataillon* RFSS – Heinrich Himmler's personal escort battalion.

IN FEBRUARY 1943, a *Führerbefehl* (a personal command from Adolf Hitler) was passed that the unit be upgraded. It was expanded to an assault brigade and began building its strength at Laibach (the German name for Ljubljana, now the capital of Slovenia). The unit was redesignated as the *SS-Sturmbrigade Reichsführer-SS* and was sent to Corsica in the summer of 1943.

The brigade consisted of three *Schützen*, or rifle, companies and a machine gun company. Artillery support was provided by one infantry gun company, a Panzerjäger company and a battery of assault guns. Flak protection was provided by one heavy battery of 8.8cm (3.5in) Flak guns and a light battery of 2cm (0.7in) weapons.

The brigade was still in Corsica in early September 1943 when the new Italian Government signed an armistice with the Allies. German troops were ordered to disarm any Italian units in their area, and the *Sturmbrigade Reichsführer-SS* occupied the Corsican city of Bastia after the Italian garrison refused to hand over their weapons.

Expanded to division size

On 15 September, the *Sturmbrigade* was shipped to northern Italy. On 3 October 1943, the *Sturmbrigade Reichführer-SS* was expanded still further to divisional size, becoming the *SS-Panzergrenadier-Division Reichsführer-SS*, incorporating a number of Hungarian and Romanian *Volksdeutsche*. It also received replacements from the 3rd SS Panzer Division *Totenkopf*'s reserve organization, which also provided much of the division's officer and NCO cadres. It began working up to operational readiness in Slovenia and northern Italy, eventually moving back to near Vienna in Austria.

The division was sent into action sooner than expected. A *Kampfgruppe* was sent south in January 1944, when the Allies attempted to outflank the Gustav Line at Cassino by mounting an amphibious

Divisional History	Formed
Begleit-Bataillon Reichsführer-SS	1941
Sturmbrigade Reichsführer-SS	1943
16 SS-Panzergrenadier-Division Reichsführer-SS	1943

Commanders

Sturmbannführer Friedrich Dern
February 1941 – ? 1941

Sturmbannführer Ernst Schützeck
? 1941

Sturmbannführer Herbert Garthe
? 1941 – February 1942

Sturmbannführer Paul Massel
February 1942

Obersturmbannführer Karl Gesele
February 1942 – September 1943

Gruppenführer Max Simon
October 1943 – October 1944

Brigadeführer Otto Baum
October 1944 – May 1945

landing between Anzio and Nettuno. The rapid German reaction to the landing stalled Allied plans until May. Elements of the *Reichsführer-SS* Division were located on the coast around Pisa, attached to the XIV Panzer Corps, commanded by *General der Panzertruppen* von Senger und Etterlin.

Occupation of Hungary

The training of the rest of the division was cut short when Hungary began looking for ways to get out of the war. To prevent the government of Admiral Miklos Horthy and Miklos Kallay from negotiating a separate armistice with the Allies, German forces, including the new *Reichsführer-SS* Division, occupied the country on 19 March 1944.

Attached to the LVIII (Reserve) Panzer Corps, the division operated alongside a battalion of the 5th SS Panzer Division *Wiking* as *Kampfgruppe Simon*, after the *Reichsführer-SS*'s commander *Gruppenführer* Max

Simon. In April, the division was at Debrecen under the orders of the *Befehlshaber Ostungarn*.

In May 1944, the division returned to Italy, where it was held in reserve to counter a possible Allied landing on Elba. In June 1944, the division was assigned to LXXXV Army Corps at Grosseto, where its constituent parts were reunited.

Its first major action was around the Tuscan hilltop town of Volterra, southeast of Livorno (Leghorn). Driven off by Allied pressure, the division retreated across the Arno to Carrera, where in August 1944 it was transferred to XIV Panzer Corps of Fourteenth Army. In the heavy fighting south of Florence, the division lost 823 officers, NCOs and men.

▶ **Sturmgeschütz Ausf B (SdKfz 142)**

Sturmbrigade Reichsführer-SS / Sturmgeschütz-Batterie

Although the *Reichsführer-SS* formations spent much of their time in anti-partisan operations, they also had a conventional combat role for which they were equipped with a small unit of assault guns.

Specifications

Crew: 4	Engine: Maybach HL120TR
Weight: 21.6 tonnes (21.1 tons)	Speed: 40km/h (25mph)
Length: 5.38m (17ft 9in)	Range: 160km (99.4 miles)
Width: 2.92m (9ft 8in)	Radio: FuG15 or FuG16
Height: 1.95m (6ft 5in)	

▶ **Panzerkampfwagen IV Ausf G (SdKfz 161/1 or 161/2)**

16.SS-Panzer-Abteilung / 3.Kompanie

The Panzer battalion attached to the *Reichsführer-SS* Division had four companies of Panzer IVs when formed. However, by June 1944 it had been re-equipped with assault guns.

Specifications

Crew: 5	Speed: 40km/h (25mph)
Weight: 25.9 tonnes (23.5 tons)	Range: 210km (130.5 miles)
Length: 6.62m (21ft 8in)	Radio: FuG5
Width: 2.88m (9ft 5in)	Armament: 1 x 75mm (3in) KwK 40/43;
Height: 2.69m (8ft 10in)	2 x 7.92mm (0.3in) MG (one hull-
Engine: Maybach HL120TRM	mounted, one coaxial)

Italy and Hungary
1944–1945

The *Reichsführer-SS* Division was the only major SS formation to spend long periods in combat in Italy, and its record in anti-partisan operations was not a good one.

T HE DIVISION'S REPUTATION dated back to the beginning of the war, when members of the *Reichsführer's Kommandostab* were accused of numerous murders in Poland. In Russia in 1943, as

the *Begleit-Bataillon* RFSS, the unit is believed to have operated alongside the notorious *Dirlewanger* Brigade in massacres at Minsk. Max Simon, the division's commander from October 1943 to October

1944, had been a concentration camp guard before the war, and a Soviet military tribunal accused him of being a key player in the slaughter of 10,000 Russian civilians at Kharkov in the summer of 1943.

In Italy, the division was engaged in bitter anti-partisan battles as it took part in the fighting retreat up the peninsula, and it showed that its behaviour in Russia had been no isolated incident.

Civilian massacre

On 12 August 1944, as part of an anti-partisan sweep through the Stazzema area of Lucca, *SS-Sturmbannführer* Walter Reder of the 16th SS Division led four columns of German Army, SS and Italian SS troops towards Sant'Anna di Stazzema. They murdered civilians in Vaccareccia, Franchi and Pero before reaching Sant'Anna. There they slaughtered the population with machine guns, hand grenades and flamethrowers. Their rampage left behind 560 dead. The youngest victim was only 10 months old and the oldest was 86.

Between 29 September and 5 October 1944, soldiers of the 16th SS Panzergrenadier Division *Reichsführer-SS*, again led by Walter Reder, attacked the small town of Marzabetto as a reprisal for partisan activity in the area. Estimates of the number of victims range from 400 to as many as 2000; among the victims, 45 were less than 2 years old, 110 were under 10, and 95 under 16.

ORGANIZATION
SS-Flk.Abt 16
St
Flk Flk Flk Flk Sw

▶ **Panzerjäger Marder III Ausf H (SdKfz 138)**
16.SS-Panzerjäger-Abteilung / Panzerjäger-Kompanie (Sf)
The division's Panzerjäger battalion had originally been raised for the 13th SS Mountain Division *Handschar*, but was transferred to the *Reichsführer-SS* Division in September 1944.

Specifications
Crew: 4
Weight: 10.8 tonnes (9.8 tons)
Length: 5.77m (19ft 11in)
Width: 2.16m (7ft 1in)
Height: 2.51m (8ft 3in)
Engine: Praga EPA 6-cylinder (140hp)
Speed: 35km/h (22mph)
Range: 240km (150 miles)
Radio: FuG Spr Ger 1
Armament: 1 x 75mm (3in) Pak 40/3 L/46 anti-tank gun; 1 x 7.92mm (0.3in) MG

▲ **2cm Flakvierling auf ZgKw 8t (SdKfz 7/2)**
16.SS-Panzer-Artillerie-Regiment / Stab / Flak-Batterie
Most of the self-propelled Flak guns operated by the 16th SS Division were single-barrel pieces, but the headquarters of the artillery regiment was protected by a battery of four 2cm (0.7in) Flakvierlings.

Specifications
Crew: 7
Weight: 1.16 tonnes (1.06 tons)
Length: 6.55m (21ft 6in)
Width: 2.40m (7ft 10.5in)
Height: 3.20m (10ft 6in)
Engine: Maybach HL62TUK 6-cylinder
Speed: 50km/h (31mph)
Range: 250km (156 miles)
Radio: None
Armament: Quad 20mm (0.7in) Flak 38

Battles in Hungary

In January 1945, the divison was rushed to Hungary as part of the ultimately futile effort to raise the siege of Budapest and to protect the Hungarian oilfields. Deployed as part of the LXXXIII Army Corps, it was sent to the area around Nagykanisza, where it was thrown into the fight to stop the overwhelming advance of the Red Army.

Badly mauled by the vastly more powerful Soviet forces, the remnants of the division were pushed back into the Steiermark in Austria, where they came under the orders of the I Cavalry Corps.

The division refused to surrender after Germany's capitulation at the end of the war. The divisional commander, *SS-Brigadeführer* Otto Baum, negotiated surrender terms in which it was agreed that some would surrender to the Americans at Klagenfurt and the remainder to the British at Graz. Baum made it clear that none of his men should be handed over to the Italian partisans, fearing for their perhaps

justifiable fate in such an event. Walter Reder was captured after the war. In May 1948, he was extradited to Italy and tried by a Italian military court in Bologna. In October 1951, Reder was sentenced to life imprisonment.

▼ 16.SS-Panzer-Artillerie-Regiment / 1.Bataillon

Early in the war, the organization of a typical light howitzer company in an artillery battalion attached to a motorized or Panzer division called for three batteries of four guns. In those early days of triumph, the use of three batteries allowed the guns to be used over a wider area during an advance. By 1944, however, the German forces were fighting on the defensive, and the need for more concentrated firepower saw the introduction of battalions with two six-gun batteries.

1.*Batterie*

2.*Batterie*

17th SS Panzergrenadier Division
Götz von Berlichingen

The 17th SS Panzergrenadier Division was raised in the south of France in October 1943. It was given the honour title *Götz von Berlichingen*.

BERLICHINGEN (1480–1562) WAS A German mercenary who nominally served the Holy Roman Empire but who was little more than a bandit. He became a folk hero after 1773 when Goethe published a popular tragedy based on his life.

The division was one of the last SS divisions to be formed from scratch. Its personnel were mostly conscripts or were transferred from SS reserve units, with numbers being made up by a significant number of Balkan and Romanian *Volksdeutche* recruits.

By March 1944, the division had largely completed its training and was assigned to LXXX Corps. Most of its units had been fully motorized, in part by using commandeered French vehicles. The Panzer battalion was equipped with assault guns.

On 10 April 1944, the formal activation ceremony was attended by a number of Nazi, SS and military dignitaries, including *Reichsführer-SS* Heinrich Himmler, *SS-Obergruppenführer* Sepp Dietrich and General Leo Freiherr Geyr von Schweppenburg.

Divisional History	Formed
SS-Panzergrenadier-Division Götz von Berlichingen	1943
17.SS-Panzergrenadier-Division Götz von Berlichingen	1943

Commanders

SS-Gruppenführer Werner Ostendorff
October 1943 – June 1944

SS-Standartenführer Otto Binge
June 1944

SS-Brigadeführer Otto Baum
June 1944 – July 1944

SS-Standartenführer Otto Binge
August 1944

SS-Oberführer Dr Eduard Deisenhofer
August 1944 – September 1944

SS-Oberführer Thomas Müller
September 1944

SS-Standartenführer Gustav Mertsch
September 1944 – October 1944

SS-Gruppenführer Werner Ostendorff
October 1944 – November 1944

SS-Standartenführer Hans Linger
November 1944 – January 1945

Oberst Gerhard Lindner
January 1945

SS-Oberführer Fritz Klingenberg
January 1945 – March 1945

SS-Oberführer Georg Bochmann
March 1945 – May 1945

▲ **Panzerkampfwagen IV Ausf H (SdKfz 161/2)**

17.SS-Panzer-Abteilung / 2.Kompanie

When originally formed, the *Götz von Berlichingen* Division's Panzer battalion was equipped with four companies of Panzer IVs. By the time the division reached Normandy early in June 1944, these had been replaced by assault guns, which the battalion was to continue to operate for the remainder of the war.

Specifications

Crew: 5

Weight: 27.6 tonnes (25 tons)

Length: 7.02m (23ft 0in)

Width: 2.88m (9ft 5in)

Height: 2.68m (8ft 10in)

Engine: Maybach HL120TRM

Speed: 38km/h (23.6mph)

Range: 210km (130 miles)

Radio: FuG5

Armament: 1 x 75mm (3in) KwK 40/43;
2 x 7.92mm (0.3in) MG (one hull-mounted,
one coaxial)

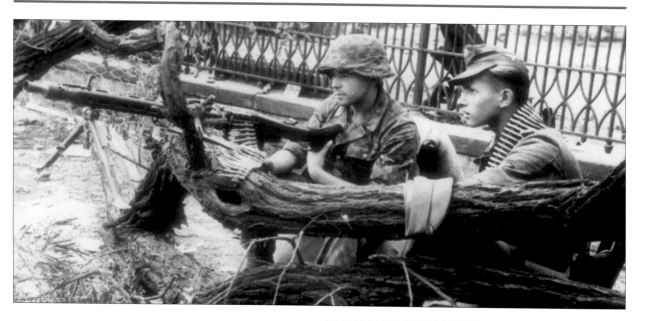

▲ **Normandy, July 1944**
Two young SS soldiers man an MG 42 while awaiting an Allied attack.

INSIGNIA

The division's insignia commemorated the fact that Götz von Berlichingen lost his arm in battle, and had an iron replacement made.

▶ **2cm Flakvierling auf Zgkw 8t (SdKfz 7/1)**

17.SS-Panzer-Artillerie-Regiment / Flak-Batterie

The division's Flak battalion was equipped with towed guns, but in May 1944 one self-propelled platoon with four quad 2cm (0.7in) guns was attached to the regimental staff of the division's artillery regiment.

Specifications

Crew: 5	Engine: Maybach HL120TRM
Weight: 24.3 tonnes (22 tons)	Speed: 38km/h (23.6mph)
Length: 5.9m (19ft 5in)	Range: 210km (130 miles)
Width: 2.9m (9ft 6in)	Radio: FuG2 and FuG5
Height: 2.76m (9ft)	

▶ **Panzerjäger 38(t) Marder III (SdKfz 138)**

17.SS Panzerjäger-Abteilung / 1.Kompanie

The division's tank-destroyer battalion had one self-propelled company with 14 tank-hunters mounting 7.5cm (3in) Pak 40s.

Specifications

Crew: 4	Speed: 35km/h (22mph)
Weight: 10.8 tonnes (9.8 tons)	Range: 240km (150 miles)
Length: 5.77m (19ft 11in)	Radio: FuG Spr Ger 1
Width: 2.16m (7ft 1in)	Armament: 1 x 75mm (3in) Pak 40/3 L/46
Height: 2.51m (8ft 3in)	anti-tank gun; 1 x 7.92mm (0.3in) MG
Engine: Praga EPA 6-cylinder (140hp)	

Battle for Normandy
JUNE 1944

The division was ordered to Normandy on 6 June 1944, arriving on the southern flank of the Allied beachhead on 10 June.

THE RECONNAISSANCE BATTALION engaged US airborne troops at Carentan on the night of 10/11 June. The Germans were driven back until reinforced by *SS-Panzergrenadier-Regiment 37*, the StuGs of the division's Panzer battalion and paratroopers of the 6th Fallschirmjäger Regiment.

Heavy losses

Throughout the remainder of June, the 17th SS Panzergrenadier Division fought in the St Lô sector. Heavy fighting in the bocage country saw the division suffer heavy losses, which were magnified when the formation found itself in the direct path of the US breakout from the beachhead.

COMBAT UNIT ORGANIZATION

17.SS-Pz.Gr.Div Götz von Berlichingen
St

SS-Pz.Gr.R 37 — SS-Pz.Gr.R 38 — SS-Art.Rgt 17
St — St — St
I II III | I II III | I II III

SS-Pzjr.A 17 — SS-Pz.Abt 17 — SS-SG.Abt 17
St — St — St
I II III | I II III | I II III

SS-Flk.Abt 17 — SS-Nach.A 17 — SS-Pz.Auf.Abt 17
St — St — St
I II III | I II III | I II III

▶ **Mittlere Lkw Opel Blitz Typ A / 2cm Flak 38**

17.SS-Panzergrenadier-Division / Stab-Begleit-Kompanie

The escort company attached to the divisional headquarters had a mix of weapons, including a Flak battery with four self-propelled 2cm (0.7in) Flak guns.

Specifications

Crew: 1	Speed: 80km/h (50mph)
Weight: 3.29 tonnes (3 tons)	Range: 410km (255 miles)
Length: 6.02m (19ft 9in)	Radio: None
Width: 2.27m (7ft 5in)	Armament: Twin or quad 20mm
Height: 2.18m (7ft 2in)	(0.7in) Flak 38 cannon
Engine: Opel 6-cylinder petrol	

▶ **Leichte Funkpanzerwagen (SdKfz 250/3)**

17.SS-Panzergrenadier-Division / Stab

Intended primarily to provide communications between Panzer and Panzergrenadier divisions and *Luftwaffe* close-support units, the SdKfz 250/3 later replaced its frame aerial with an extending pole aerial.

Specifications

Crew: 4	Engine: Maybach HL42TRKM 6-cylinder
Weight: 5.35 tonnes (4.87 tons)	Speed: 60km/h (37.3mph)
Length: 4.56m (14ft 11.5in)	Range: 320km (199 miles)
Width: 1.95m (6ft 5in)	Radio: FuG Spr Ger 1
Height: 1.66m (5ft 5in)	Armament: 1 x 7.92mm (0.3in) MG

On 6 August, the remnants of the division were attached to the *Das Reich* battle group, which was under the orders of Seventh Army's XLVII Panzerkorps. On the 7th, the *Kampfgruppe* was at Mortain and took part in the failed offensive against the US Third Army. The SS unit was split into four smaller *Kampfgruppen*. These managed to avoid being caught in the Falaise pocket, eventually retreating towards Chartres. On 28 August, the survivors were ordered to Metz, where the division was to be rebuilt.

▼ 17.SS-Panzer-Abteilung, Panzer-Kompanie, May 1944

In an ideal table of organization and equipment, Panzergrenadier divisions in 1944 usually had a single battalion of tanks divided into four companies. The tanks were generally Panzer IVs, though shortages of Panzers meant that divisions were often equipped with much cheaper assault guns instead. The *Götz von Berlichingen* Division was formed with Panzer IVs, but by the time it reached combat these had been replaced by assault guns.

Stab

1.Zug

2.Zug

3.Zug

▶ **7.5cm Sturmgeschütz Ausf G (SdKfz 142/1)**

SS Panzer Abteilung 17 / 1. Kompanie

The last production series of the StuG III assault gun was the Ausf G. More than
7700 examples were produced between
March 1943 and March 1945.

Specifications

Crew: 4	Speed: 40km/h (25mph)
Weight: 26.3 tonnes (23.9 tons)	Range: 155km (96.3 miles)
Length: 6.77m (22ft 2in)	Radio: FuG15 and FuG16
Width: 2.95m (9ft 8in)	Armament: 1 x 75mm (3in) StuG
Height: 2.16m (7ft 0in)	L/48 cannon
Engine: Maybach HL120TRM	

 # Metz and Lorraine

SEPTEMBER 1944 – MAY 1945

Early in September 1944, the division was reinforced when it absorbed the 49th and 51st SS Panzergrenadier Regiments, though its Panzer battalion was still understrength.

O N 8 SEPTEMBER, THE DIVISION returned to action, attacking a US bridgehead over the Moselle River held by the US 5th and 80th Infantry Divisions on 10 September. By 12 September, the rest of the division had completed refitting and had joined the attack, which was driven off. After heavy fighting, the division pulled back to the Saar and joined the defenders of Metz.

The division was pulled back to the Maginot Line in mid-November after the divisional headquarters had been destroyed in an Allied air attack. By this time, divisional strength had fallen to 4000 men and

20 armoured vehicles. Through December, the division's infantry regiments were brought up to full strength, although the ethnic German (*Volksdeutsche*)

ORGANIZATION

SS-Pz.Gr.Rgt 38

St

| I | II | III | 13 | 14 | 15 |

conscripts were of much lower quality than the original divisional personnel.

During this period, the division was assigned to the XIII SS Corps, under the command of *SS-Gruppenführer* Max Simon. The XIII Corps took part

▶ **Flakpanzer 38 (SdKfz 140)**

38.SS-Panzer-Abteilung / Flak-Batterie

In June 1944, the threat of Allied air power meant that all German formations in Normandy had increased Flak protection. The *Flakpanzer* 38 was issued to the Flak platoons of tank regiments in Panzer and Panzergrenadier divisions.

Specifications

Crew: 4	Engine: Praga AC, 6 cylinder petrol
Weight: 9.8 tonnes (9.64 tons)	engine
Length: 4.61m (15ft 2in)	Speed: 42km/h (26mph)
Width: 2.15m (7ft 0.5in)	Range: 210km (130 miles)
Height: 2.25m (7ft 4in)	Armament: 2cm (1.8in) Flak 38

in Operation *Nordwind*. This was an offensive designed to take pressure off the German offensive in the Ardennes, which had bogged down at the end of December 1944. *Götz von Berlichingen* was teamed with the 36th Volksgrenadier Division. Together the two divisions launched an attack on the US 44th and 100th Infantry Divisions at Rimling in Lorraine. Significant reinforcements had been added to the division, notably a company of Panther tanks, two companies of flamethrowing tanks and a detachment of heavy Jagdtiger tank-destroyers from *schwere Panzerjäger-Abteilung* 653.

Nordwind fails

Although the German attacks inflicted significant losses on the US Seventh Army, they could not break through the American defences. By 5 January, it was clear that Operation *Nordwind* had failed. On 10 January, the 17th SS Division's commander, *SS-Standartenführer* Hans Linger, was captured by an American patrol. The division continued fighting elements of XV US Corps until 25 January 1945, when Operation *Nordwind* was officially brought to an end.

The division retreated to the defences of the *Westwall*, where it would continue to hold out until March 1945. On the 18th of that month, elements of Lieutenant-General Alexander Patch's US Seventh Army broke through. On 22 March, the division abandoned all its vehicles and began a retreat across the Rhine into Germany. Three days later, it was north of the Neckar River, defending the Odenwald.

By 1 April, the division had been reduced to a strength of 7000 men. It fell back to Nuremberg and continued fighting until 24 April. It retreated to Donauwörth on the Danube and the last organized engagement fought by the division was on 29 April at Moosburg. On 7 May 1945, what remained of the 17th SS Panzergrenadier Division *Götz von Berlichingen* surrendered near the Achensee.

▶ **Mittlere Pionierpanzerwagen Ausf D (SdKfz 251/7)**

17.SS-Panzer-Pionier-Abteilung / 1.Pionier-Kompanie

The combat engineer companies in the divisional pioneer battalion had light assault bridges mounted on half-tracks. There was also a bridging column which was used to build larger or more permanent bridges.

Specifications

Crew: 7 or 8	6-cylinder (100hp)
Weight: 8.9 tonnes (8.6 tons)	Speed: 50km/h (31mph)
Length: 5.80m (19ft 0in)	Range: 300km (186 miles)
Width: 2.10m (6ft 11in)	Radio: FuG Spr Ger 1
Height: 2.70m (8ft 10in)	Armament: 1/2 x 7.62mm
Engine: Maybach HL42TUKRM	(0.3in) MG

▶ **Flakpanzer IV 2cm Vierling Wirbelwind**

SS Panzer Abteilung 17 / Stab Kompanie / Flak Zug

Issued to the Flak platoons of Panzer regiments late in the war, the Whirlwind was a conversion of old Panzer IVs in which the main turret was replaced by an open-topped quad 2cm (0.7in) mount. The 17th SS took delivery of four early in 1945.

Specifications

Crew: 5	Engine: Maybach HL120TRM
Weight: 24.3 tonnes (22 tons)	Speed: 38km/h (23.6mph)
Length: 5.9m (19ft 5in)	Range: 210km (130 miles)
Width: 2.9m (9ft 6in)	Radio: FuG2 and FuG5
Height: 2.76m (9ft)	

Stab

Flak-Batterie

1.Kompanie

2.Kompanie

3.Kompanie

◀ **17.SS-Panzer-Abteilung, December 1944**

The division had suffered heavy losses in the fighting around Metz in November 1944. Withdrawn from the line, the division had its Panzergrenadier units brought up to strength by the end of December, but its armoured vehicle inventory was still only at half-strength. More StuGs were on their way to the division, but at the end of the year the Panzer battalion had only 17 guns to equip its three companies. The division was temporarily reinforced by Army Panzer units when it took part in Operation *Nordwind* in January 1945.

18th SS Freiwilligen Panzergrenadier Division *Horst Wessel*

The 18th SS Division was supposed to have been a completely National Socialist formation, raised from the brown-shirted Stormtroopers of the Nazi party's *Sturmabteilung*, or SA.

IN JANUARY 1944, ADOLF HITLER ordered *Reichsführer-SS* Heinrich Himmler to raise a *Waffen-SS* division from a cadre of *Sturmabteilung* reservists. In fact, the 18th SS Freiwilligen Panzergrenadier Division *Horst Wessel* was cobbled together from 1.*SS-Infanterie-Brigade (mot)* – an SS motorized brigade created from elements of two *Totenkopf-Standarten* – together with elements from the 6.*SS-Gebirgs-Division Nord* and large numbers of Hungarian and Yugoslav *Volksdeutsche*.

Nazi 'hero'

The division was named after one of the Nazi party's heroes, portrayed in National Socialist mythology as a young Berlin Stormtrooper who was killed in a streetfight with Communists before the Nazis came to power. In fact, although Horst Wessel was indeed an SA man killed by a Communist, he was actually a street thug and pimp who was killed in a fight over

INSIGNIA

The symbol of the 18th SS Division commemorated Horst Wessel's membership of the SA by using a representation of a Stormtrooper dagger.

who would benefit from the income of Wessel's prostitute girlfriend.

As formed, each of the division's component regiments had their own pioneer companies and Flak companies. These were later merged to form divisional Flak and pioneer battalions, and a Panzerjäger battalion was attached.

The division was assembled at the Stablack training area in East Prussia. In January 1944, it was transferred to Zagreb in Croatia. From there, it was deployed to the Agram area on the Hungarian–Yugoslav border, where it went into action against Tito's partisans.

Commanders

Brigadeführer Wilhelm Trabant *January 1944 – January 1945*	Oberführer Georg Bochmann *January 1945 – March 1945*
Gruppenführer Josef Fitzthum *January 1945*	Standartenführer Heinrich Petersen *March 1945 – May 1945*

Divisional History	Formed
1.SS-Infanterie-Brigade (mot)	1941
18.SS-Panzergrenadier-Division	1944
18.SS-Freiwilligen-Panzergrenadier-Division Horst Wessel	1944

▶ **7.5cm Sturmgeschütz 40 Ausf G (SdKfz 142/1)**

18.SS-Sturmgeschütz-Abteilung / 1.Kompanie

Late-model assault guns based on the Panzer III were identifiable from their revised roof line and the Panzer-style commander's cupola equipped with all-round periscope vision blocks.

Specifications

Crew: 4	Speed: 40km/h (25mph)
Weight: 26.3 tonnes (23.9 tons)	Range: 155km (96.3 miles)
Length: 6.77m (22ft 2in)	Radio: FuG15 and FuG16
Width: 2.95m (9ft 8in)	Armament: 1 x 75mm (3in) StuG
Height: 2.16m (7ft 0in)	L/48 cannon
Engine: Maybach HL120TRM	

Specifications

Crew: 3	Muzzle Velocity (AP): 990m/s (3248fps)
Weight: 1.5 tonnes (1.37 tons)	Range: AP: 2000m (2190 yards), HE: 7.5km
Length: 3.7m (12ft 1.5in)	(4.66 miles)
Calibre: 75mm (3in)	Ammunition: Armour-piercing, high explosive

▲ **7.5cm Panzerabwehrkanone (Pak 40)**
SS Panzerjäger Abteilung 18 / 2. Kompanie (mot)

By the time the *Horst Wessel* Division was formed in 1944, the 7.5cm (3in) Pak 40 was the standard anti-tank gun in most German divisions. It equipped the 18th Panzerjäger Battalion and was also used by the anti-tank platoon of the divisional headquarters company.

⚔ Ukraine, Poland and Hungary
1944–1945

The division gained some combat experience in the anti-partisan war in the Balkans, but it was soon to participate in full-scale combat against the Red Army on the Eastern Front.

IN MARCH, THE DIVISION was moved into Hungary for Operation *Margarethe* alongside the 8th SS Cavalry Division *Florian Geyer*. Here the division was used as a threat to control the Hungarian Government, at that time showing signs of trying to find a way out of the war.

In July, the bulk of the division was sent, under the command of *Obersturmbannführer* Ernst Schäfer, to form a *Kampfgruppe* operating under XXIV Panzerkorps in the Ukraine. The formation took under its command elements of the 8.SS-Sturmbrigade Frankreich, formed after the dissolution of the *Légion des Volontaires Français*.

Under intense Soviet pressure, the *Horst Wessel* battle group retreated through Podhajce and Lipica to the Dniester River, then back through Baliezne, Podrozne and Siechow. One unit was detached in August, and for the next three months it was used alongside the notorious *Dirlewanger* Brigade in the crushing of the Slovak National Uprising.

In September, the rest of the division was moved into Hungary, where it fought the advancing Soviets in the area around Jasz and Ladany. As the Soviet juggernaut pushed on towards Budapest, the division was involved in heavy fighting. It was driven aside and forced to retreat northwards, allowing the Soviets

▶ **2cm Flak 38 / leichte Zugkraftwagen 1t (SdKfz 10/5)**
39.SS-Panzergrenadier-Regiment / 16.Kompanie

The 16th Company in each of the *Horst Wessel*'s two Panzergrenadier regiments was a self-propelled Flak unit, equipped with 12 light anti-aircraft guns divided between three batteries.

Specifications

Crew: 7	(100hp)
Weight: 5.5 tonnes (5 tons)	Speed: 65km/h (40mph)
Length: 4.75m (15ft 7in)	Range: 300km (186 miles)
Width: 2.15m (7ft 1in)	Radio: None
Height: 3.20m (10ft 6in)	Armament: Twin 20mm (0.7in)
Engine: Maybach HL42TRKM 6-cylinder	Flak 38 L/112.5

to encircle the Hungarian capital. The *Florian Geyer*, *Maria Theresia* and 33rd SS (Hungarian) Cavalry Divisions were trapped in the city.

Horst Wessel was used in the attempt to break the Soviet siege of Budapest. On 1 January 1945, the Germans launched the first of three offensives intended to lift the siege. German Army troops attacked through hilly terrain north of Budapest. Simultaneously, *Waffen-SS* forces struck from the west. The Soviets replied by sending four more divisions to meet the threat, stopping the offensive less than 20km (12.5 miles) from the city. On 12 January, the German forces were forced to withdraw.

Meanwhile, the Germans launched a second offensive from Esztegom towards Budapest airport,

COMBAT UNIT ORGANIZATION

▲ 15cm schwere Infanterie Geschütz (sIG33)

40.SS-Panzergrenadier-Regiment / 17.Kompanie

One company in each battalion of the Panzergrenadier regiment was equipped with light 7.5cm (3in) infantry guns; the heavy 15cm (5.9in) weapons were concentrated into a single company.

Specifications

Crew: 5	Muzzle Velocity: 241m/s (783fps)
Weight: 1.75 tonnes (1.71 tons)	Range: 5504m (6000 yards)
Length: 1.64m (64.57in)	Ammunition: High explosive or smoke
Calibre: 150mm (5.9in)	

trying to capture it in order to allow the city to be supplied from the air. The Soviets stopped the drive before it could reach the airport.

On 17 January 1945, the last offensive was launched. German forces attacked from the south of Budapest in an attempt to encircle 10 Soviet divisions. The encirclement attempt failed.

Final days

After the failure of the Budapest offensives, the *Horst Wessel* Division was split into two *Kampfgruppen*. One was used around Karlsbrunn and Ratibor before surrendering to the Red Army at Mährisch-Ostrau.

The other *Kampfgrupe* moved to Zobten in April, where it came under the control of VIII Army Corps. There was no serious fighting in the area, and after the final German surrender small groups moved westwards to surrender to the Americans.

▶ 7.5cm Pak 40 auf PzKpfw 38(t) (SdKfz 138)

18.SS-Panzerjäger-Abteilung / 1.(Sf) Kompanie

Although it had entered service early in 1943, the first version of the self-propelled Pak 40 mounted on a Panzer 38 chassis remained operational until the end of the war.

Specifications

Crew: 4	Speed: 35km/h (22mph)
Weight: 10.8 tonnes (9.8 tons)	Range: 240km (150 miles)
Length: 5.77m (19ft 1in)	Radio: FuG Spr Ger 1
Width: 2.16m (7ft 1in)	Armament: 1 x 75mm (3in) Pak 40/3 L/46
Height: 2.51m (8ft 3in)	anti-tank gun; 1 x 7.92mm (0.3in) MG
Engine: Praga EPA 6-cylinder (140hp)	

▼ **18.SS-Panzerjäger-Abteilung, 1945**

Although the division was intended to have a tank-destroyer battalion from the time it became operational in March 1944, *Horst Wessel* did not in fact form *SS-Panzerjäger-Abteilung* 18 until February 1945. By that time, the division was retreating after German failure to relieve Budapest in January.

Stab

1.Zug

2.Zug

3.Zug

19th Waffen Grenadier Division der SS

The Germans were seen as liberators by many Latvians. Initially they had the full support of Latvian right-wing nationalists, and the SS Latvian Legion was formed in 1942.

THE 19TH WAFFEN GRENADIER DIVISION der SS was the second division of Latvian volunteers raised by the *Waffen-SS*. As in the case of its sister unit – the 15th Waffen Grenadier Division der SS – German troops formed the nucleus of the 19th SS Division, the *2.SS-Infanterie-Brigade (mot)* also providing the bulk of the NCO and officer cadre.

Divisional History	Formed
Lettische SS-Freiwilligen-Brigade	1943
2.Lettische SS-Freiwilligen-Brigade	1943
19.Lettische SS-Freiwilligen-Division	1944
19.Waffen-Grenadier-Division der SS (lettische Nr. 2)	1944

Strength was made up by the addition of a large number of Latvians who had been serving in the *SS-Schutzmannschaft* battalions.

The first large unit of the new Latvian Legion was formed at the Leningrad Front from three police battalions, later reinforced by three further battalions.

Initially known as the *Lettische SS-Freiwilligen-Brigade*, it was redesignated as *2.Lettische SS-Freiwilligen-Brigade*. It was expanded to division size, eventually becoming 19.*Waffen-Grenadier-Division der SS (lettische Nr. 2)* in the summer of 1944. The division found itself in combat in June, only a month after its formation, when the Soviet summer offensive got under way. Over the next six months, it formed part of the heavily outnumbered German force in the Baltic States which managed to hold back a series of offensives by the Red Army.

The 19th SS Division fought at the long-drawn-out Battle of Narva along with many other Germanic and volunteer SS units. It was later trapped in the Courland pocket as the German forces in the Baltic

States retreated from the advancing Soviet juggernaut. Little has been documented about the division's record in the last months of the war, but there are rumours that some divisional units may have mutinied at the end of 1944.

Commanders

Standartenführer Hinrich Schuldt
May 1943 – July 1943

Oberführer Fritz Freitag
August 1943

Brigadeführer Hinrich Schuldt
September 1943 – March 1944

Standartenführer Friedrich-Wilhelm Bock
March 1944 – April 1944

Gruppenführer Bruno Steckenbach
April 1944 – May 1945

COMBAT UNIT ORGANIZATION

INSIGNIA

The symbol of the 19th SS Division was simply an 'L' for Latvia together with the Roman numeral 'II' to indicate that it was the second Latvian division.

▲ **2cm Fliegerabwehrkanone (Flak 38)**

52.SS-Panzerjäger-Abteilung / Flak-Kompanie

The 19th SS Division was supposed to have had its own Flak battalion, but though the 52.*Flak-Abteilung* was formed it was never incorporated into the division. The only Flak unit in the division was a company in the *Panzerjäger-Abteilung*.

▲ **Leichte Personenkraftwagen VW (Kfz 1)**

42.Waffen-Grenadier-Regiment der SS / Stab-Kompanie

Waffen Grenadier divisions, as distinct from Panzergrenadier divisions, were equipped as ordinary infantry formations. Motorization was limited to staff units and some tank-hunter and support units, including a supply troop which had two truck companies and two horse-drawn companies.

Specifications

Crew: 4

Weight: 420kg (920lb)

Length: 2.25m (7ft 5in)

Calibre: 20mm (0.7in)

Muzzle Velocity (HE): 900m/s (2953fps)

Rate of fire: 420–480rpm

Range (ceiling): HE: 2200m (7218ft)

Ammunition: High explosive

Projectile weight: 0.119kg (0.262lb)

Specifications

Crew: 1

Weight: 0.64 tonnes (0.58 tons)

Length: 3.73m (12ft 3in)

Width: 1.60m (5ft 3in)

Height: 1.35m (4ft 5in)

Engine: Volkswagen 998cc petrol (24hp). Later
Volkswagen 1131cc petrol (25hp)

Speed: 100km/h (62mph)

Range: 600km (375 miles)

Radio: None

20th Waffen Grenadier Division der SS

Following the German occupation of the Baltic States, large numbers of Estonians volunteered to fight against the hated Soviets. Some were later to join the *Waffen-SS*.

THE 20. *WAFFEN-GRENADIER-DIVISION* der SS (*estnische Nr. 1*) was formed from the 3. *Estnische SS-Freiwilligen-Brigade* and was directly descended from the Estonian Legion, authorized by Adolf Hitler in August 1942.

Soon after the occupation of Estonia, the Germans began to allow the formation of Estonian units, variously called security, police or defence battalions or companies. The primary purpose of these units was to provide security in German rear areas, which came to mean fighting partisans. Volunteers were plentiful, and by March 1942 there were 16 Estonian battalions and companies, with 10,000 men on active duty in Russia. Eventually more than 50 such units were to be formed, with as many as 25,000 Estonians under arms.

Their experience of Soviet oppression at first hand meant that the Baltic States were seen by the SS as potentially valuable recruiting grounds for foreign volunteer legions to take part in the 'crusade' against Communism. On 28 August 1942, the *Waffen-SS*

Commanders	
Brigadeführer Franz Augsberger *October 1942 – March 1945*	Brigadeführer Berthold Maack *March 1945 – May 1945*

INSIGNIA

The symbol of the 20. *Waffen-Grenadier-Division der SS* (*estnische Nr. 1*) was a stylized letter 'E' (for Estonia) overlaid with a dagger or shortsword.

announced the intended formation of the *Estnische Freiwilligen-SS-Legion*. By the end of the year, 1280 men were under training at Debica in Poland as the 1. *Estnische SS-Freiwilligen-Grenadier-Regiment*.

Estonian grenadiers

The regiment-sized legion took some time to organize, becoming operational in the spring of 1943. Formed as a motorized infantry regiment, the legion was referred to in German orders as the 1. *Estnische SS-Freiwilligen-Grenadier-Regiment*. It quickly grew to brigade size, however. In March

▲ **10.5cm leichte Feldhaubitze (leFH18)**

20. SS-Artillerie-Regiment / I.Bataillon / 1.Batterie

The Estonian division had a four-battalion artillery regiment. Three of the battalions were equipped with towed leFH18s, while the fourth operated 15cm (5.9in) heavy field howitzers.

ORGANIZATION

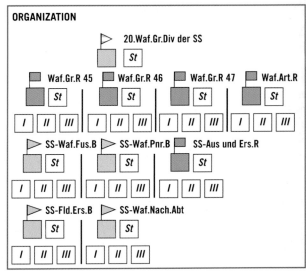

Specifications	
Crew: 5	Muzzle Velocity: 540m/s (1770fps)
Weight: 1.95 tonnes (1.85 tons)	Range: 12,325m (13,480 yards)
Length: 3.3m (10ft)	Ammunition: High explosive or smoke
Calibre: 105mm (4.1in)	

▶ Estonian tank riders

Detached from the *Estnische SS-Freiwilligen-Brigade* in 1943, the *Narva* Battalion was assigned to the crack *SS-Panzergrenadier-Regiment Nordland*, part of the 5th SS Panzer Division *Wiking*.

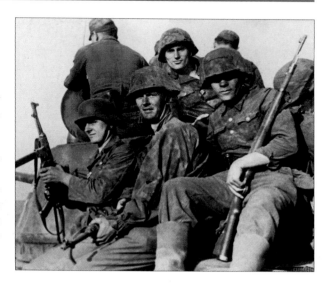

1943, one battalion was detached as the *Estnische SS-Freiwilligen-Bataillon Narva*, replacing the disbanded Finnish battalion as the third battalion of the *Nordland* regiment of the *Wiking* Division.

At the same time, continuing manpower shortages led to reinforcements being conscripted in Estonia, around 12,000 men being called into service. Some 5300 were sent to the legion battalions training at Debica, which were reinforced and organized as the 3.*SS-Freiwilligen-Brigade*. The remaining conscripts were sent to German Army units.

Estonian SS division

The 20.*Estnische SS-Freiwilligen-Division* was established in January 1944. Its component units were engaged in action at the front during the three-month campaign known as the Battle of the Narva, which meant that formation took longer than expected. In May 1944, the division was some 5000 men understrength, and its build-up was expedited under Himmler's orders. However, it did not reach combat strength until July 1944.

In September, many Estonian troops were released from German service, and the remnants of the division were evacuated from Estonia along with the rest of the German forces. The division was reconstructed at *Truppenübungsplatz* Neuhammer from October 1944. In Estonian it was known as the 20.*SS-Relvagrenadieride Diviis (Eesti Esimene)*. In February 1945, the formation was so weakened that

it was now referred to as a battle group (*SS-Kampfgruppe*) rather than a division, possibly named *Kampfgruppe Augsberger* after the divisional commander. It continued fighting in Silesia and later in Czechoslovakia until the end of the war, when parts of the formation surrendered to the Western Allies while the main body of the division surrendered to the Soviets north of Prague.

Divisional History	Formed
Estnische Freiwilligen-SS-Legion	1942
Estnische SS-Freiwilligen-Brigade	1943
3.Estnische SS-Freiwilligen-Brigade	1943
20.Estnische SS-Freiwilligen-Division	1944
20.Waffen-Grenadier-Division der SS (estnische Nr. 1)	1944

▶ Mittlere Zugkraftwagen 3t (SdKfz 11)

20.SS-Panzerjäger-Abteilung / 1.(mot) Panzerjäger-Kompanie

The SdKfz 11 was the standard 3-tonne (2.94-ton) tractor used by the *Wehrmacht*. It towed a variety of light and medium artillery pieces, including the 7.5cm (3in) Pak 40 and the 10.5cm (4.1in) leFH18.

Specifications

Crew: 1 plus 8 troops
Weight: 7.1 tonnes (6.46 tons)
Length: 5.48m (18ft 0in)
Width: 1.82m (5ft 11.5in)
Height: 1.62m (5ft 4in)
Engine: 6-cylinder petrol (100hp)
Speed: 53km/h (32.9mph)
Range: 122km (75.8 miles)
Radio: None

Chapter 4

Late-War Divisions

Even though the war had turned decisively
against Germany in 1943 and 1944, nothing could stop
Heinrich Himmler's ambitions for the SS. More and more
divisions were formed, but the nature of the organization had
changed. The most committed of the foreign volunteers
found a home in the *Waffen-SS*, until large parts of it were
more like a German 'Foreign Legion' than the elite of the
German race, which it had been in the earlier days
of the Third *Reich*.

◀ **Belgian volunteers**

SS volunteers parade in Brussels, July 1944. Even at this late stage of the war, with German forces being
pushed back both in France and on the Eastern Front, fresh volunteers were found to fill the ranks of
Himmler's rapidly expanding SS.

21st Waffen Gebirgs Division der SS *Skanderbeg*

On 17 April 1944, *Reichsführer-SS* Heinrich Himmler approved the formation of an Albanian *Waffen-SS* division. The SS Main Office envisioned an Albanian formation of 10,000 troops.

A REINFORCED BATTALION OF approximately 300 ethnic Albanians serving in the Bosnian Muslim 13th Waffen Gebirgs Division der SS *Handschar* were transferred to the newly forming division. To this Albanian core were added veteran German troops from Austria plus *Volksdeutsche* officers, NCOS and enlisted men, as well as a number of *Kriegsmarine* sailors who no longer had ships. The total strength of the Albanian *Waffen-SS* division would be 8500–9000 men.

The 21.*Waffen-Gebirgs-Division der SS Skanderbeg* did not acquire a good reputation. Intended to combat partisans, it was used in its earliest days to massacre Orthodox Serb civilians in Kosovo-Metohija. Over 10,000 Serbian families were forced to flee Kosovo. Albanian colonists and settlers from northern Albania took over their lands and homes. The goal of many members of the *Skanderbeg* Division was not to fight for the Germans; rather it was to advance Albanian nationalism by deporting and killing the non-Albanian populations of Western Macedonia, creating an ethnically pure and homogeneous region of Greater Albania, free of Serbs, Jews and Roma (Gypsies). The *Skanderbeg* Division targeted all of these groups when the formation occupied Tetovo and Skopje and other towns and cities in Western Macedonia.

Commanders

Brigadeführer Josef Fitzhum	Oberführer August Schmidthuber
April 1944 – May 1944	*May 1944 – January 1945*

In October 1944, the *Skanderbeg* Division occupied Skopje, the capital of Macedonia. By November 1944, the Germans were withdrawing their forces from the Aegean islands and from Greece. Called on to fight in something other than their own private war, many of the division's members deserted – so many, in fact, that the unit could not function as a division. The formation's remnants were reorganized into *Regimentgruppe 21.SS-Gebirgs-Skanderbeg*, which was concentrated at Skopje. The *Kampfgruppe Skanderbeg*, in conjunction with the 7th SS Volunteer Mountain Division *Prinz Eugen*, defended the valley of the Vardar River in Macedonia to allow *Generaloberst* Alexander Löhr's Army Group E to retreat from Greece and the Aegean. The Vardar Valley was crucial as an escape corridor.

By January 1945, remnants of the *Skanderbeg* Division had retreated to Kosovska Mitrovica in Kosovo and then to Brcko in Bosnia-Herzegovina. The *Skanderbeg* remnants would reach Austria in May 1945, when Germany surrendered following the military and political collapse of the regime.

INSIGNIA

The divisional symbol of the *Skanderbeg* Division was the double-headed eagle of Albania, mounted on the Gebirgs-style SS shield.

Divisional History	Formed
Waffen-Gebirgs-Division der SS Skanderbeg (albanische Nr. 1)	1944
21.Waffen-Gebirgs-Division der SS Skanderbeg (albanische Nr. 1)	1944

ORGANIZATION

▲ **3.7cm Panzerabwehrkanone (Pak 35/36)**
21.SS-Aufklärungs-Abteilung / 1.Kompanie (mot) / Panzerjäger-Zug

Although obsolete, the 3.7cm (1.5in) Pak 35/36 was an effective weapon against partisans. With a weight of about 430kg (946lb), it was also a relatively light and handy weapon more suited to operations in mountainous terrain than were larger anti-tank guns.

Specifications

Crew: 3	Muzzle Velocity: 762m/s (2500fps)
Weight: 0.43 tonnes (0.39 tons)	Range: 600m (656 yards)
Length: 1.67m (5ft 5.5in)	Ammunition: Armour-piercing
Calibre: 37mm (1.5in)	

▲ **Mittlerer Nachrichten Kraftwagen (Kfz 15)**
21.SS-Freiwilligen-Nachrichten-Abteilung

The 21st Mountain Signals Battalion was made up of three companies – two mountain telephone companies and a mountain radio company. The Kfz 15 medium car was standard equipment in communications units, at least 30 being in the standard table of equipment of a battalion.

Specifications

Crew: 1	Engine: Skoda 3.1L petrol (80–85hp)
Weight: 2.4 tonnes (2.2 tons)	Speed: 100km/h (62mph)
Length: 4.8m (15ft 9in)	Range: 400km (250 miles)
Width: 1.80m (5ft 9in)	Radio: None
Height: 1.72m (5ft 3in)	

22nd SS Freiwilligen Kavallerie Division *Maria Theresia*

The SS formed a second cavalry division in the spring of 1944. The idea was that the new formation would serve with the *Florian Geyer* Division as part of an SS cavalry corps.

THE *MARIA THERESIA* DIVISION was formed in May 1944. Assembled at Kisber, Hungary, it was based on a nucleus provided by the 17.*SS-Kavallerie-Regiment* transferred from the 8.*SS-Kavallerie-Division Florian Geyer.*

The bulk of the strength of the division was provided by Hungarian *Volksdeutsche*, who had originally been drafted by the Hungarian Army but had been transferred to the *Waffen-SS* following an agreement between the German and Hungarian Governments.

The symbol of the division was a cornflower, adopted since it was the favourite flower of the Empress Maria Theresa (Theresia in German) of Austria, after whom the division had been named.

In September 1944, a detachment from *Maria Theresia*, consisting of 52.*SS-Kavallerie-Regiment*, was assigned to a *Kampfgruppe* commanded by *SS-*

ORGANIZATION

22.SS-Fre.Kav.Div Maria Theresia

SS-Kav.Rgt 52 SS-Kav.Rgt 53 SS-Kav.Rgt 54 SS-Kav.R 17

SS-Pz.Auf.Abt SS-Pzjr.A 22 SS-Art.Rgt 22

Hauptsturmführer Toni Ameiser. *Kampfgruppe* Ameiser was deployed to Romania. It was unable to reach its designated positions because of the advance of the Red Army, and after fighting alongside Hungarian troops it was encircled by the Soviets.

Break out

One section of the *Kampfgruppe*, commanded by *SS-Hauptsturmführer* Harry Vandieken, fought its way to the Harmas River, swimming across to the safety of the German-held bank. The second part of the *Kampfgruppe*, commanded by Ameiser himself, remained in the trap for a month, eventually fighting its way through to the German lines south of Budapest on 30 October.

Battle for Budapest

The rest of the *Maria Theresia* Division was still in training when it was sent to reinforce Budapest in November 1944.

When the Red Army closed a ring of iron around the Hungarian capital, the formation was destroyed along with most of the rest of the German defenders.

Commanders
Brigadeführer August Zehender
April 1944 – February 1945

Divisional History	Formed
22.SS-Freiwilligen-Kavallerie-Division Maria Theresia	1944

INSIGNIA

The divisional symbol of the *Maria Theresia* Division was the cornflower, the favourite bloom of the empress (1717–1780) after whom the division was named.

Only 170 men managed to make it through the Soviet lines to safety. The survivors, along with those parts of the Maria Theresia Division that had not been sent into Budapest, were used as the core of the newly formed 37.SS-Freiwilligen-Kavallerie-Division Lützow. What was left of the divisional Flak units was transferred to 32.SS-Freiwilligen-Grenadier-Division 30 Januar.

23rd Waffen Gebirgs Division der SS *Kama*

Approval was given for the raising of a second Croatian *Waffen-SS* division on 17 June 1944, even though the reliability of many of the personnel intended for the unit was questionable.

THE 23.*WAFFEN-GEBIRGS-DIVISION* der SS *Kama* *(kroatische Nr. 2)* was recruited from Croatian volunteers, including both *Volksdeutsche* anti-Communist Croats and Bosnian Muslims. In common with many volunteer divisions, the formation was stiffened by a German cadre of senior NCOs and officers.

Further strength was supplied by its sister formation, the 13th SS Division *Handschar*, which provided its reconnaissance battalion and a number of Croat officers and NCOs. Like the *Handschar*, the new division was named after a traditional weapon from the region – in this case, a short Turkish sword or long fighting knife known as a *kama*.

Commanders	
Standartenführer Helmuth Raithel	Oberführer Gustav Lombard
July 1944 – September 1944	*September 1944*

Divisional History	Formed
23.Waffen-Gebirgs-Division der SS Kama (kroatische Nr. 2)	1944

Kama never reached anything like its planned strength. At its peak, in September 1944, it had a total of 3793 men in training to play their part in the anti-partisan war. That training was taking place at Backa in Hungary, far enough from the main areas of partisan action as to be safe from attack.

They were not safe from the Red Army, however, which by the end of September was advancing perilously close to the divisional training grounds in southern Hungary. The SS wanted the division to be ready for combat by the end of September, but as the troops still had not completed basic training this was never a realistic prospect.

Disbanded without combat

On 1 October 1944, as the Red Army advanced into Hungary, the SS decided to disband the *Kama* Division, transferring already formed units as replacements to other divisions. Most of the division's personnel were used to form the 31.*SS-Freiwilligen-Grenadier-Division*.

The Muslims of *Kama* were transferred to the *Handschar* Division. Most reported for duty, but a large minority, who had signed on primarily to fight for their homeland, deserted en route. The divisional designation '23' was assigned to the newly forming SS volunteer Panzergrenadier division being created from Dutch volunteers.

ORGANIZATION

▲ 7.5cm Panzerabwehrkanone (Pak 40)
Panzer-Aufklärungs-Abteilung 23

Although the divisional Panzerjäger battalion had become fully self-propelled over the winter of 1943/44, the Panzerjäger platoon of the reconnaissance battalion's heavy company was equipped with three towed Pak 40s.

Specifications

Crew: 3
Weight: 1.5 tonnes (1.37 tons)
Length: 3.7m (12ft 1.5in)
Calibre: 75mm (3in)

Muzzle Velocity (AP): 990m/s (3248fps)
Range: AP: 2000m (2190 yards), HE: 7.5km
(4.66 miles)
Ammunition: Armour-piercing, high explosive

▶ Leichter Einheits Pkw Stoewer 40 (Kfz 2)
SS-Gebirgs-Nachrichten-Abteilung 23

Although the division began forming with a full table of organization, few of its component units were even partially manned or equipped. The divisional communications battalion would have operated a few communications cars before the formation was abandoned.

Specifications

Crew: 1
Weight: 1.81 tonnes (1.65 tons)
Length: 3.58m (11ft 9in)
Width: 1.57m (5ft 2in)
Height: 1.78 (5ft 10in)

Engine: Stoewer AW2 or R180W petrol (50hp)
Speed: 100km/h (62mph)
Range: 500km (311 miles)
Radio: Various

23rd SS Freiwilligen Panzergrenadier Division *Nederland*

In 1943, when it was clear that the national legions within the SS would never achieve great success, Dutch Nazi leader Anton Mussert suggested that a Dutch SS division be formed.

Howe ver, finding 20,000 men in the time scale envisaged proved to be impossible. Nevertheless, a brigade-sized formation was possible, and the *SS-Freiwilligen-Panzergrenadier-Brigade Nederland* was formed in October 1943 as part of the further expansion of the *Waffen-SS*. Some 2500 veteran legionnaires joined the brigade with an additional 3000 volunteers from the SS *Nordland* Regiment. The 23.*SS-Freiwilligen-Panzergrenadier-Division Nederland (niederlandische Nr. 1)* was formed on 10 February 1945, when the *SS-Freiwilligen-Panzergrenadier-Brigade Nederland* was upgraded to divisional status.

The *Nederland* Brigade had been composed of two regiments: the *General Seyffardt* (named after the first legion commander, who had been assassinated by the Dutch resistance earlier that year) and the *De Ruyter* Regiment (named after the seventeenth-century Dutch admiral Michael de Ruyter).

The *Nederland* Brigade had been in action in the Baltic States from the end of 1943, and had shared in the retreat from Leningrad to the Narva Line and back to the Courland pocket. Along with the rest of

INSIGNIA

The 23rd SS Freiwilligen Panzergrenadier Division *Nederland* adopted a variant of the ancient runic sumbol for 'O' as its divisional symbol.

Commanders

Sturmbannführer Herbert Garthe *November 1941 – February 1942*	Standartenführer Josef Fitzthum *July 19423 – May 1943*
Oberführer Otto Reich *February –March 1942*	Brigadeführer Jürgen Wagner *October 1943 – May 1945*
Obersturmbannführer Arved Theuermann *April–May 1942*	

Divisional History	Formed
SS-Freiwilligen-Verband-Niederlande	1941
SS-Freiwilligen-Legion-Niederlande	1941
4.SS-Freiwilligen-Panzergrenadier-Brigade Nederland	1943
SS-Freiwilligen-Panzergrenadier-Brigade Nederland	1944
23.SS-Freiwilligen-Panzergrenadier-Division Nederland (niederlandische Nr. 1)	1945

Specifications

Crew: 3

Weight: 9.4 tonnes (8.53 tons)

Length: 5.98m (19ft 7in)

Width: 2.83m (9ft 4in)

Height: 2.07m (6ft 10in)

Engine: Maybach HL42TUKRM

Speed: 53km/h (33mph)

Range: 300km (186 miles)

Radio: FuG Spr Ger 'f'

Armament: 1 x 75mm (3in) KwK L/24 gun

▲ **Mittlerer Schützenpanzerwagen Ausf C 7.5cm (SdKfz 251/9)**

SS Frw Pzg Regt 49 / III Bataillon / 12. (schwere) Kompanie

The 49th Volunteer Panzergrenadier Regiment, known as the de Ruyter Regiment, was named after the Dutch seventeenth-century admiral Michael Adriaenszoon de Ruyter. The 3rd Battalion was equipped with half-tracks.

III SS-Korps, *Nederland* was evacuated by sea to Stettin, where the brigade was to form part of the defensive line on the Oder.

The SS had originally intended for the Dutch soldiers to be assigned to the *Nordland* Division, but after protests from the Dutch Nazi party, the *Nationaal Socialistische Beweging* (NSB), it was decided that they would form their own division. *Nederland* was given the number '23' when the *Kama* Division was disbanded.

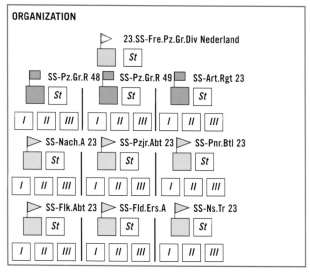

Last battles in the East

Nederland, together with the SS Divisions *Nordland*, *Wallonien* and *Langemarck*, was responsible for the defence of the Oder Front between the towns of Stettin and Neustadt.

In April 1945, Nederland was split up. The 48th Regiment General Seyffardt was destroyed near Hammerstein while fighting with the 15th SS Grenadier Division. The 13 soldiers that were captured were executed by the Soviets.

At the end of April, the 49th Regiment *De Ruyter*, which had remained on the Oder Front, was forced to withdraw to the west, around the north of Berlin.

On 3 May 1945, near the village of Parchim, the regiment destroyed an attacking Red Army tank unit, and then its members heard more tanks approaching – from the west. These proved to be Americans, and the 49th Regiment was happy to surrender to them. The *23.SS-Freiwilligen-Panzergrenadier-Division Nederland* had had little more than 1000 effective combatants when it fought its last battles on the Eastern Front.

Specifications

Crew: 6	Speed: 42km/h (26mph)
Weight: 26.5 tonnes (24 tons)	Range: 215km (133.6 miles)
Length: 7.17m (23ft 6in)	Radio: FuG Spr 1
Width: 2.97m (9ft 8in)	Armament: 1 x 150mm (5.9in) sFH 18/1 L/30;
Height: 2.81m (9ft 2in)	1 x 7.92mm (0.3in) MG
Engine: Maybach HL120TRM (265hp)	

▲ **15cm schwere Panzerhaubitze auf Geschützwagen III/IV (SdKfz 165)**

SS Artillerie Regiment 23 / I Abteilung / 1. Batterie

The 1st Battalion of the 23rd Artillery Regiment was equipped as a standard late-war self-propelled unit, with one battery equipped with 15-cm (6in) Hummels and two batteries with smaller 10.5-cm (4.2in) Wespe self-propelled guns. Each battery had six guns. The other two battalions were equipped with towed guns and howitzers.

24th Waffen Gebirgs (*Karstjäger*) Division der SS

Descended from a unit formed to fight Italian and Yugoslav partisans in the highest peaks of the Dolomites, the *Karstjäger* was a division in name only.

THE *SS-KARSTWEHR-BATAILLON* had been fighting partisans in northern Italy and the Dolomites since 1942. On 1 August 1944, it was upgraded to become 24.*Waffen-Gebirgs-(Karstjäger-) Division der SS*, though it was never more than brigade-sized. It was redesignated as the *Waffen-Gebirgs-(Karstjäger-) Brigade der SS* on 5 December 1944 but once again upgraded to division on 10 February 1945.

Originally under the control of the *Höheren SS- und Polizei-Führers Adriatisches Meer* (Higher SS- and Police- *Führer* Adriatic), it was manned mainly by Italian volunteers but also contained volunteers from Slovenia, Croatia, Serbia and the Ukraine. *Karstjäger* mainly fought partisans in Istria, with considerable success, but at the end of the war it found itself facing the Western Allies advancing through Italy. On 8 May 1945, *Karstjäger* surrendered to the British.

ORGANIZATION

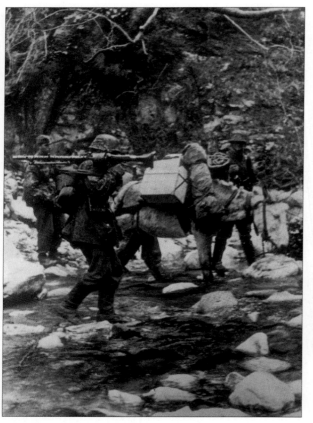

Divisional History	Formed
SS-Karstwehr-Kompanie	1942
SS-Karstwehr-Bataillon	1942
24.Waffen-Gebirgs-(Karstjäger-) Division der SS	1944

Commanders

Standartenführer Dr Hans Brand
November 1942 – 1943

Sturmbannführer Josef Berschneider
1943 – August 1944)

Obersturmbannführer Karl Marx
? August 1944 – 5 December 1944

Sturmbannführer Werner Hahn
5 December 1944 – 10 February 1945

Oberführer Adolf Wagner
10 February 1945 – 8 May 1945

◀ Mule carriers

SS troops ford a stream in the Dolomite Mountains, early 1944. Mules were essential transport for divisions operating in the mountainous Balkans.

25th Waffen Grenadier Division der SS *Hunyadi*

The Hungarian Government originally forbade Germany from recruiting amongst its citizens, but in 1943 Hitler pressured Prime Minister Miklos Kallay to permit conscription of *Volksdeutsche*.

AFTER IT BECAME CLEAR that the Germans were on the retreat in Russia, the Regent, Admiral Horthy, and Prime Minister Kallay sought to negotiate a separate armistice for Hungary with the Western Allies. To keep Hungary (and its vital oil reserves) in the Axis fold, the Germans occupied the country on 19 March 1944.

Horthy was permitted to remain Regent, but Kallay was replaced by General Dome Sztojay, head of the Hungarian Arrow Cross fascists and fanatically pro-German. Sztojay's appointment freed the SS to recruit actively among the Hungarian population.

Hungarian SS division

Towards the end of October 1944, the SS and police commander in Hungary asked the Hungarian Government to provide the manpower for two SS divisions. The Hungarians agreed – on condition that they would fight in Hungary only, and only against the Soviets.

Himmler ordered that the 25th Waffen Grenadier Division der SS *Hunyadi* be raised. By the end of November, strength had reached 16,700 men, most being former members of the 13th *Honvéd* Light Infantry Division. It included 1000 men from *Kampfgruppe Deák*, the first Hungarian SS unit, who were used to form the 61.*SS-Grenadier-Regiment*. *Kampfgruppe Deák* had been raised from Hungarian Army and police volunteers in August 1944 and had seen action in the Banat. *Waffen-Schibataillon der SS 25* was created from Hungarian Army mountain troops. Some divisional troops were transferred from *Waffen-SS* training schools, but the bulk of the manpower came from Hungarian recruiting depots.

Commanders

Standartenführer Thomas Müller *November 1944*	Gruppenführer Josef Grassy *November 1944 – 8 May 1945*

INSIGNIA

The main image on the *Hunyadi* Division's symbol was the 'Arrow Cross' of the *Nyilaskeresztes Párt* – Hungary's pre-war fascist movement.

Transferred to the *Truppenübungsplatz* (training ground) at Neuhammer in Germany, the division was still far from operational when the Red Army entered Silesia. With over 22,000 men in the camp, together with many wives and families, Neuhammer was seriously overcrowded, and it was a relief when orders were given that the division should retreat to Bavaria. The 25.*Waffen-Grenadier-Division der SS Hunyadi (ungarische Nr. 1)* surrendered to the Americans after a brief firefight at Salzkammergut in Austria.

▲ **15cm schwere Infanterie Geschütz sIG33**

SS Waffen-Grenadier-Regiment 61 / Infanterie Geschütz Kompanie
Waffen-Grenadier Regiment der SS 61 was one of three such formations attached to the first Hungarian SS division. The 'Grenadier' designation was applied to standard infantry divisions and regiments in the later years of the war.

Divisional History	Formed
25.SS-Freiwilligen-Grenadier-Division	1944
25.Waffen-Grenadier-Division der SS Hunyadi (ungarische Nr. 1)	1944

Specifications

Crew: 5	Muzzle Velocity: 241m/s (783fps)
Weight: 1.75 tonnes (1.6 tons)	Range: 5504m (6000 yards)
Length: 1.64m (64.57in)	Ammunition: High explosive or smoke
Calibre: 150mm (5.9in)	

26th SS Panzer Division

The 26th SS Division was the Panzer division that wasn't. Created primarily as a propaganda and disinformation exercise, it never reached divisional strength.

SHORTLY AFTER THE NORMANDY invasion began on 6 June 1944, the *SS-Kampfgruppen* 1, 2, 3 and 4 (composed for the most part of emergency battalions from SS schools and replacement units) were mobilized. Only two of these formations were sent to the front, however. These were *SS-Kampfgruppe* 1 (later to become *SS-Panzergrenadier-Brigade* 49) and *SS-Kampfgruppe* 3 (later *SS-Panzergrenadier-Brigade* 51). Considered sister units, the two brigades would fight on the same sector of the Western Front.

SS-Panzergrenadier-Brigade 49 was a battalion stronger than its sibling, *SS-Panzergrenadier-Brigade* 51, and it lasted for a few days longer in the extremely destructive combat action. The two brigades were designated 26.*SS-Panzer-Division* and 27.*SS-Panzer-Division* respectively, for a very short time, in an attempt to mislead the Allies into thinking that they were much larger formations.

The 26th SS Panzer Division was ostensibly formed on 10 August 1944 and was disbanded on 8 September 1944 after combat in Champagne. Surviving elements of the formation, which never reached divisional strength, were absorbed by the 17th SS Panzergrenadier Division *Götz von Berlichingen*. A similar fate befell the 26th SS Division's sister formation.

ORGANIZATIONS

SS-Pz.Gr.Brig 49
St
I II III Art Flk Pnr Kfr

Commanders

Sturmbannführer Markus Haulhaber
June 1944 – August 1944

Divisional History	Formed
SS-Kampfgruppe 1	1944
49.SS-Panzergrenadier-Brigade	1944
26.SS-Panzer-Division	1944

26th Waffen Grenadier Division der SS *Hungaria*

The second SS division raised in Hungary was the 26th Waffen Grenadier Division der SS *Hungaria*. Its formation was ordered at the end of November 1944.

THE 26.*WAFFEN-GRENADIER-DIVISION* der SS *Hungaria (ungarische Nr. 2)*, sometimes referred to as the *Gombos* Division, was formed under the authority of the Hungarian defence minister, at the request of *Reichsführer-SS* Heinrich Himmler. *Waffen-Schibataillon der SS* 26, raised from the Hungarian Army, was ordered to join the new division. Late in December 1944, 5000 civilian

ORGANIZATION

26.Waf.Gr.Div der SS Hungaria
St

Waf.Gr.R 64   Waf.Gr.R 65   Waf.Gr.R 85   W.Art.R 26
St   St   St   St
I II III   I II III   I II III   I II III

INSIGNIA

Hungaria used the same symbol as the *Hunyadi* Division, an 'Arrow Cross' surmounted by two crowns, possibly signifying the dual monarchy of Austria-Hungary.

raftees brought the strength up to 8000. By January, divisional strength was up to more than 16,000, and the formation had been moved to Siederatz in Poland for training. The formation was short of equipment and food – weapons were issued early in January, just in time to allow foraging parties to fight off attacks by Polish partisans.

Fighting retreat as training

Forced to retreat by the Soviet winter offensive (minus mortars and machine guns, which had been taken by the German Ninth Army), the partially trained division reached the Oder after suffering over 2500 casualties. Plans to refit at Neuhammer were dashed on 8 February, when the Soviets attacked the training ground. This forced the still untrained

division to make a headlong retreat towards southern Germany. The more experienced members served as a rearguard while the rest retreated westwards.

As part of XVII. *Waffen-Armee-Korps der SS (ungarisches)*, the *Hungaria* Division retreated into Austria, where it surrendered to the Western Allies at Attersee. Many of the division's surviving troops were turned over to the Soviets, and were destined for the *gulag* or the firing squad.

27th SS Panzer Division

The 27th SS Panzer Division was the name given to *SS-Panzergrenadier-Brigade* 51 in an attempt to mislead the Allies into thinking that it was a much larger formation.

THE *SS-PANZERGRENADIER-BRIGADE* 51 was formed in March 1944 as *SS-Kampfgruppe* 3. Much of its personnel came from the SS NCO school at Lauenberg, Pomerania. It was not fully activated until after the Allied landings in Normandy. On 18 June 1944, *SS-Kampfgruppe* 3 officially became *SS-Panzergrenadier-Brigade* 51 and was deployed to Denmark to relieve the 363rd Infantry Division, which was sent to Normandy.

On 4 August, the 51st SS Brigade was ordered to France. Commanded by *SS-Sturmbannführer* Walter Jöckel, the brigade's 3000 troops headed for Troyes. On 10 August 1944, the brigade assumed the title of 27.*SS-Panzer-Division*, though internally it still used its old title. It was also referred to by official sources

as the *Stamm Regiment/27.SS-Panzer-Division* – that is, the 27th's 'nucleus' regiment.

Into combat

The *SS-Panzergrenadier-Brigade* 51 first saw action on 22 August at Sens, when one battalion served alongside a battalion of Army Security Regiment 199. On 23 August, Allied pressure forced them to withdraw to the Seine. Briefly cut off in Troyes by resistance attacks, the brigade headquarters ordered the other units of the formation to fight their way to the Seine independently.

The 1st battalion was all but destroyed on 25 August in a series of running battles at St Savine and Fontvannes. The brigade staff was captured by the Americans on 28 August; only the 2nd Battalion was reasonably intact.

The disintegrating brigade could do little else but retreat towards Verdun and Metz to the northeast, reaching safety with the 3rd Panzer Division near St Dizier. After the fighting in Champagne, the formation was disbanded on 9 September 1944. The brigade's surviving troops and equipment were absorbed by the 17.*SS-Panzergrenadier-Division Götz von Berlichingen*.

Divisional History	Formed
SS-Kampfgruppe 3	1944
51.SS-Panzergrenadier-Brigade	1944
27.SS-Panzer-Division	1944

27th SS Freiwilligen Grenadier Division *Langemarck*

The division was formed on 19 October 1944, when the 6.*SS-Freiwilligen-Sturmbrigade Langemarck* was upgraded to divisional status.

THE *LANGEMARCK* DIVISION, named after a village near Ypres which saw some of the bloodiest fighting in the Great War of 1914–1918, descended directly from the SS Flemish Legion, the original Flemish volunteer unit in the *Waffen-SS*.

The Flemish Legion had been less than impressive in its early actions on the Eastern Front, but experience had shown that the volunteers from Flanders could fight – and fight hard. Although the legion had been withdrawn from combat by the beginning of 1943, it was expanded to form the *Sturmbrigade Langemarck* with the addition of fresh recruits from Flanders, a Finnish battalion and several German artillery and support units. The *Sturmbrigade* was attached to the *Das Reich* Division in the Ukraine, before being sent to the Leningrad Front as part of *SS-Obergruppenführer*

Felix Steiner's III.*SS-Panzerkorps* (*Germanisches*).

The *Langemarck* Brigade took part in the fighting retreat from the Baltic, and played its part in the long

INSIGNIA

The division's insignia was a triskelion, claimed by the Nazis to be an ancient Celtic symbol and so suitable for a division made up from 'Celtic' volunteers.

ORGANIZATIONS

27 SS-Fri-Grn-Div Langemarck — St

SS-PzGrn 66 — St | SS-PzGrn 67 — St | SS-PzGrn 68 — St | SS-Art 27 — St

I | II | III   I | II | III   I | II | III   I | II | III

SS-Pzjr 27 — St | Kmp-Sch — St

I | II | III   I | II | III

Commanders

Sturmbannführer Michael Lippert
September 1941 – April 1942

Oberstumbannführer Hans Albert
von Lettow-Vorbeck *April 1942 – June 1942*

Hauptsturmführer Hallmann
June 1942

Oberstumbannführer Josef Fitzthum
June 1942 – July 1942

Oberstumbannführer Conrad Schellong
July 1942 – October 1944

Standartenführer Thomas Müller
October 1944 – May 1945)

▲ **7.5cm Sturmgeschütz Ausf G (SdKfz 142/1)**

Sturmbrigade Langemarck / Sturmgeschütz-Batterie

The *Langemarck* Brigade had a battery of assault guns attached when the formation was created around members of the disbanded Flemish Legion in the summer of 1943.

Specifications

Crew: 4

Weight: 26.3 tonnes (23.9 tons)

Length: 6.77m (22ft 2in)

Width: 2.95m (9ft 8in)

Height: 2.16m (7ft 0in)

Engine: Maybach HL120TRM

Speed: 40km/h (25mph)

Range: 155km (96.3 miles)

Radio: FuG15 and FuG16

Armament: 1 x 75mm (3in) StuG L/48 cannon

Divisional History	Formed
SS-Freiwilligen-Legion Flandern	1941
SS-Sturmbrigade Langemarck	1943
6.SS-Freiwilligen-Sturmbrigade Langemarck	1943
27.SS-Freiwilligen-Grenadier-Division Langemarck (flämische Nr. 1)	1944

▲ **Leichter Personenkraftwagen VW (Kfz 1)**

27.SS-Füsilier-Bataillon / Stab

Fusilier battalions were infantry units with reconnaissance capability, introduced mid-war when the standard infantry regiment reduced from nine battalions to six.

Specifications

Crew: 1

Weight: 0.64 tonnes (0.58 tons)

Length: 3.73m (12ft 3in)

Width: 1.60m (5ft 3in)

Height: 1.35m (4ft 5in)

Engine: Volkswagen 998cc petrol (24hp). Later Volkswagen 1131cc petrol (25hp)

Speed: 100km/h (62mph)

Range: 600km (375 miles)

Radio: None

sequence of fierce battles on the Narva. In the autumn of 1944, the brigade was refitting on the Lüneburg Heath when it was upgraded to become *27.SS-Freiwilligen-Grenadier-Division Langemarck (flämische Nr. 1)*, though it never really approached divisional size. In February 1945, it went into action with the Eleventh Army and then with the Third Panzer Army in Pomerania. Most of the division surrendered at Mecklenburg, though a battle group that had been detached was used in the final defence of Berlin.

28th SS Panzer Division

The Soviet summer offensive in 1944 threatened to cut off large numbers of German troops in the Courland. The 28th SS Panzer Division was ordered to be established in the area.

THE SOVIET SUMMER OFFENSIVE had overwhelmed the garrisons at Mitau and Tuckum, and the division was intended to maintain a corridor to Riga in the Baltic States. It incorporated two training units based in Latvia – the SS Training and Replacement Regiment at Dondangen and the SS Panzer Personnel Training Regiment *Seelager* at Ventspils.

Two Panzergrenadier regiments (identified as the 66th and 67th but in some sources recorded as the 70th and 71st) were to be formed at the Seelager training ground, but Soviet advances meant that the area had to be abandoned. The training regiments were instead formed into *SS-Panzer-Brigade Gross*, under *SS-Sturmbannführer* Martin Gross.

The brigade took only three days to be assembled from 8 August and was organized into two infantry battalions, a mixed Panzer battalion with around 15 Panzer IIIs and IVs, which were later joined by seven Tigers, a reconnaissance battalion and an assault gun battalion. Two artillery batteries were transferred from the 19th SS Division.

The brigade went into action on 20 August as part of *Panzer-Division Strachwitz*. Over the next month,

Commanders

Obersturmbannführer Martin Gross
August 1944 – November 1944

Divisional History	Formed
37.SS-Panzergrenadier-Regiment	1943
SS-Panzer-Brigade Gross	1944
28.SS-Panzer-Division	1944

it was in constant action in Latvia and Estonia. By the middle of September, the brigade had only 300 active troops, and its vehicle strength had fallen to three Panzer IIIs, two Panzer IVs, two StuGs, one captured T-34 and four armoured half-tracks.

In November, survivors were withdrawn to Sennelager in Westphalia, where they were used to train front-line replacements.

Other units that were intended for the 28th SS Panzer Division were used to rebuild the 37th SS Panzergrenadier Regiment, and formation of the 28th SS Panzer Division was cancelled in September 1944.

28th SS Freiwilligen Grenadier Division *Wallonien*

The *SS-Freiwilligen-Grenadier-Division Wallonien* was formed when *SS-Sturmbrigade Wallonien* was upgraded to divisional status, though it never actually reached divisional size.

WALLOON (FRENCH-SPEAKING BELGIAN) troops had served as volunteers in the German Army since 1941, but many transferred to the *Waffen-SS* in 1943. The new *SS-Sturmbrigade Wallonien* fought on the Dnieper bend and was trapped in the Cherkassy pocket while serving with the 5th SS *Wiking* Division. The Walloons escaped from the pocket with 632 men of the approximately 2000 who had originally been trapped by the Red Army.

Divisional status

The 28.*SS-Freiwilligen-Grenadier-Division Wallonien* was created in October 1944, eventually as a reduced-size 'Type 45' division. In February 1945, the division was assigned to III.*SS-Panzerkorps* (*Germanisches*) in Pomerania, where it fought the Soviets until the end of the war. Some divisional units managed to retreat to Denmark; most of the rest surrendered to the Soviets in Brandenburg in May 1945.

▶ Leon Degrelle, after escaping from the Cherkassy pocket, spring 1944.

▼ 15cm schwere Infanterie Geschütz sIG33

SS-Freiwilligen-Grenadier Regiment 69 / I Bataillon / IG. Kompanie

The 28th Division's three grenadier regiments each had a motorized infantry gun company, which was equipped with two 15cm (5.9in) heavy infantry guns and four 7.5cm (3in) light infantry guns.

INSIGNIA

Walloon volunteers in the German Army wore an armshield with the Belgian flag. When transferred to the SS, the Walloons adopted the insignia shown here.

Divisional History	Formed
373.Wallonisches-Infanterie-Bataillon (Heer)	1941
SS-Sturmbrigade Wallonien	1943
5.SS-Freiwilligen-Sturmbrigade Wallonien	1943
28.SS-Freiwilligen-Grenadier-Division Wallonien	1944

ORGANIZATION

Commanders

Sturmbannführer Lucien Lippert
October 1943 – February 1944

Standartenführer Léon Degrelle
February 1944 – April 1945

Specifications

Crew: 5

Weight: 1.75 tonnes (1.6 tons)

Length: 1.64m (64.57in)

Calibre: 150mm (5.9in)

Muzzle Velocity: 241m/s (783fps)

Range: 5504m (6000 yards)

Ammunition: High explosive or smoke

29th Waffen Grenadier Division der SS

The 29.*Waffen-Grenadier-Division der SS (russische Nr. 1)* was to be formed from the Russian volunteer unit *Waffen-Sturm-Brigade* RONA commanded by Bronislav Kaminski.

DESCENDED from one of the first Russian formations to fight for the Germans, it had possibly the worst reputation of any SS unit. Disbanded before its formation got under way, the number '29' was given to an Italian SS Waffen Grenadier Division (see below).

Divisional History	Formed
Lokot Militia	1941
Russkaya Osvoboditelnaya Narodnaya Armiya (RONA)	1942
Volksheer-Brigade Kaminski	1943
Waffen-Sturm-Brigade RONA	1944
29.Waffen-Grenadier-Division der SS (russische Nr. 1)	1944

Commanders

Waffen-Brigadeführer der SS Bronislav Kaminski
1941 – August 1944

SS-Brigadeführer Christoph Diehm
August 1944

29th Waffen Grenadier Division der SS

The 29.*Waffen-Grenadier-Division der SS (italienische Nr. 1)* was descended from the Italian Volunteer Legion formed by Italian fascists after the fall of Mussolini.

THE DIVISION WAS CREATED in September 1944, when the *Waffen-Grenadier-Brigade der SS (italienische Nr. 1)* was upgraded to a division. It was given the number '29' when the formation of the first Russian SS division was cancelled.

The Italian SS division never reached full divisional strength, though it came closer than many foreign SS divisions formed late in the war. It was primarily used on anti-partisan operations in northern Italy, but at the end of the war it saw some action against the British and the Americans. Some parts of the division surrendered to the Allies; members of those divisional units that surrendered to the Italian resistance were mostly executed.

Commanders

Obergruppenführer Karl Wolff
March 1944 – September 1944

Brigadeführer Pietro Mannelli
September 1944

Brigadeführer Peter Hansen
September 1944 – October 1944

Standartenführer Gustav Lombard
October 1944 – November 1944

Oberführer Constantin Heldmann
November 1944 – March? 1945

Oberführer Erwin Tzschoppe
March? 1945 – April 1945

INSIGNIA

The bundles of sticks known as fasces were symbols of the classical Roman Republic. They were adopted by the Italian fascists and gave the movement its name.

Divisional History	Formed
Italienische Freiwilligen-Legion	1943
1.Italienische Freiwilligen-Sturm-Brigade Milizia Armata	1943
1.Sturmbrigade Italienische Freiwilligen-Legion	1943
Waffen-Grenadier-Brigade der SS (italienische Nr. 1)	1944
29.Waffen-Grenadier-Division der SS (ital. Nr. 1)	1944

ORGANIZATION

▶ **Autocarro Fiat/Spa 38R**

29.Waffen-Grenadier-Division / Versorgungsdienst

The standard 2.5-tonne (2.45-ton) truck of the Italian Army was manufactured between 1936 and 1944, and was used by German as well as Italian fascist units.

Specifications

Crew: 1	Engine: 4-cylinder petrol (43bhp)
Weight: 3.5 tonnes (3.4 tons)	Speed: 65km/h (41mph)
Length: 4.7m (15ft 5in)	Range: not known
Width: 1.94m (6ft 4in)	Payload: 1.25 tonnes (1.2 tons)
Height: 2.5m (8ft 3in)	

30th Waffen Grenadier Division der SS

The 30.*Waffen-Grenadier-Division der SS (russische Nr. 2)* was formed in August 1944 in Poland from *Schutzmannschaft-Brigade Siegling*.

THE *SIEGLING* BRIGADE had been assembled from several small Russian volunteer formations withdrawn from the front following the Soviet summer offensive. Germans provided the officer cadre; most of the rest of the division was Russian. The division transferred to France, where it immediately came under attack by the French resistance. Some divisional units avoided action, though others did engage the resistance fighters with enthusiasm. It was disbanded in December 1944; reliable Russian troops were used in *Waffen-Grenadier-Brigade der SS (weissruthenische Nr. 1)*.

Divisional History	Formed
Schutzmannschaft-Brigade Siegling	1944
30.Waffen-Grenadier-Division der SS (russische Nr. 2)	1944

Commanders

Obersturmbannführer Hans Siegling
August 1944 – December 1944

▲ **15.2cm K433/I(r) (152mm M1937 gun-howitzer)**

30.Waffen-SS-Artillerie-Regiment / I.Bataillon

The two battalions of the 30th Artillery Regiment were each equipped with three batteries of captured Soviet guns and howitzers.

Specifications

Crew: 5	Muzzle Velocity: 655m/s (2149fps)
Weight: 7.9 tonnes (7.6 tons)	Range: 17,265m (18,880 yards)
Length: 4.925m (16ft 2in)	Ammunition: High explosive or smoke
Calibre: 152mm (6in)	Projectile weight: 43.5kg (96lb)

ORGANIZATION

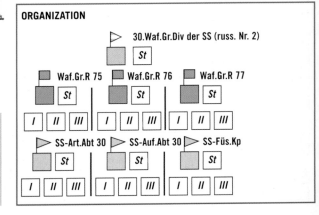

31st SS Freiwilligen Grenadier Division

Orders for the formation of the 31.*SS-Freiwilligen-Grenadier-Division* were issued in October 1944, and by the beginning of December 1944 some 11,000 recruits were in training.

MANY OF THE RECRUITS were Czech or Slovak *Volksdeutsche.* These recruits were bolstered by the attachment of parts of the disbanded 23. *Waffen-Gebirgs-Division der SS Kama* and by the addition of the *Polizei-Regiment Brixen.* The division fought briefly against the Soviets around its Hungarian training area but was soon forced to retreat into Germany, where it was intended to complete its formation at Marburg.

In January 1945, the division was converted into a reduced-strength Type 45 unit. In February, it was assigned to Army Group Centre. By the war's end, a *Kampfgruppe* was operating around Königsgrätz, where survivors surrendered to the Soviets.

INSIGNIA

Stags were popular *Wehrmacht* divisional emblems. This version is thought to have been assigned to the 31st Division but was probably never used.

Commanders

Brigadeführer Gustav Lombard	Brigadeführer Wilhelm Trabandt
October 1944 – April 1945	*April 1945 – May 1945*

Divisional History	Formed
Böhmen-Mähren-Division	1945
Batschka-Division	1945

32nd SS Freiwilligen Grenadier Division *30 Januar*

The 32nd SS division was formed in just five days from recruiting depots in Courland.

ALTHOUGH MADE UP of raw recruits and remnants from *Kampfgruppe Schill,* the division entered combat in April 1945. Attached to the Ninth Army, the division was defending the Seelowe Heights, east of Berlin, when it was destroyed in the Halbe 'kettle'. Survivors surrendered to the Americans on 3 May.

INSIGNIA

The ancient runic symbol for the letter 'T' symbolized the spear of Tiwaz, or Tir, the god of war in Norse mythology.

Commanders

Standartenführer Rudolf Mühlenkamp	Oberführer Adolf Ax
January 1945 – February 1945	*February 1945 – March 1945*
Standartenführer Joachim Richter	Standartenführer Hans Kempin
February 1945	*March 1945 – May 1945*

ORGANIZATION

33rd Waffen Grenadier Division der SS *Charlemagne*

The 33.*Waffen-Kavallerie-Division der SS (ungarische Nr. 3)* was intended to be formed from Hungarian volunteers, mostly from the scattered remnants of Hungarian Army cavalry units.

THE FORMATION NEVER reached anything close to divisional size and was destroyed in the fighting near Budapest in January 1945. The number '33' was given to the *Charlemagne* Division.

The 33.*Waffen-Grenadier-Division der SS Charlemagne (französische Nr. 1)* was formed on 2 February 1945 when the decision was taken to expand the *Waffen-Grenadier-Brigade der SS Charlemagne (französische Nr. 1)* to full divisional status. As might be expected from the name, the *Charlemagne* Division was a largely French formation, but it also had on its strength transfers from the 18th SS Division *Horst Wessel* and volunteers from other countries. Some French sources suggest that the division had Swedish, Swiss, Laotian, Vietnamese and Japanese members.

On deployment to Pomerania on 25 February, the Frenchmen were scattered by tanks of the Soviet 1st Belorussian Front as they unloaded. They gathered into three ad hoc battle groups. One made it to the Baltic coast, eventually being shipped via Denmark to Mecklenburg. A second group ran straight into one of the main thrusts of the Soviet winter offensive, and was never seen again. The third group took heavy casualties at the railhead before making a fighting retreat westwards to the German lines.

About a third of the 1100 survivors were released from their SS vows of allegiance. The remainder were

enough to make up a single Waffen grenadier regiment. This was among the last units to enter Berlin before the Soviets completed their enclosure of the German capital. On 2 May 1945, after the general order of surrender announced by General Weidling, some 30 surviving Frenchmen went into Soviet captivity near the Potsdamer station.

Commanders

Roger Labonne (LVF)
August 1941 – March 1942

Major Lacroix/Major Demessine
April 1942 – May 1943

Edgar Puaud (LVF)
June 1943 – August 1943

SS-Obersturmbannführer
Paul Gamory-Dubourdeau
August 1943 – July 1944

SS-Hauptsturmführer Erich Kostenbader
August 1944

Oberst/SS-Oberführer Edgar Puaud
August 1944 – February 1945

SS-Brigadeführer Gustav Krukenberg
March 1945 – April 1945

SS-Standartenführer Walter Zimmermann
April 1945 – May 1945

INSIGNIA

The *Charlemagne* Division's symbol combines half of the imperial eagle of the Holy Roman Empire with the fleur-de-lys of France.

Divisional History

Divisional History	Formed
Légion des Volontaires Français (Heer)	1943
Französische SS-Freiwilligen-Grenadier-Regiment	1943
Französische SS-Freiwilligen-Regiment 57	1943
Französische Freiwilligen-Sturmbrigade	1944
Waffen-Grenadier-Brigade der SS Charlemagne (französische Nr. 1)	1944
33.Waffen-Grenadier-Division der SS Charlemagne (französische Nr. 1)	1945

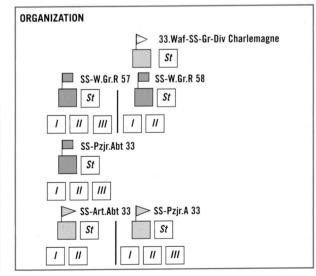

ORGANIZATION

▶ **Jagdpanzer IV (SdKfz 162)**

33.Waffen-Grenadier-Division Charlemagne / Grenadier-Regiment / schwere Bataillon

In April 1944, the *Charlemagne* Division was little more than a regiment in size. The heavy battalion of the regiment had a Panzerjäger company, a Flak company and a Jagdpanzer company with a handful of vehicles.

Specifications

Crew: 4	Speed: 35km/h (21.7mph)
Weight: 25.8 tonnes (23.48 tons)	Range: 210km (130.5 miles)
Length: 8.50m (27ft 10.5in)	Radio: FuG5
Width: 3.17m (10ft 5in)	Armament: 1 x 75mm (3in) PaK 42
Height: 2.85m (9ft 4in)	L/70 anti-tank gun; 1 x 7.92mm
Engine: Maybach HL120TRM (300hp)	(0.3in) MG

34th SS Freiwilligen Grenadier Division *Landstorm Nederland*

The *Landstorm Nederland* Division came into existence when the *SS-Freiwilligen-Grenadier-Brigade Landstorm Nederland* was upgraded to a division.

A DIVISION IN NAME ONLY, it was formed from the *Landstorm Nederland* unit plus Dutch Stormtroopers and other Dutch collaborationist organizations. The division saw little conventional action against Allied forces. It started life (originally as *SS-Grenadier-Regiment* 1 *Landwacht Niederlande*)

in March 1943 as a territorial defensive unit. The name was changed to *SS-Grenadier-Regiment* 1 *Landstorm Nederland* that October.

Landstorm Nederland troops fought against the Dutch resistance in northwest Holland and played a small part in the battle against British paratroopers at

Commanders

Oberführer Viktor Knapp	Standartenführer Martin Kohlroser
March 1943 – March 1944	*May 1944 – February 1945*
Obersturmbannführer Albert Doerheit	Oberführer Martin Kohlroser
April 1944 – May 1944	*February 1945 – May 1945*

▶ **Schwerer Kommandokraftwagen Horch (Kfz 21)**

SS-Freiwilligen-Grenadier-Brigade Landstorm Nederland / Stab

By the time the *Landstorm Nederland* Brigade was redesignated as a division, non-fighting elements of the formation were equipped with whatever their transport companies could lay their hands on.

Specifications

Crew: 1	Engine: Horch 6-cylinder petrol (90hp)
Weight: 2.4 tonnes (2.2 tons)	Speed: 88km/h (55mph)
Length: 4.44m (14ft 7in)	Range: 400km (250 miles)
Width: 1.68m (5ft 6in)	Radio: None usually fitted
Height: 1.73m (5ft 8in)	

Divisional History	Formed
SS-Grenadier-Regiment 1 Landwacht Niederlande	1943
SS-Grenadier-Regiment 1 Landstorm Nederland	1943
SS-Fre.Gr.Brigade Landstorm Nederland	1944
34.SS-Freiwilligen-Grenadier-Division Landstorm Nederland	1945

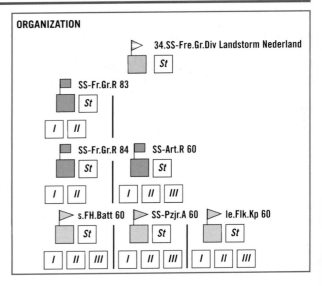

ORGANIZATION

Arnhem in September 1944. *Landstorm Nederland* troops also saw combat against Dutch soldiers, in an encounter with the 'Princess Irene Brigade', a unit of Dutch volunteers serving with the Allies.

In November 1944, the *SS-Wachbataillon Nordwest* was combined with two *Landstorm* battalions to form the *SS-Freiwilligen-Grenadier-Brigade Landstorm Nederland*. Although nominally part of the *Waffen-SS*, the *Wachbataillon* had much lower physical entry standards.

It also included a company of Ukrainian volunteers transferred from the Eastern Front. The reason for the lower physical standards was simple: *SS-Wachbataillon Nordwest* was responsible for guarding the perimeters of German concentration camps in the Netherlands.

The 3000 or so members of the *Landstorm Nederland* included fanatical Nazis who used terror to persuade the population to acquiesce in their demands. Troops from the 84th SS Volunteer Grenadier Regiment in particular, the former prison camp guards of *SS-Wachbataillon Nordwest*, were quite happy to shoot Dutch civilians who refused to obey their commands.

The last major combat fought by *Landstorm Nederland* was against the advancing Canadians around the villages of Oosterbeek and Otterlo in March 1945. The *Landstorm Nederland* went on to fight against Dutch resistance members right up to 7 May, when the division was disarmed by the British 49th (West Riding) Infantry Division.

▲ **3.7cm Panzerabwehrkanone (Pak 35/36)**
60.SS-Panzerjäger-Abteilung
The *Landstorm* Division's anti-tank battalion included the original Panzerjäger company of the *Landstorm* Brigade, which was joined by the 1st and 2nd *Nordwest* Panzerjäger Companies.

▲ **3.7cm Fliegerabwehrkanone (Flak 36/37)**
34.Waffen-SS-Flak-Abteilung
When the *Landstorm* Brigade was redesignated as a division, it created a Flak battalion by incorporating the personnel and equipment of the former *Clingendaal* Battery, a fixed defensive unit that had been based on the Atlantic Wall.

Specifications
Crew: 3
Weight: 0.43 tonnes (0.39 tons)
Length: 1.67m (5ft 5.5in)
Calibre: 37mm (1.5in)
Muzzle Velocity: 762m/s (2500fps)
Range: 600m (656 yards)
Ammunition: Armour-piercing

Specifications
Crew: 5
Weight: 1.5 tonnes (1.4 tons)
Length: 3.5m (11ft)
Calibre: 37mm (1.5in)
Muzzle Velocity: 820m/s (2690fps)
Range: 4800m (5250 yards)
Ammunition: High explosive or smoke

35th SS und Polizei Grenadier Division

Formed in the spring of 1945, the 35th SS Division received its personnel when *Ordnungspolizei* Regiments 14, 29 and 30 were transferred from the police to the *Waffen-SS*.

THROWN INTO ACTION only partially formed in April 1945, the division was sent to the Niesse River. As part of the German Ninth Army, it was badly mauled defending Berlin during the Battle of the Seelowe Heights, and was destroyed during the Halbe breakout when the divisional hedquarters was overrun. Survivors surrendered to the Americans or the Soviets near the demarcation line of the Elbe.

Commanders

Oberführer Johannes Wirth
February 1945 – March 1945

Standartenführer Rüdiger Pipkorn
March 1945 – May 1945

Divisional History	Formed
Polizei-Regiment z.b.V. 1	
Polizei-Regiment z.b.V. 2	
SS-Polizei-Brigade Wirth	1945
35.SS- und Polizei-Grenadier-Division	1945

INSIGNIA

The unit used a variant of a late-war symbol of the 4th SS Division, with a second bar to indicate that it was the second SS division drawn from police personnel.

ORGANIZATION

36th Waffen Grenadier Division der SS

The 36.*Waffen-Grenadier-Division der SS* was the most notorious of *Waffen-SS* units, serving under perhaps the most sadistic of all commanders of World War II.

OSKAR DIRLEWANGER was a highly decorated veteran of World War I, but he was also a drunk and a sadist, who had been imprisoned in the 1920s for sexual assaults on children. Dirlewanger led a special punishment unit that quickly earned a reputation for barbarity. It cemented its reputation with the part it played in the brutal suppression of the Warsaw uprising in the autumn of 1944. Reclassified as a 'paper' division in February 1945, the unit was never more than the size of an understrength brigade.

INSIGNIA

Also known as the Dirlewanger emblem, the symbol of the *Dirlewanger* Brigade and Division was a pair of crossed 'potato-masher' hand grenades.

Commanders

Oberführer Dr Oskar Dirlewanger
March 1945

Brigadeführer Fritz Schmedes
May 1945

Divisional History	Formed
Wilddiebkommando Oranienburg	1940
SS-Sonderkommando Dirlewanger	1940
SS-Sonderbataillon Dirlewanger	1940
Einsatz-Bataillon Dirlewanger	1943
SS-Regiment Dirlewanger	1943
SS-Sonderregiment Dirlewanger	1943
SS-Sturmbrigade Dirlewanger	1944
36.Waffen-Grenadier-Division der SS	1945

▶ **Panzerkampfwagen T-34 747(r)**

36. Waffen-SS-Panzer-Abteilung

The *Dirlewanger* Brigade included many Russians in its number, some of whom had deserted from the Red Army with their tanks.

Specifications

Crew: 4	Engine: V-2-34 V12 diesel
Weight: 26 tonnes (25.5 tons)	Speed: 55km/h (34mph)
Length: 5.92m (19ft 5in)	Range: 186km (115 miles)
Width: 3m (9ft 10in)	Armament: 1 x 76.2mm (3in)
Height: 2.44m (8ft)	cannon; 2 x 7.62mm (0.3in) MG

37th SS Freiwilligen Kavallerie Division *Lützow*

The *37.SS-Freiwilligen-Kavallerie-Division Lützow* was formed near Marchfeld on the Hungarian–Slovakian border in February 1945.

RAW MATERIAL FOR THE DIVISION came from the remnants of the *Florian Geyer* and *Maria Theresia* Divisions, both of which had been shattered in the battles around besieged Budapest. The division was to be brought up to strength as far as possible by drafts of Hungarian *Volksdeutsche*.

In March 1945, the division was far from combat-capable, not all of its units having been formed. However, a *Kampfgruppe* from *Lützow*, consisting of all veteran and battle-ready elements of the division, was sent to *6.SS-Panzerarmee*. Commanded by *SS-Obersturmbannführer* Karl-Heinz Keitel (the son of *Wehrmacht* high command chief *Generalfeldmarschall* Wilhelm Keitel), the *Kampfgruppe* arrived on 4 April. Subordinated to I.*SS-Panzerkorps Leibstandarte Adolf Hitler*, *Kampfgruppe* Keitel

experienced some fierce combat in the retreat through Hungary to Austria. In May 1945, a number of units were taken by the Soviets, while others moved west to surrender to the advancing Americans. Some men from the *Lützow* Division took part in a mass breakout from the Altheim prisoner of war camp on 13 May, after watching the release of regular *Wehrmacht* units while they and other SS men remained in custody.

Commanders

SS-Oberführer Waldemar Fegelein *February 1945 - March 1945*	SS-Standartenführer Karl Gesele *March 1945 - May 1945*

INSIGNIA

Fitted in the cavalry/mountain-style SS shield (with a central notch at the top), the 37th Division's insignia was based on the Gothic script letter 'L' for *Lützow*.

ORGANIZATION

Divisional History	Formed
37.SS-Freiwilligen-Kavallerie-Division Lützow	1945
SS-Kampfgruppe Keitel	1945

38th SS Grenadier Division
Nibelungen

Although it was designated a division, the last SS formation to be created was never more than brigade-sized, with a strength of around 6000 men.

T HE DIVISION WAS FORMED around the students and staff at the *SS-Junkerschule* (Officer Training School) at Bad Tölz in Bavaria. Other troops were provided by the *Begleit-Bataillon Reichführer-SS*, the Customs Police, the 6th SS Mountain Division *Nord*, the 7th SS Mountain Division *Prinz Eugen*, a battalion-size draft from the Hitler Youth, and officers from the 30th SS Waffen Grenadier Division.

Although told to prepare for battle early in April 1945, combat units were not declared operational until 24 April. Deployed to defend the Danube Line from Vohlburg to Kelheim, the task proved too much for the understrength formation faced with heavy American pressure. By 28 April, *Nibelungen* had

withdrawn across the Danube and over the next two days continued to retreat towards Landshut.

Caught by the Americans as it crossed the Isar River, the division fought a short but fierce battle with troops of the US 14th Armored Division. By 1 May, in constant contact with two American divisions, *Nibelungen* was no longer combat-capable.

INSIGNIA

In keeping with its Wagnerian title, the *Nibelungen* Division used an ancient Germanic helmet as its divisional symbol.

Divisional History	Formed
SS-Junkerschule Bad Tölz	1945
SS-Division Junkerschule	1945
38.SS-Grenadier-Division Nibelungen	1945

Commanders

Standartenführer Hans Kempin
March 1945

Obersturmbannführer Richard Schulz-Kossens
April 1945

Brigadeführer Heinz Lammerding
April 1945

Brigadeführer Karl Reichsritter von Oberkamp
April 1945

Gruppenführer Martin Stange
April 1945 – May 1945

ORGANIZATIONS

38.SS-Gr.Div Nibelungen
St

SS-Pz.Gr.R 95   SS-Pz.Gr.R 96   SS-Art.Rgt 38
St   St   St

I II III   I II III   I II III

SS-Pzjr.Abt 38   SS-Flk.Abt 38
St   St

I II III   I II III

▶ **Jagdpanzer 38(t) Hetzer (SdKfz 138/2)**

38.SS-Panzerjäger-Abteilung

The division's *Panzerjäger-Abteilung* received about 10 Jagdpanzer 38s late in April 1945. It also had some 7.5cm (3in) Pak 40 towed anti-tank guns.

Specifications

Crew: 4

Weight: 14.5 tonnes (14.2 tons)

Length: 6.2m (20ft 4in)

Width: 2.93m (9ft 7in)

Height: 1.96m (6ft 5in)

Engine: Maybach HL120 petrol

Speed: 35km/h (22mph)

Range: 214km (133 miles)

Armament: 1 x 75mm (3in) Pak 39 cannon; 2 x 7.92mm (0.3in) MG

SS Organizational Structure

Day-to-day management of the SS was through a number of *Hauptamter*, or main offices, which were responsible for controlling a particular aspect of the SS.

Reichsführer-SS und Chef der Deutschen Polizei Heinrich Himmler

Persönliche Stab RFSS (Personal Staff of the Reichsführer)
SS-Obergruppenführer und General der Waffen-SS Karl Wolff
Ahnenerbe – SS Ancestral Heritage
Lebensborn – SS maternity/breeding programme

SS-Hauptamt (SS Main Office)
SS-Obergruppenführer Gottlob Berger
SS Registration Office
Waffen-SS replacement personnel

SS-Personalhauptamt (SS Personnel Office)
SS-Obergruppenführer Maximilian von Herff
Personnel records
Officer records

SS-Führungshauptamt (SS Operations Department)
SS-Obergruppenführer und General der Waffen-SS Hans Jüttner
Kommandoamt der Allgemeinen-SS (General SS command department)
Kommandoamt der Waffen-SS (Armed SS command department)
Waffen-SS units
SS-Totenkopf-Sturmbanne

Wirtschaft- und Verwaltungshauptamt (WVHA) (Main Economics and Administration Office)
SS-Obergruppenführer Oswald Pohl
Concentration camps
Buildings
SS economic interests
Military administration
Waffen-SS supplies

Hauptamt SS-Gericht (SS Legal Office)
SS-Obergruppenführer Franz Breithaupt
SS and police courts

Hauptamt Ordnungspolizei (Order Police Main Office – Uniformed Police)
SS-Obergruppenführer und Generaloberst der Polizei Kurt Daluege
Kommandoamt (Uniformed Police command)
Colonial policing
Fire services
Emergency and civil defence organizations

Reichssicherheitshauptamt (RSHA) (Main State Security Office)
SS-Obergruppenführer Reinhard Heydrich
SS-Obergruppenführer Ernst Kaltenbrunner (from 1943)
Inland-Sicherheitsdienst (SD) (SS Security Service – German intelligence)
SS-Brigadeführer Otto Ohlendorf
Ausland-Sicherheitsdienst (SD) (SS Security Service – Foreign intelligence)
SS-Brigadeführer Walter Schellenberg
Geheime Staatspolizei (*Gestapo*) (Secret Police)
SS-Gruppenführer Heinrich Müller
Kriminalpolizei (*Kripo*) (Criminal Police – plainclothed/detective)
SS-Gruppenführer Artur Nebe
SS-Gruppenführer Friedrich Panziger (from 1943)
Personnel and training
Ideological research
Budget and administration

Heissmeyeramt
SS-Obergruppenführer August Heissmeyer
Political education
SS schools

Hauptamt Volksdeutsche Mittelstelle (VoMi) (Ethnic German Liaison Department)
SS-Obergruppenführer Wernher Lorenz
Resettlement organization and technical assistance
German Race Department

Reichskommissar für die Festigung
   Deutschen Volkstums
   (Reich Commissar for Strengthening
   German-ness)
SS-Obergruppenführer Ulrich Greifelt
Resettlement planning and execution

Rasse- und Siedlungshauptamt
   (Race and Settlement Main Office)
SS-Obergruppenführer Richard Hildebrandt
Racial purity
Marriage permits

SS-Führungshauptamt

Although SS units came under *Wehrmacht* control in combat, in all other aspects the SS was independent of the Army. The *SS-Führungshauptamt* (SS-FHA) was the administrative and operational headquarters for the Waffen SS, responsible for the organization, equipment and orders of battle of SS combat units. The SS-FHA was also responsible for the administration of SS officer schools, medical services and logistics.

Amtsgruppe A
Organisation, Personal, Versorgung
(Organization, Personnel and Supply)

Amt I *Kommandoamt der Allgemeinen-SS*
   (Command Department of the *Allgemeine-SS*)
Amt II *Kommandoamt der Waffen-SS*
   (Command Department of the *Waffen-SS*)
Amt III *Zentralkanzlei* (Central Chancellery)
Amt IV *Verwaltungsamt*
   (Administration Department)
Amt V *Personalamt* (Personnel Department)
Amt VI *Reit- und Fahrwesen*
   (Horsemanship and Driver Training)
Amt VII *Nachschubwesen* (Logistics Planning)
Amt VIII *Waffenamt* (Weapons Office)
Amt IX *Technische Ausrüstung und Maschinen*
   (Technical and Mechanical Development)
Amt X *Kraftfahrzeugwesen*
   (Motor Vehicle Organization)

Amtsgruppe B
Ausbildung (Training)

Amt XI *Führer-Ausbildung und SS-Junkerschulen*
   (Officer Training and Officer Cadet Schools)
Amt XII *Unterführer-Ausbildung und
SS-Unterführerschulen*
   (NCO Training and NCO Training Schools)

Amtsgruppe C
Inspektionen (Inspectorates)

Inspektion 2 *Infanterie- und Gebirgstruppen*
   (Infantry and Mountain Troops)
Inspektion 3 *Kavallerie* (Cavalry)
Inspektion 4 *Artillerie* (Artillery)
Inspektion 5 *Pioniere/Techniker*
   (Engineers/Technicians)
Inspektion 6 *Panzertruppen* (Armoured Troops)
Inspektion 7 *Nachrichtentruppen* (Signals Troops)
Inspektion 8 *Feldzeug- und Instandsetzungstruppen*
   (Field Maintenance Troops)
Inspektion 9 *Versorgungstruppen*
   (Service and Support Troops)
Inspektion 10 *Kraftfahrparktruppen*
   (Motor Pool Troops)
Inspektion 11 Not known
Inspektion 12 *Technische Lehrgänge*
   (Technical Training)
Inspektion 13 *Flakartillerie* (Anti-Aircraft Artillery)

Amtsgruppe D
Sanitätswesen der Waffen-SS
(Waffen-SS Medical Services)

Amt XIII *Verwaltung* (Administration)
Amt XIV *Zahnwesen* (Dental)
Amt XV *Versorgung* (Supply)
Amt XVI *Ärztliche Behandlung*
   (Medical Treatment)

Index

Page numbers in *italics* refer to illustrations.